REASONABLE
Ethics

REASONABLE
Ethics

A Christian Approach
to Social, Economic,
and Political Concerns

ROBERT BENNE

CONCORDIA PUBLISHING HOUSE · SAINT LOUIS

To those readers through the years
who have encouraged me to write social commentary

Published by Concordia Publishing House
3558 S. Jefferson Avenue, St. Louis, MO 63118-3968

Copyright © 2005 Robert Benne.

Cover illustration by Paine Proffitt, copyright © 2005 Concordia Publishing House.

Manufactured in the United States of America

Library of Congress Cataloging-in-Publication Data

Benne, Robert.
  Reasonable ethics : a Christian approach to social, economic, and
political concerns / Robert Benne.
    p. cm.
  Includes bibliographical references.
  ISBN 0-7586-0492-0
  1. Christian ethics.   I. Title.
BJ1251.B395 2006
241'.0441--dc22

2005031603

1   2   3   4   5   6   7   8   9   10   15   14   13   12   11   10   09   08   07   06

CONTENTS

Preface   7

Abbreviations   10

Part 1: Personal Basics
    My Story   13
    The Sometime Prodigal Son   18
    Brushes with the Great and Near Great   30
    If I Had It to Do over Again   39
    Lent in Summer   48

Part 2: Basic Lutheran Ethics
    Lutheran Ethics   57
    The Paradoxical Vision   89
    Ordinary Saints   104
    Radical Orthodoxy   111
    The Lake Wobegon Factor   118
    Living the Wholly Christian Life   125

Part 3: Politics
    Religion and Politics   133
    Religious Faith and Political Office   143
    Faith-Based Organizations as Instruments of Public Policy   152
    The Persistence of Civil Religion   163
    Can Liberalism Be Totalitarian?   167
    A Christian Realist Approach to the Events of 9/11   172
    Beware of the Foreign Policy Opinions
        of Religious Professionals   175

Part 4: Economics

    Less Enthusiasm, Please, I'm Lutheran   181

    The Calling of the Church in Economic Life   186

    Am I Righteous or What?   211

Part 5: Christian Higher Education

    The Darkness before the Dawn?   217

    Integrity and Fragmentation   227

    Reconnecting   242

    Christian Colleges and Civil Society   250

Part 6: Sexual Ethics

    Reinventing Sexual Ethics   259

    God's Holy Ordinance   266

    Magic's Moment   277

Part 7: Culture and Entertainment

    The Play's the Thing   283

    Does God Favor the Yankees?   287

    Viewing Movies through Christian Eyes   291

    Green Shoots in America   298

    Down with Diversity   308

    The Burden of Cultural Correctness   314

    Music Matters   321

    Whatever Happened to Accountability?   325

    America the Okay?   329

    The Objective Worth of Human Life   335

Preface

REASONABLE ETHICS

In 1793, the famous philosopher Immanuel Kant wrote an influential book entitled *Religion within the Limits of Reason Alone*.
He believed that true human enlightenment meant that religion
should be based on strictly rational grounds. The religion of
Deism followed from his argument, as did several sorts of rational
ethics. Both religion and ethics were then distanced from the revelation of the triune God in Holy Scripture. Religion and ethics
became detached from the Bible and theology.

The title of this book may lead some people to think that
the ethical reflection herein follows this rationalist model. Nothing could be further from the truth. It would be truer to say that
the exercise of reason in this book—the "reasonable ethics" of the
title—follows the path of the contemporary philosopher Nicholas
Wolterstorff, whose book *Reason within the Bounds of Religion* is
a direct counter to the earlier claims of Kant. Wolterstorff argues
that much of our reasoning proceeds from deep-running assumptions that are conveyed to us by living religious traditions. Rather
than being autonomous, reason is dependent on something that is
supra- or nonrational. For Christians, that something is the reve-

lation of God, and the reasoning of Christians follows upon the premises of that revelation.

Lutherans, however, do believe that autonomous reason does have a place in human affairs. Reason is placed in the minds of all humans by God. It can be an instrument of truth in secular life. It can grasp scientific truth. It can lead to reasonable judgments in social, economic, and political concerns. But for the Christian, those judgments cannot be completely detached from the deeper truths of Christian revelation. God's truth is one, and ultimately the truths of revelation and reason cannot be contradictory, though in this life we may not see how they fit perfectly together.

This book operates from Christian assumptions—Lutheranly construed—but also employs the capacities of reason that Christians share with all humans. The elaboration of basic Lutheran convictions in the second part of the book is more directly dependent on Scripture and Lutheran theology and perhaps is more stable and less debatable. But even in those sections, my reasoning about God's revelation and the Lutheran understanding of that revelation might be faulty. While I seek it, I claim no complete or infallible understanding of these important matters.

As I reason outward from those basic convictions to judgments about social, economic, and political matters in the following sections of the book, I know that Christians of goodwill and intelligence can and will disagree with my assessments. That is because with each step outward, many other judgments are made that employ differences in the readings of the situations, in the relevant principles of justice, in the ordering of values, and in synthetic judgments. Thus though I hope that my judgments on these "secular" issues are reasonable, I fully admit that Christians can come to other conclusions.

I'm afraid that the first part of the book—the autobiographical—is more of a personal account than an argument about ethics. Early in life I became convinced that God called me to work in the church. At first I thought that call was to parish ministry, but later it became a call to teach and write in and for the church. Also, quite early in life I became fascinated with how religion affects culture. That was to be the pervasive interest that runs through my calling. I believe that God has called me to try to understand how Christianity influences society and to communicate those understandings to students, pastors, and the wider church.

I have spent more than fifty years responding to this call. I am still excited about it and look forward to pursuing it until I can do so no more. God has blessed me deeply by giving me purpose in life, and I hope that I have responded to His blessing with faithfulness and devotion. The first part of this book is an autobiographical account—from different perspectives—of this long journey. The second part of the book is centered upon the distinctly Lutheran themes of Law and Gospel, the calling of the Christian, and the role of the church in society.

The rest of the book is a collection of applications of Lutheran theological ethics to politics, economics, higher education, sexual ethics, culture, and entertainment. They are wide ranging, which may prompt some readers to think that a fool rushed in where angels feared to tread. Because most of these essays and articles were written since 1990, the examples and allusions in them should be recognizable. In cases where they weren't, I have updated the essays.

I wish to thank Concordia Publishing House for publishing this collection of short writings, as well as the journals and newspapers that originally printed them. But I am most grateful to the readers who have encouraged me to write by offering appreciative comments. They must take some of the blame for the following.

Robert Benne
August 2005

ABBREVIATIONS

ACLU	American Civil Liberties Union
CTS	Chicago Theological Seminary
ELCA	Evangelical Lutheran Church in America
LCA	Lutheran Church in America
LCMS	The Lutheran Church—Missouri Synod
LSTC	Lutheran School of Theology (Chicago)
LW	Luther, Martin. *Luther's Works*. American Edition. General editors Jaroslav Pelikan and Helmut T. Lehmann. 56 vols. St. Louis: Concordia, and Philadelphia: Muhlenberg and Fortress, 1955–86.
ULC	United Lutheran Church

Part 1

PERSONAL BASICS

MY STORY

I heard the call of God to be His own in a normal and unexciting way. My parents were young when I was born toward the end of the Depression. But when they had a youngster on their hands, they brought him for Baptism right after his birth (he was "re-born" on July 22, 1937) and to Sunday school at an early age. At the same time they began to increase their attachments to and activities in the church. In our little all-German town, you were either Lutheran or Catholic. Those churches spent considerable effort on the formation of their young. Lutheran Sunday schools and youth groups were large and active. Our Sunday school featured a common assembly that was held before we were sent to our specific classes. Mrs. Thompson led the assembly with rousing Gospel songs that owed more to the Methodist movement on the frontier than our Lutheran tradition of hymnody. I learned those Gospel songs by the score.

We preschoolers wailed when we were "promoted" from our comfortable little room in which Jesus' disputation with the elders peered down on us from among the steam pipes. Kindly teachers told us the Christian story and embodied Christian virtue through their loyalty, forbearance, and affection for children. In later high school years teachers were even intellectually stimulating. One, Mrs. Beckenhauer, bet me a milkshake that humans would be able to control the weather in twenty years. I collected my winnings years ago.

Sunday school was always followed by compulsory attendance at church in the large nave above the Sunday school rooms. There the presence of God was deeply sensed. The moods of the church year, closely intertwined with the seasons, are still instantly retrievable to my memory. The expectation and preparation of Advent. The pristine winter purity of Christmas; Mrs. Hasebrook singing "Star of the East" at the midnight candlelight Communion. The somberness of Lent—no movies but plenty of midweek services. The triumphant spring of souls—Easter. On through the long season of Trinity with strong preaching by Pastor Krebs. Communion with grape juice was offered only four times a year, but laypeople received the elements with utmost seriousness.

Confirmation brought a vivid encounter with the Holy Spirit, which was palpably present as we took our first Holy Communion in white robes. That time was also appropriate for getting serious about the Christian life. A young person was to become a model Christian in life outside the church. The Christian way was starkly clear and sometimes at painful odds with the ways of the world. Although that way was legalistic and tempted to self-righteousness, it provided a good starting point for the Christian life. A particularly important part of my early formation as a Christian was the experience of a "call to the ministry," as it was termed in those days. This had not only to do with who (or whose) I was as a child of God but also with what I should do with my life.

Now the last thing I wanted to do with my life was become a pastor. Pastors were "unmanly" and definitely not a model for young athletes, which I tried to be. Most of my "heroes" were athletes and coaches. Men were devout Christians in our church and town, but religion was never talked about nor were their religious "affections" ever worn on their sleeves. Pastors did both, and while respected for their necessary leadership, they were not particularly to be emulated.

Against these odds a strange thing happened while I was working as a gardener for one of the most prestigious and well-educated women in our church. I overheard her talking on the phone with one of her friends. During the conversation, she opined that indeed Bobby Benne would make an excellent minister. I was nailed! I was offered my earthly destiny. After that "word" I was never able completely to shake the notion that I was called to work in the church. That call came against most of my surface inclinations. After it, however, I secretly prepared for the kind of course work and college program that conventionally led toward ordination.

The call of God to be His own and to do His bidding came to me through the church in that particular time and place. The orderliness and reliability conveyed by that early formation in the faith have communicated a sense of trust deeper than mere intellectual assent. Faith and life fit together hand and glove. Despite absurdities and painful setbacks, life—and the power behind it— is basically for us, not against us. One can have a basic confidence in things. God is our rock.

That early faith did not lack a sense of sin. Although rather legalistically conceived, our failures and flaws led to the conviction that we were disobedient sinners. We needed the forgiveness offered by God in Christ. So we came with repentant hearts to the Lord's Supper. Receiving forgiveness, we resolved to live upright lives—sexual restraint, soberness, honesty, and hard work—and to be charitable and kindly to those less fortunate than we.

Formation in the faith also meant that one was here on earth for a purpose, that is, to do God's will in one's work. One was not simply here to enjoy oneself or to support one's family, but to discern what it was that God wanted you to do and then do it as best you could. The call to enter the work of the church has been a great blessing for me. It gave me purpose in life that has sustained me through a whole life.

Finally, there was a sense of gratitude for the fact that life was as good as it was. We were not raised on high expectations and were constantly surprised that eventualities outran expectations. One praised God for those blessings and faced the future with a modicum of hope.

This simple posture of Christian faith and life was "caught" from the adults of family and church. We were formed into the Christian tradition in that time and place. The practice of the Christian faith and life in that place shaped my outlook and way of life powerfully. The dependencies of our early life "make" us what we are to a much greater extent than we would like to admit. The persons who embodied the Christian tradition for us can well be counted as God's special gifts to us.

Formation into the church's tradition was certainly not the only conditioner of my life. As for most people, the immediate family was powerful. Parents from Nebraska farms and small towns bore strong virtues of the frontier. Self-reliance, uncomplaining endurance, loyalty, and compassion for the "deserving" poor and unfortunate were emphasized. Above all, "doing the best one can" without complaint or excuse was prized. This trait was most vividly admired in athletes, but for me it was quickly channeled into academics and music as well.

Such an upbringing blossomed under the conditions of small-town Nebraska life. There the American Dream was a reality. We were free to shake off the limits of the past, to engage in a struggling ascent, and to live in confident hope that such efforts would be embraced by a gracious future. The land and society were open.

Everyone started from roughly the same starting point and the rules of the game were generally fair. One could rise according to ability, choice, and ambition. In the distinctly human scale of the small town, one could participate in a wide variety of activities—drama, debate, sports of each season, vocal and instrumental music, journalism, Scouts—as well as the prescribed schooling. Because it was such a small pond, "excellence" was not reserved for specialists but was accessible to the relatively gifted and strongly motivated generalist. Such an environment breeds an appreciation for the variety of life's activities, a thirst for participation, and a confidence that excellence is a lively possibility.

The fond backward glance just given exaggerates the goodness of the past and, no doubt, the benign imprint of that past on my life and character. Unfortunately, there are negative limits as well as positive. My surrounding culture was emotionally unexpressive, parochial, judgmental toward others, utterly uncompassionate toward those who "deserved" their plight, and defensive about its own smallness and anonymity. The accentuation of small-town American values carries with it a dark side, a disregard for values that necessarily complement them—interdependence, cosmopolitanism, and a sense of ambiguity.

Religion did not suffocate these other sources of identity. Indeed, in many cases it merely sanctified those small-town American values. But in other cases it reminded us of a larger world, of higher values, and of divine purposes that certainly transcended our lives in that time and place. Above all, it placed the world in which we dwelled into an ultimate context that gave meaning and sanctity to all of it—the good, the bad, and the indifferent. The Christian faith provided the canopy of meaning that responded clearly to the central questions of life: Who am I? What is going on? What should I do?

THE SOMETIME PRODIGAL SON

A THEOLOGICAL AUTOBIOGRAPHY

What happened to you, Bob?" was the poignant question of a revered woman who had known me in my '60s incarnation. The distinct implication was that I had fallen from an admirable state to one that should best be left undescribed. In other words, she feared that I had become a conservative. And, alas, she was right, though I don't have quite the negative view of that state that she has.

My first inclination in reflecting over my journey of almost sixty years was to focus on my changes in social interpretation. That is, I would chronicle how my judgments on politics, economics, and society had changed. That was what the woman was interested in. On second thought, that approach would not wash. For one thing, that would fall into a trap that I worry about: that mainstream Protestantism is basically more interested in politics than the Christian faith itself. For another, this series is on theological biographies, not political ones.

Originally published in *Dialog*, vol. 35 (Fall 1996).
Amended and reprinted with permission.

So I was pressed into reflecting more deeply on the relation of my fundamental theological convictions to the dynamic social milieu of my sixty years in a rapidly changing America. The two poles are closely related, of course, but it is the former that is the focus of the following essay. The need to think things through from this more theological perspective was, for me, an important and illuminating process.

THE FORMATIVE YEARS: 1937–1958

I was born and raised in West Point, Nebraska, the home of many Lutherans of note, among them Martin Marty, Walter Wick, Ralph Bohlmann, and Frederick Niedner. It was an all-German burg, evenly divided between huge Lutheran and Catholic communities. The Lutherans were also divided between the United Lutheran Church (ULC), my church, and the Missouri branch. The churches and the surrounding culture were symbiotic—each reinforced strong religious and moral norms that, even when violated, were widely shared and sanctioned.

The piety of the ULC had many characteristics of frontier Methodism: moralistic, anti-Catholic, and low church (Communion four times a year with grape juice) but also nonfundamentalist and effective. The Sunday schools were huge and the teachers patient and caring. In my teenage years an alert Sunday school teacher actually stimulated us intellectually. Our pastor delivered solid Lutheran fare.

In about my twelfth year, a prominent townswoman, for whom I was gardening, remarked to me that I would make a good minister. That little word felled me because after that I could not get such a calling out of my mind, though I desperately wanted to. Religion, after all, to our lower middle-class way of thinking, was a woman's thing. But when I look back, almost all the people who dramatically influenced my life at that stage were women. Indeed, the families I knew were all centered in strong women who tended to be more intelligent and directive than the men. (This has made me suspicious of some feminist interpretations that have accentuated the victimization of women. The West Point women certainly weren't that way. The women *were* strong, though the men were not particularly good looking. To insist differently is to take an ideological sledgehammer to the real filaments of history.)

The American Dream worked in our town. My parents were uneducated children of the Depression and we had a small income. But the schools, churches, and civic organizations opened the way to improvement of our lot, and each member of my little high school class has enhanced his or her position in life. Christopher Lasch, in his various works, but particularly in *The True and Only Heaven*, accurately describes the lower middle-class populism of that little town. Doing things well (without any particular obsession about success), self-reliance, modest expectations of life, the capacity for uncomplaining endurance, and gratitude for the good things one already had been given were virtues deeply ensconced in that culture. When combined with the steady piety of the Lutheran tradition, it made for a once-born kind of Christianity, to use William James's category. Its underlying themes emphasized reliable and steady promise-making and promise-keeping, adherence to religious and moral tradition, trust in and gratitude for the providence of God, and faithfulness to the end. It had many weaknesses, of course, but chief among them was the judgmentalism that left little room for grace and new beginning.

THE "PROPHETIC" YEARS: 1958–1970

I went off to Midland College in 1955 and pretty much followed conventional patterns. There was a coterie of bright young students at Midland who were cultivated by a handful of dedicated faculty. One of the faculty, Alan Hauck, introduced me to Søren Kierkegaard and Reinhold Niebuhr in my senior year. The Kierkegaard of *Attack on Christendom* and the Niebuhr of *A Christian Interpretation of Ethics* fired the imagination of one who had grown restless with the complacency, stability, and homogeneity of the Midwestern culture of the late 1950s.

A Fulbright Grant got me to Erlangen, where I received my first introduction to Lutheran ethics (Walter Künneth), and a Woodrow Wilson Fellowship took me to the University of Chicago Divinity School, where things really began to happen. I entered the Ethics and Society Program and studied under Gibson Winter and Alvin Pitcher, both of whom exercised powerful critiques of American church and society. More of that a bit later.

The Chicago of that period—1960–1965—was characterized by an imposing array of Lutheran faculty and students. I was taught by Jaroslav Pelikan, Paul Tillich, Jerald Brauer, Martin Marty, Joseph Sittler, and Richard Luman among the faculty, but I learned perhaps even more from the gifted Lutheran students who were in the doctoral program at the university. Especially Phil Hefner, Robert Wilken, Paul Sponheim, Thomas Droege, Vern Faillettaz, Nelvin Vos, Paul Heyne, Gerald Christianson, and Peter Kjeseth come to mind. Such a concentration of bright Lutherans in both the faculty and student body brought about a direct challenge to the liberal Protestant heritage of the school, especially its strong strand of Whiteheadian thought. There were great intellectual exchanges in the classroom and the coffee shop. In such ongoing debate I found out why and how I was a Lutheran. I armed myself with classic Lutheran theology and ethics to do battle with the Protestant liberals. The Chicago of that era provided us with an intellectual environment that I have rarely experienced before or since.

However, the powerful and exciting liberal Protestantism of the Ethics and Society Program won the battle for my heart and mind at that particular time. I didn't jettison my Lutheranism; I just put it on the back burner in favor of more spicy fare. Gibson Winter taught us H. Richard Niebuhr's theology and ethics and drove home his own critique of the burgeoning suburban Christianity that came with the religious expansion of the 1950s. In contrast to *The Suburban Captivity of the Churches*, Winter proposed a *New Creation as Metropolis*. But Al Pitcher had even more influence on many of us. He taught us Reinhold Niebuhr the Chicago way—disciplined, in-depth attention to key texts. At the end of Pitcher's three-course sequence, I knew how to think like Niebuhr, a capacity I have continued to use in my social-ethical writings. Al was also an inveterate social activist who got us in tune with the civil rights and community organization movements, both of which were at white-hot intensity in the Chicago of the early 1960s. Al's firsthand reports and analyses made our classes electric.

At the end of my residence at the University of Chicago in 1965, the Lutheran School of Theology (LSTC) offered me a position at its Rock Island campus. I was to be a two-year replacement for Frank Sherman, who was slated to become the LSTC professor of ethics after completing his term as tutor to Lutheran students at Oxford.

The Rock Island campus of LSTC to which I came was a fairly quiet and insular seminary. But I was armed with the exciting idealism of cosmopolitan, early '60s, liberal Protestantism. I was bursting to get out the call to the church to get involved in urban ministry, civil rights, and community organization. I coupled this with a sharp Niebuhrian critique of American society and culture. Michael Harrington's *The Other America*, Harvey Cox's *The Secular City*, Hannah Arendt's *The Human Condition*, and Winter's works were my favorite texts of the day.

Wow! Instead of struggling to find my way as a new, young (28!), lay professor in a resistant seminary, I blew in like a whirlwind. The students were extraordinarily responsive (two thirds of the senior class requested inner-city calls upon graduation), and the faculty was tolerant and supportive. My impact was sufficient to persuade LSTC to create a position in church and society for me, and I was kept on the faculty when the seminaries merged in Chicago in 1967.

My liberal idealism continued to run delightfully wild at the new LSTC. Large incoming classes of students ready to encounter the challenges of the late 1960s continued to respond to my exhortations to transform church and society. It was a heady time. A large faculty in a new building in a new location with loads of idealistic students. A great time was had by all. Unfortunately, that time was quite brief, but that's getting ahead of the story.

This period of my journey was characterized by what I thought were "prophetic" teaching and writing, and to a certain extent that was true, though I have become reluctant to use the word *prophetic* in relation to anything I have done. My teaching and writing moved with the "triumphant" liberal Protestant idealism of the day. It focused attention on "structural" sin and evil, of which it thought American society had a massive amount, and argued that the main mission of the church was to transform these structures, including the church. It assumed the mainstream Protestant churches would continue to flourish and their progeny would be firmly formed in Christian faith and ethics. Thus they could afford to be "prophetic" with regard to both church and society and focus their attention on a new church's transformation of society. I firmly struck these themes in my own work, and, given the character of the time, I believe they conveyed an important message to the seminary and the church.

TIMES OF CRISIS: 1970–1980

The Lord does not allow such "good times" to tarry. I need not detail the upheavals of the sixties, which really began about 1965 and extended until about 1975. It was the last five years of that period that confronted me with a genuine fork in the road, both ideologically and theologically.

Ideologically, my idealistic liberalism was soon outflanked by the radicals who popped up among the students and the faculty. "As a liberal institution, LSTC isn't even worth bombing," opined one of our student radicals, a Lutheran wrestler from the University of Iowa who had been radicalized by the revolutionary student movement. My reformism looked tame and compromising to such radicals. I was no longer on the cutting edge.

But what to do? For a while I tried to join the radicals and get back on the front lines. But it didn't work. Protest trips to Washington and revolutionary rallies in the neighborhood turned me off. The radical interpretation of American society and its institutions, including the church, seemed grossly exaggerated, if not downright wrong. "Power to the people," I thought, would mean the election of Richard Nixon rather than a revolutionary upheaval.

After undergoing serious cognitive dissonance at a neighborhood rally that featured every imaginable revolutionary group, I vowed to be more honest with myself and my students. I announced to Dean Sherman that he was going to see some changes in me. I would begin "calling them as I saw them," not posturing as the radical I was not.

Such a decision began to put me more and more "out of sync" with the seminary in general and the students in particular. (Is it possible to be a conservative and teach Church and Society at an LCA seminary? My experience suggests not.) I resisted the radical politics of the day and found myself on the "wrong side of history," to use the Marxist phrase. I had politically incorrect opinions on Central American politics, capitalism, strategies to end Apartheid in South Africa, the Cold War, and sexual and gender politics. East Coast neoconservatives—Kristol, Podhoretz, Neuhaus, Novak—were articulating publicly the positions that I had come to hold. A great shift in my social, economic, and political opinion was taking place. Or was it that the older liberalism had disintegrated and it was the radicalism of the sixties that I found abhorrent?

At any rate, my membership in the religious left, which by then encompassed the intellectual and ecclesial leadership of mainstream Protestantism, came to an end. Mainstream Protestantism, which had been so much inclined to see the hand of God in the transforming impulses of sixties radicalism, now turned with contempt on the American project it had so much stake in shaping. The key element in this shift, I think, was a reversal in its perception of the American project. The myth of American innocent progress—shaped by transformist Protestantism—had turned into the myth of American guilty regress. Because it had been complicitous in this oppressive American history, it now had to dissociate itself from this history of oppression and aim at transforming America from new sources that had not been contaminated by its own dominant past. It looked to Marxism, feminism, ecologism, multiculturalism—"voices from the periphery"—to purge and restore its transformist vision.

Not only did I depart from this assessment and prescription, at a deeper theological level I found out how deeply I disagreed with the transformist vision, that is, the persisting view that the mission of the church is to transform society toward the kingdom of God. But it took the collapse of my liberal idealism through the wrenching of the sixties to open my eyes to the dubiousness of the transformist project itself.

The books I wrote in the decade of 1970 to 1980 trace my movement away from the trajectory of mainstream Protestantism. *Wandering in the Wilderness: Christians and the New Culture* (1972) was an effort to appropriate critically some of the impulses of the sixties. Its inordinately existentialist interpretation of the Christian faith at least maintained a critical distance from those movements, though I now think it treated them too benignly. Philip Hefner and I wrote *Defining America: A Christian Critique of the American Dream* (1974) to struggle with the questions of whether and how one could be both Christian and American, questions that had real significance at that time in history. We adopted a dialectical approach that proposed some constructive theological moves to get us through the impasse. But *The Ethic of Democratic Capitalism: A Moral Reassessment* (1981) definitely put me "on the other side," that is, with the neoconservatives. In that book I argued that the combination of market economic arrangements and political democracy could constitute not only a morally defensible political economy, but could provide a model for developed and developing nations alike. I used a Niebuhrian/Rawlsian perspective to make such a judgment and to propose policies for refining and extending justice. (When I revisit this topic now, I tell my audience that it took only eight years before the effect of my book brought down the Soviet empire in 1989!)

RETURN TO TRADITION: 1980–1996

The decade of the 1980s began with vigorous involvement on my part in the neoconservative movement. I was active enough to be warned by a high official of the Lutheran Church in America that I had no future in official LCA church and society concerns if I did not cease and desist. But my focus on economics and politics began to wane naturally as I discerned a more menacing threat than mere secular politics. The radical critique of America that came out of the sixties was now being trained on the church and the Christian tradition itself. What I had experienced as a church and society professor in the seventies was then in the eighties being experienced by those who taught the core disciplines of church history, Bible, and theology. The biblical and theological roots of the tradition itself were being challenged by liberationism, feminism, ecologism, and multiculturalism. (Sorry about the -isms, but it is the only way to point efficiently to rather complex and variegated movements.)

This deconstruction of tradition obviously seemed to be happening in mainstream Protestantism and insofar as the emerging new Lutheran church (Evangelical Lutheran Church in America [ELCA]) participated in this process, it, too, seemed under threat. These trends were particularly disturbing because they were combined with a general weakening of the capacity of religious traditions to pass on their convictions to a new generation. Religious individualism was running amuck, and the mainstream denominations had few weapons to combat it. In fact, they were aiding and abetting it by their dalliance with militant revisionist parties.

I was awakened to this rampant religious individualism by teaching the mainstream young at Roanoke College in Salem, Virginia, where my family and I moved in 1982. The mainstream Protestant and Catholic college students I found there were weakly connected to their own religious traditions. (The evangelical students were another matter.) Moreover, the college I came to was as weakly connected to its Christian heritage as the students were to theirs.

In recent years my attention has been directed to three fronts: the struggle over the direction of the ELCA; the effort to make our Lutheran Christian vision publicly relevant to the institutions of the church, particularly its colleges; and the pressing need to articulate and communicate the Lutheran ethical tradition to a new generation.

Let me begin with the third, a central focus of my lifelong calling as a Christian teacher. It would be an essential concern of my more mature years, even if I weren't convinced of its absolute importance in light of my analysis above. But I am convinced that the living Lutheran tradition is under severe challenge. It is a mature tradition slowly accommodating itself to the cultures of the day, one step behind the Protestant mainline.

At the level of grassroots popular culture, it is being dissolved by the individualism that idolizes choice as the first principle of religious and moral life. At the upper levels it accommodates to the going concerns of the American secular elite. It mirrors the "progressive" movements of secular liberalism. This pincer movement from above and below has well-nigh squeezed out the substance of living Lutheran tradition. So my teaching and writing have been devoted to communicating our tradition's core moral vision. In the Lutheran tradition, of course, that moral perspective cannot be separated from its larger theological vision, both of which I have tried to articulate.

Ordinary Saints: An Introduction to the Christian Life (1988) is a Lutheran interpretation of the Christian's calling. [A second edition has now been published.] Moreover, the book elaborates the key theological themes out of which the doctrine of vocation rises. It is meant to be a college text as well as a study book for adult laypersons. My fervent hope is that it gives a clear and alluring vision of the Christian life that might aid Lutherans and other Christians in finding their bearings as they move through the journey of life.

The Paradoxical Vision: A Public Theology for the Twenty-first Century (1995) is a complement to *Ordinary Saints*. It contains my effort to elaborate a Lutheran framework for Christian social ethics. It interprets the doctrine of the two kingdoms to a Christian readership that sorely needs alternatives to the dominant transformist perspectives that have led us to religionized politics and politicized religion at both ends of the political and religious spectrums. It also includes a typology of how in fact religious traditions do affect the public world.

Both books embody an attempt in my teaching, lecturing, and writing to clarify the core elements of the Lutheran heritage. They represent a return to the wells that have nourished our church's moral teaching for hundreds of years. At the same time, they have been written with an increasing conviction that these nourishing currents make sense only in the larger river of catholic Christianity, the Great Tradition that draws more and more serious Christians to its treasures.

Moving outward from the center, I find myself strongly moved to call our church-related institutions to their proper role in the mission of the church. The Lutheran colleges are inheritors of a great tradition, what I call "dialectical Lutheran humanism," that can give them character and mission in the tough years ahead. But so many of the colleges, as well as other institutions related to the church, are in the process of selling their spiritual souls for a mess of secular pottage. The public relevance of the Lutheran religious and moral heritage has waned considerably in the past decades, and it is time to reassert that heritage honestly and persuasively or get out of these institutions altogether. The coming years will be a test of our clarity and courage on these matters. I have written a book on how church-related colleges and universities "keep the faith" in their institutional life. *Quality with Soul—How Six Premier Colleges and Universities Keep Faith with Their Religious Traditions* (2001) is my constructive effort at showing that the secularization process need not be inevitable.

Finally, the ELCA remains an object of great interest. It is the part of the living body of Christ into which I was born and within which I continue to live and move and have my being. It is the concrete Christian context within which my calling, my church life, and many precious friends are to be found. To think of myself without it is almost impossible, though a surprising number of my acquaintances have survived in new church homes.

Yet I have ambivalent feelings toward it, as my occasional writings have certainly made clear. Its founding documents have built flaws into the body that guarantee unending struggle and stalemate. They ensure that wholesome authority will remain elusive in a time when that is what is needed most. "Diversity" at the top levels and "choice" at the grass roots offer themselves as pathetic vestiges of a Protestant principle that is already dangerously bereft of catholic substance. The controversy over homosexuality could well split the church and force many of us to consider whether we can remain in it. But we watch and pray with hope for constructive signs in the ongoing life of the church.

I have retired from full-time teaching and now devote my time to running Roanoke College's Center for Religion and Society, which continues my lifelong calling to understand the relation of Christ to culture. That quest will not end until God brings it to a *finis* in His own good time. Then, God willing, I will at last be shown precisely and truly how it should be.

BRUSHES WITH THE GREAT AND NEAR GREAT

FIFTY YEARS OF THEOLOGICAL REMINISCENCES

Having lived and taught for many years now, I want to offer some anecdotes about theological and philosophical figures I have encountered. When I regale younger folks with some of these tales, their eyes grow wide with disbelief. Could anyone have lived long enough to have met Rudolph Bultmann in person? I want to emphasize that most of these are reminiscences of a bystander. The name-dropping I will be doing is not done to inflate my importance; I had very little influence in these brushes. Mostly I was just lucky enough to have been on the scene as an observer or at most as a minor participant in the encounter. Nevertheless, I offer the following for your amusement.

NEBRASKA ROOTS

Although I didn't know it at the time, the most important church people in my early life sprang from The Lutheran Church—

Originally published in *Dialog*, vol. 42, no. 1 (Spring 2003).
Amended and reprinted with permission.

Missouri Synod in my hometown of West Point, Nebraska. Although we couldn't claim as many worldly celebrities as Wahoo, Nebraska—Howard Hansen (composer and conductor), George Wells Beadle (Nobel Prize-winning geneticist and president of the University of Chicago), and "Wahoo Sam" Crawford (Hall of Fame baseball player), we did all right with religious figures. Martin Marty grew up in West Point, the son of the local Missouri Synod parochial school principal and teacher. He enjoys a similar fondness for our background as I do, and we've chatted about it periodically over many years. I played ball with Victor Bohlmann, the brother of Ralph Bohlmann, whose father was the pastor of the local Missouri Synod parish. Ralph became president of the Missouri Synod. Further, Walter Wick, president of the Indiana-Kentucky Synod of the LCA, grew up in rural West Point.

When I was a senior at Midland Lutheran College, I won a Fulbright Scholarship to study theology at Erlangen University in Germany. I was also taking Greek at the time from a seminary professor (Central Lutheran Seminary was then located in Fremont, Nebraska, where the college was). Upon receiving notification that I had won the scholarship, I excitedly told this news to my professor after Greek class. He deflated me immensely by telling me I wasn't ready to study at a German university. I should turn down the Fulbright, he said. Determined to go anyway, I wrote Philip Hefner, an earlier Midlander who had also been a Fulbright scholar, to get his opinion. He wrote back immediately, telling me that what the professor told me amounted to cow chips ... or something like that! After all, he said, your government isn't sending you to Germany to get a full theological education but to be a good representative of your country. His advice: Immerse yourself in the culture and enjoy yourself! If you get a bit of theological education, so much the better.

German Shoots

Therefore one week after we were married in the fall of 1959, my wife and I embarked with two hundred other Fulbright scholars on the *MS Berlin* to Germany. We were seated at a table with a one-armed philosopher from Texas. When the conversation turned to politics, I offered some negative opinions about Adlai Stevenson. I had heard from my dad that if a man can't keep a marriage together (Stevenson had been divorced), it was unlikely that he could keep the country together. I tossed that into the hopper, unaware that I would get a blistering rebuttal that made me feel as stupid as the opinion I offered. That fiery person was John Silber, who became a rather distinguished philosopher and then the controversial president of Boston University. Later, when my wife, Joanna, was secretary to the philosophy department of the University of Chicago, she misread his name and sent a letter addressed to John Sillier. His response was as blistering as the one he aimed at me some years earlier. In the argot of today, we might say that he should have "lightened up."

When we finally arrived at Erlangen, where I was to be a Fulbright student, we met many interesting Lutherans who became well-known figures. William Weiblen, who was finishing his dissertation, became president of Wartburg Seminary. John Damm became a professor at Concordia Seminary in St. Louis and later a pastor of St. Peter's in New York City. John and other liturgical Missouri Synod pastors introduced me to a Missouri Synod that I never knew existed, the church of Arthur Carl Piepkorn.

During the year at Erlangen, Bill Weiblen offered to drive a group of us to other German and Swiss universities to hear more famous theologians than we had at Erlangen. Erlangen wasn't so shabby, however. Although Werner Elert had died by that time, I did hear Paul Althaus, Walter Künneth, Wilhelm Maurer, and Ethlebert Stauffer. Stauffer, a distinguished New Testament scholar, arrived at his lecture hall in formal attire, allowed an obsequious student to take off his coat and hang it up, gave his lecture, closed his notebook, had the same student put on his coat, and departed without a conversational word. Those early postwar days in Germany were the days of the weekly Saturday bath. On Mondays, the big swinging windows of the lecture halls were tightly closed but by Friday were wide open. But I digress.

MEETING BULTMANN

Our intrepid group arranged personal meetings with Bultmann in Marburg, Barth in Basel, and a group of Lutherans—Schlink, Bornkamm, and Brunner—in Heidelberg. A theological joke of the day likened the various theologians to church bells. Bultmann and Barth went "BOOM, BOOM, BOOM," while Schlink, the Lutheran confessionalist, went "tinkle, tinkle, tinkle."

The meeting with Bultmann was the most memorable. He invited us to his study, where we sat in a circle, drinking coffee and puffing on pipes (all theologians smoked pipes in those days). The conversation proceeded smoothly until a question was put by a conservative student who had just moved from the Wisconsin Synod to the Missouri Synod. He thought Bultmann was a heretic, and we knew he would pose an incendiary question sometime in the encounter. Sure enough, throughout the conversation he grew redder by the moment until he blurted out this accusative question: "Ist es wahr, Herr Doktor Professor Bultmann, dass Ihre Theologie ist eine Theologie ohne Gott und ohne Ewigkeit?" ["Is it true, Professor Bultmann, that yours is a theology without God or eternal life?"] We all slunk down in our chairs, wondering what Bultmann's response would be. After a few quiet puffs on his pipe, Bultmann said simply, "Das wurde Ich nicht sagen," ["I wouldn't say that."] and passed on to the next question. A pretty cool guy.

We met Barth in Basel but did not have such an intimate exchange. We went to an evening seminar at which a Scottish student was holding forth in English about the internal life of the Trinity. I thought the subject odd for a disciple of a theologian who emphasized that we know nothing about God except that which He chooses to reveal in Christ. Heidelberg offered few juicy tidbits.

During that year, I drove Bill Weiblen's family to England for a visit while he worked on his dissertation. While in London, we saw Bertrand Russell lead a huge "Ban the Bomb" march, replete with "Better Red Than Dead" placards. Such is the political wisdom of most philosophers.

CHICAGO BLOSSOMS

After the year in Germany, we were off to the University of Chicago Divinity School, where I studied under many famous theologians and with many students who went on to various degrees of stardom in academe. My church history sequence was taught by a quartet of luminaries: Robert Grant (early church), Jaroslav Pelikan (medieval), Richard Luman (Reformation), and James Hastings Nichols (modern). Nichols received a standing ovation from the students following the course's last lecture (read formally from a manuscript). Pelikan lectured brilliantly with no notes. One day in class he grew morose because it was his 35th birthday and he hadn't achieved as much as Mozart, who died at age 35.

Markus Barth, the son of Karl, was my New Testament teacher and, oddly enough, played an important role in my development as a student. (I did not specialize in New Testament but in ethics and society. Gibson Winter and Alvin Pitcher were my main teachers. At the end of my stay at the Divinity School, Winter went to study phenomenology in Europe while I was writing my dissertation for him. This turned out to be a nightmare because he wanted me to incorporate phenomenological thought into my dissertation and I resisted.)

Back to Markus Barth. The second term of my first year featured a New Testament survey course taught by Barth. He was a tall, gawky figure with coke-bottle glasses and a passionate nature for his subject matter. I was terrified when he assigned a research paper on St. Paul as our major assignment. Actually, I was terrified most of the time that first year, surrounded by seminary graduates and students from Harvard, Yale, etc. I was from Midland College. I had a default plan to transfer to Maywood Seminary when the Divinity School found out how weak I was.

Barth had each of us come into his office for personal conferences after he read our papers. Mine was on "Paul and Mysticism." When my turn came to go into his office, I could barely prevent my knees from knocking. My heart sank when his first words were: "I fear for your soul, Mr. Benne." I thought he was worried that my despondency over a flunking grade could lead to a self-destructive act, which could indeed endanger my soul. Then he said, "You have done such a fine job that I have given you an A+, and I fear that you will become proud and haughty." Wow. After that I never felt inferior in intellectual capacity to those students who seemed so much brighter than I. It made a world of difference for my confidence.

TILLICH AND PANNENBERG

Paul Tillich came to Chicago after he retired from Harvard after he retired from Union. I had three memorable encounters with Tillich—two of them a bit embarrassing. The first was during his lectures in the history of Christian thought, which were held in a large hall that was filled with several hundred listeners. He asked students to write out questions, which he would then answer at the beginning of the next lecture. I wrote what I thought was a nifty question on the differences in theological method between him and the Lundensians, a Swedish school of theologians headed by Gustaf Aulén and Anders Nygren. Tillich read my question aloud, then said, "This is a terribly confused question. Does the person who wrote it have the courage to identify himself and try to explain it?" I was in the first row, and a friend sitting next to me knew I had written the question. So, I gulped and rose to full height. We seemed to muddle through to some bit of clarity.

The second encounter involved Wolfhart Pannenberg, who at that time was a rising young German theologian who was invited as a guest professor to Chicago. In a seminar Tillich held, he asked if anyone knew anything about Pannenberg. (There was a suspicion among us that Tillich never read theologians who wrote after the close of the nineteenth century, and this, as well as the episode on Lundensian theology, seemed to bear that out.) I had heard a bit about Pannenberg, so I piped up: "I have heard that he is a neo-Hegelian." To that Tillich exclaimed: "*Ach, mein Gott*, we have no need for any more Hegelian theologians."

In that same seminar another embarrassing event happened. Tillich would have a glass of wine at lunch and often grew sleepy in his afternoon seminars—not unusual for a man in his 80s. At any rate, he fell asleep in mid-sentence one lazy afternoon. We students didn't know what to do. He slept a few moments, then woke up with a start. "Where were we?" he asked. We told him what topic he was on, and he continued without a hitch.

LSTC, KING, AND JACKSON

When I moved on to teach at the Lutheran School of Theology (LSTC) in 1965, I had the opportunity to be around a number of major figures in theology. Anecdotes of two figures from those years may be interesting. The Hyde Park Cluster of Theological Schools featured fine disciplinary discussion groups. I belonged to one in Christian ethics to which James Gustafson also belonged. After years of being encouraged to develop his own constructive theological ethic, he shared with us the manuscript of what became *Ethics from a Theocentric Perspective*. In a discussion of the manuscript, I remarked about the absence of a Christology in which Christ mediated the forgiving grace of God. No such notion seemed to be present in the volume. Instead of the genial response we were accustomed to from Jim, he sternly shook his finger at me and said; "I do not want too friendly a God!"

During those early years at LSTC, I became involved in Operation Breadbasket, which was the northern initiative of Martin Luther King Jr. Besides participating in King's rallies and marches, we had a chance to meet him personally. King came to preach every month at a weekly Saturday morning breakfast, and I was able to meet him. The young Jesse Jackson, then a student at Chicago Theological Seminary, was selected to head that operation. Each Saturday morning I got to hear those two preach, plus many prominent black pastors from the South Side. What preaching! What exhilaration! When the Saturday morning breakfast outgrew the CTS cafeteria, we moved it to LSTC. It stayed there until the rise of Black Power led Jackson to disaffiliate from "white" institutions.

During those LSTC years, I can recall two memorable encounters with Richard John Neuhaus, who was then a Missouri Synod pastor in a poor area of Brooklyn. When he came to Chicago as a delegate to the 1968 Democratic Convention, he regaled us with tales of marches and jailings. In a long nighttime conversation fueled by much bourbon and scotch, he allowed as how a small group of determined men could sway the course of history at such a tumultuous time. Soon thereafter he joined a neoconservative movement that indeed made its mark on American history.

In another late-night conversation at some long forgotten conference, Richard told the late Paul Heyne and me about an opportunity he might have to follow William Sloan Coffin as chaplain at Yale. Heyne and I argued that this was not his calling; instead, he was to become a first-class religious journalist. Whether that conversation affected Richard's decision to found and edit first *This World* and then *First Things,* only the Lord knows.

Toward the end of my stay at LSTC, I was struggling with a decision about whether to leave for Roanoke College. I went for counsel to Joseph Sittler, who had been an acquaintance for many years and was something of a prophetic figure. By this time (around 1981), Joe was nearly blind. He had baptized our last child and liked my wife, Joanna, very much. The thought of leaving was a painful one because I had been with the same colleagues since the beginning of the school in Hyde Park in 1967. I said: "Joe, to leave would feel like a betrayal and a kind of death. I will be the first of the colleagues to jump ship and I feel like I would become no one . . . it would be a kind of death."

Joe peered through his thick glasses and said to me: "Benne, you'll feel bad for about three weeks but you will resurrect after that. Besides, if it is better for Joanna that you go, do it. She is more important to you than your work here!" So we went.

The Ripe Roanoke Fruit

Since my arrival at Roanoke College in 1982, I have directed the college's Center for Religion and Society. I have invited many well-known theologians and church leaders to our campus. Two stories about one theologian will suffice. In 1985, we held a major conference on the relation of West Germany and the United States. We invited Helmut Schmidt, Arthur Burns (the U.S. ambassador to West Germany), Michael Nauman (editor of *Die Zeit* and recently a minister in the Schroeder government), and Wolfhart Pannenberg. Schmidt told us his health would permit him to speak only ten minutes, but he spoke for more than an hour to a gym full of listeners. Such are the promises of politicians.

Besides giving a fine lecture on the differences between the German and American churches' response to the Cold War (the American response was wiser because it had Niebuhrian realism to draw upon while the German church was under Barth's influence), Pannenberg was also invited to preach at our Sunday morning college worship service. We excised the Eucharist to give him more time. Upon learning that, he demanded we put the Eucharist back in. He then preached a beautiful, uncomplicated sermon of about ten minutes, and we celebrated the Eucharist.

While Pannenberg and his wife, Hilke, were in Salem, we arranged for one of our retired professors to lead them on a hike on the Appalachian Trail. The professor was steeped in the lore of the Appalachians—their flora and fauna. He charmed the Pannenbergs so much with his narrated tour that they continued to exchange Christmas greetings for many years.

One of the great oddities of my theological story is that I neither met nor heard Richard or Reinhold Niebuhr, the great American theologians, though I met and heard many great Europeans. The irony is that the two Niebuhrs influenced my thinking far more than the great Europeans. Those I didn't hear personally had more impact than those I did. Nevertheless, I am grateful for a life full of brushes with the great and near great. It's been almost too much for a Lutheran boy from West Point, Nebraska.

IF I HAD IT TO DO OVER AGAIN

I.

At the sixtieth wedding anniversary of my parents, we children and grandchildren pulled out all the stops. We wined and dined them at a nice restaurant, then regaled them with toasts, tributes, and happy stories. Glasses were raised as often as compliments were offered. It was a grand occasion. At the end of the festivities, we looked expectantly to the parents to see what response they might have. We no doubt secretly wanted to be complimented by them as lavishly as they had been by us. But we had overestimated our ability to make them respond as we wished. They looked at each other and Dad—as usual—took the lead. "Yes," he said, "things have worked out pretty well. None of you are in jail!" With that flash of Nebraska understatement, attention was redirected to where it belonged—on them.

To continue the understatement, things have worked out pretty well with our four children; none of them are in jail. In fact, two of our children are happily married with homes and children

Part I of this essay originally published in *The Cresset* (Easter 2001).
Amended and reprinted with permission.

of their own. A third is serious about a divorced woman with two children. All three families participate in church life at what one could call a moderate level. The appearance of children in their lives did the trick. They began connecting with the church.

The youngest is repeating the trajectory of the older three. He is not hostile to the church, but he rarely goes. High holidays are sure things, but ordinary Sundays are not his cup of tea. He is not married yet, so the magic of marriage and family has not had its chance to work up to this point.

All of them are really nice kids. They are affectionate and loyal. Two have solid marriages and are wonderful parents. It is clear that our extended family life means a lot to them. My three sons are avid athletes and sports fans, which leads me to the uneasy suspicion that those values were the really serious ones in my life and I communicated them particularly well. But despite such misgivings, I think it safe to say that most of our cherished values have been transmitted at a fairly profound level. The two younger sons are finding their way into the world with varying degrees of difficulty. We are deeply grateful that things have turned out so well.

But I wonder about the depth of their religious values, which for my wife and me were the most important ones to communicate. Their religious values seem to be somewhat peripheral to the important and pressing things in life. Although brought up surrounded by a myriad of Christian practices—prayer, devotions, church-going, hospitality, Christian symbols, sacramental meals, religious conversation—they do not seem to practice them themselves. Christian faith and life seem like one more option or preference in their lives that they have not ranked all that highly. I wonder if they are looking at the world through Christian eyes and I wonder if they are self-consciously living out the Christian virtues of faith, love, and hope.

It could be, of course, that their faith is stronger and more central than I think. It could be that as life unfolds their maturity in the faith will grow. Their Christian faith may become more comprehensive, central, and unsurpassable. But I worry about both the present and the future. While I don't accept full responsibility for the status of their religious convictions, I do accept some responsibility and often wonder what I would do differently if I had it to do over again.

II.

One thing I would do differently would be to adapt a more accurate—and disturbing—assessment of the power and pervasivity of the cultural changes that were going on in my children's growing up years: the 1970s and the 1980s. Of course I was aware of the wrenching nature of cultural change in the 1960s. As a young professor, I was an enthusiastic participant in those changes. Later, I reached a much more ambivalent estimation of those times. But the changes initiated by the 1960s continued in the 1970s and 1980s. Further, even deeper trends than those in the 1960s—whose dynamics were in many cases only symptomatic of those deeper trends—continue to shape our society. Those deeper changes are shaped by vast economic and political transitions that seem beyond the control of great nations, let alone ordinary citizens.

Without going into further detail about these vast changes, we can talk about some of their effects on the culture in which our children are growing up. It was Daniel Bell who first noticed the division between the imperatives of the economic and social spheres. In *The Cultural Contradictions of Capitalism*, Bell argued that the economic sphere demanded disciplined utilitarian work, while the social sphere encouraged hedonistic self-expression. He thought these "cultures" were contradictory and would bring trouble in the years ahead. Robert Bellah, in *Habits of the Heart*, picked up similar signals when he suggested that two new lifestyles—utilitarian individualism and expressive individualism—were fast overtaking the older traditions of biblical and republican virtue. The former was a calculating approach to life that instrumentalized all other values for the sake of personal success, particularly in the economic sphere. The latter was something of a romantic revolt against the former. Expressive individualism valued the spontaneous expression of internal states, the more individualized and intense the better. In its milder forms expressive individualism encouraged people to "be who they are" and "to follow their bliss." More extreme versions enjoined them to "make their lives an artistic statement," to become a roman candle shot off in the dark.

Bellah suggested that the "new" American culture actually combines the two. People can be utilitarian individualists in their daytime or workaday lives and expressive individualists in their leisure. A culture of affluence allows both to occur in the same people. Further, Bellah argues, this new American culture enshrines "freedom" or "autonomy" as the primary regulative or formal value. "Freedom" means the absence of any internal or external restraints on the choices one makes to realize one's individual success or to express oneself. This is a distinctly truncated version of freedom in comparison to the older traditions of biblical and republican virtue, which had substantive notions about what freedom was for. Both forms of individualism are corrosive of traditions, as well as the narratives and practices that constitute traditions. In both sorts of individualism, persons have weak connections to others and make up their own narratives, if they have any at all.

David Brooks carries this sort of analysis further in *Bobos in Paradise: The New Upper Class and How They Got There*. Brooks argues that the emerging affluent classes combine a bohemian lifestyle with the bourgeois values of discipline, achievement, and common sense. In other words, they express their "subversive and off-beat desires" within measured bounds and within a basically achievement-oriented way of life. Bohemianism has been tempered by bourgeois imperatives, but bourgeois values have been spiced with "counter-cultural" flavors. In Bellah's language, utilitarian individualism has combined with expressive individualism under the imperial sway of the individual's free choice.

It seems to me that this is the cultural world into which our children are born and nurtured. It envelopes them in the pop culture of the media, in school, in their peer culture, and especially in the exploding electronic culture that increasingly will be the shaper of our young. This culture is profoundly antitraditional and anti-institutional. It produces free, "sovereign" individuals who make up their own identities and projects based on self-generated choices. For such persons strong commitments to demanding realities outside themselves are unlikely. They make partial commitments limited by their own utilitarian or expressive choices. Rigorous moral or religious duties are scarcely thinkable. Such persons can easily say, as my daughter once told me: "But, Dad, we're very spiritual even though we aren't religious."

If this characterizes the emerging culture in which children are nurtured, the challenge before us as Christians is serious, far more serious than I thought when we were raising our children. The pressures of this culture are toward forming unencumbered selves—free from strong connections to anything outside the self, including the Christian community, its ethos and worldview. Perhaps we see such masses of persons already appearing in the radically secularized countries of Europe. We are shielded from such a scene for the moment by the extensive but rather superficial participation of most Americans in religious communities.

Thus I do not think we were intentional and intensive enough in the Christian formation of our children, especially given the strength of the cultural challenge that surrounded them and us. If I had it to do over again, I would try to give them a stronger formation in the faith. I say "try" because I, too, am infected with the modern commitment to freedom from too strenuous commitments. Perhaps even now I wouldn't be ready for the kind of training in Christian virtue that it would take to counteract the pushes and pulls of this culture. To paraphrase Oscar Wilde: "Christianity would be fine but it leaves too few free evenings." (He said that about socialism.)

III.

One of the things that I would do—had I the chance to do things over—would indeed cut down on my free evenings. I would engage my children in more intensive and extended conversation about the religious values we wanted to transmit. In retrospect, we relied far too much on the power of example. We both felt that if we modeled good religious values that our kids would emulate them. So we engaged in many Christian practices in our home that we simply thought would catch on with them. Prayer is a good example. We prayed at meals and had daily devotions before dinner. We would sing a hymn and end with prayer. But we never talked about the meaning of prayer and the necessity for it in the Christian life. Moreover, we never instructed them in how and what to pray. We didn't insist that they pray openly in the family rituals. I could give many other examples, the most important of which is continuing conversations about the meaning and relevance of our Christian convictions. We thought that all this would simply be absorbed in their lives by osmosis. But now we see that it didn't work that way. Much more time for intensive engagement has to be devoted in the formation of the young.

Another thing we would consider had we another chance would be getting rid of the television. Although we restricted the time and controlled the content of what our children could watch, there is little doubt that popular American culture became powerfully influential in their lives through TV. We adults watched the news and high-quality programs on public TV. (To be honest, I must admit a passion for sports on TV!) But again, except for sports, our example went nowhere. The kids sneaked in MTV, as well as a lot of awful network TV, when we weren't looking. Moreover, three out of four of our children took up the rock music fads of their day. While we listened to classical music, the example didn't take. And we had constant debates—you might call them running skirmishes—about the loudness and content of what they were listening to. By and large, then, TV and pop music did a lot to undermine what we were trying to instill. One of our children, particularly, fell under the spell of a rock band that indirectly cost him painful setbacks in life. Banishing the TV would also have given much more time for the kind of intensive engagement I mentioned above.

Given another chance, I believe we would seek out serious Christian schools for the elementary and high school education of our kids. In the 1960s and 1970s, we were urban idealists committed to the public school system of Chicago and kept our kids in public schools while many of my colleagues headed for the private institutions. We also were pressed enough economically to think twice about private schools. But knowing what I do now, I would argue for sending them to nearby Catholic schools or perhaps Lutheran or Christian Reformed schools farther away. What I would look for in those schools, besides compassionate and qualified teaching in a small-scale, disciplined setting, would be serious attention to learning the Bible and basic Christian doctrine, to a Christian ethos supported by worship according to the Christian year, and to a public affirmation of Christian identity and mission in the world. At the secondary level I would hope to see some critical grappling from a Christian point of view with secular claims to knowledge and with contemporary culture.

Coupled with Christian schools, we would seek out Lutheran churches with good youth ministry programs, no matter how far away they were. (There go more free evenings!) We were altogether too committed to joining our local parish, which, in our case, had virtually no youth ministry to speak of. Indeed, it boasted of being an adult parish while it played down family and youth concerns. At any rate, I am firmly convinced that in this challenging cultural situation, families need a lot of help from the local parish in the formation of the young. Families can't do it alone. But neither can church or church school do it alone. Formation must be a cooperative effort. I would want a disciplined confirmation program and a supportive youth ministry. The kids needed first-rate instruction in the faith and a Christian peer group to counter the view of the world they were getting in the media and the various pathologies they were encountering in their peer culture. When we needed help, the local parish couldn't or wouldn't give it. If I had it to do over again, I would look beyond our local parish.

Perhaps with a stronger formation in the faith, our children might have gone to more intensively Christian colleges than they did. Two went to a Lutheran college and two went to two different Methodist schools. The Lutheran college was not a total wash; the kids at least had the opportunity to take courses in the Christian tradition and to participate in worship and devotional life. They did little of that, though they received a pretty decent liberal arts education in a supportive environment. The Methodist schools were pretty much a total wash. There was scarcely a whiff of Christianity in them, let alone of Wesleyanism. That is not to say there weren't serious Christians at those Methodist schools. There indeed were, but they kept their convictions private. The public face of the school was pervasively secular. A straight course in Christian thought could not be found. The chaplain would not utter the name of Christ at the school's baccalaureate service because it wouldn't be "inclusive."

With a stronger formation perhaps they would have been more inclined to go to a Valparaiso or a St. Olaf, which are more forthrightly and aggressively Christian than the colleges they attended. It would then have been far more likely that their faith would have been deepened and enriched. That is, such might have happened *if* they would have already been predisposed to follow the Christian path. If they would have gone to Valparaiso or St. Olaf with their relatively weak formation, they may well have fallen though the cracks as so many young people do. But it would have been nice to have had them go to such schools. It may have been even better to have gone to a Calvin or a Wheaton, where there is not so much chance of falling through the cracks. But, at any rate, with another chance at forming our children, we might have disposed them to go to more full-blooded Christian schools than they did.

What conclusions to make of this intensely personal story? First, do not think I have given up hope for my children or that they are hostile to the faith. I pray daily that the Holy Spirit will enflame their faith even as I pray that He will enflame mine. The Holy Spirit will work in His own time and place and manner. It was and is not up to me to make my children Christian. That gift comes from a power beyond me.

But this set of reflections does suggest that Christians must become a more distinct people again, a counter-cultural people that drinks from its own wells of biblical and traditional wisdom. Our own culture no longer supports the Christian agenda; we cannot rely on it to do our work for us. Christians must become more intense in their efforts at formation. We must spend our free evenings teaching our young about the faith, about prayer and worship, about love and compassion, about obedience to the commands of God, about the Christian worldview, and thereby draw them into a grand moving train whose head is Christ. In aiming for this, we do not reject nor deny the world. Indeed, if we are formed properly as Christians we will add much salt and leaven to a world that needs those ingredients badly.

LENT IN SUMMER

The Gospel Lesson is written in Luke 12:16–21 (RSV):

He told them a parable, saying, "The land of a rich man brought forth plentifully; and he thought to himself, 'What shall I do, for I have nowhere to store my crops?' And he said, 'I will do this; I will pull down my barns and build larger ones; and there I will store all my grain and my goods. And I will say to my soul, Soul, you have ample goods laid up for many years; take your ease, eat drink, be merry.' But God said to him, 'Fool, this night your soul is required of you; and the things you; have prepared, whose will they be?' So is he who lays up treasure for himself, and is not rich toward God."

The Word of the Lord.

Grace be unto you and peace, from God our Father, and the Lord Jesus Christ.

If Lent is a season of participating in the passion journey of Christ, it sometimes reminds us of our own journeys that are times of suffering, humiliation, and abandonment. Our own journeys often do not mean much except in retrospect. Hard times are too turbulent to give much meaning to them immediately. Later we see meaning in them and connect them with Lent, though we must be careful that we don't equate them with Christ's suffering. Our own journeys don't save anyone, but perhaps they do prepare the soul for deeper meaning. Often these journeys occur at times of great pride and complacency in our lives. Our barns are full, and we are full of pride. We are not aware that, like the rich farmer, our lives could be altered at any moment.

In the spring of 2000, my barn was full and we were literally preparing to build a new house for our retirement years in Salem, Virginia. We were completing a sabbatical year at Valparaiso University in Indiana. I was Senior Lilly Fellow there and had just completed a successful year of writing and research. I had completed a book on Christian higher education that I knew would sell well and get me plenty of invitations to speak about a cause that I hold dear. Joanna and I were enjoying our first year alone after forty years with children in the house—close to the all-time record in the Guinness Book of Records. It was something of a second honeymoon, and we enjoyed it. For the first time in all those years, we had money in our account at the end of the month. Our first grandson had just been born to our son and his wife, and we were looking forward to seeing him in Virginia. Not least, I was in great tennis form. I play tennis fanatically, and during that year, I found many good players to play. All were younger than me, but through the year, I succeeding in beating them consistently. Being a fitness buff and an aspiring athlete, that winning year was deeply satisfying. I remember saying to myself: I must be the most robust 63-year-old on the face of the earth, and I think I will keep this up until about 85, when no doubt things will start to deteriorate. But I will face that in about twenty years.

My barn was full, and my soul was taking its ease. I thought I could control the future.

We arrived in Salem on May 10, and I had an appointment with an allergist on May 12 because I had experienced some congestion and wheezing in Valpo. The allergist gave me several tests—including one for lung function—and quietly announced that I had adult onset asthma. What a shock! I'd never had respiratory problems in my life, even when we lived in Chicago for twenty years. A chronic disease that I never expected.

Soon thereafter my anxieties were increased by the beginning of back pains. I had had severe back problems three or four times in my life and had come out okay, though I knew I had a badly deteriorated disk between two vertebrae. The pains became worse and soon I was on my back, unable to walk or sit without pain. My orthopedist sent me for an MRI, which indicated arthritic spurring around the diskless vertebrae. The MRI picture looked awful.

I don't know how many of you have been totally incapacitated by severe back problems, but it is one of the most depressing experiences—pain, forced inactivity, a trapped feeling, and no tennis for the foreseeable future! Here I was, stuck with two chronic conditions after I had just decided I would flourish for another twenty years. Pride goeth before the fall.

I began to think of my future with these two chronic problems. I saw myself soon carrying an oxygen tank to help my failing lungs. I fantasized that with such a damaged back I would never be able to be active or free of pain again. Because of my asthma, I couldn't tolerate the anti-inflammatory drugs that had been so helpful during my earlier bouts with back troubles. I felt trapped. I felt that the life I so enjoyed was coming to an end. More than that, my idolatrous image of myself was in shambles. My former self was dying.

I got so worked up that I began spending sleepless nights, sometimes three or four days without any sleep at all. Even in the daytime I couldn't nap—I would get close to falling asleep and would wake up with a traumatic start. My doctor's best sleeping pills had no effect on my sleeplessness. I had an anxiety attack that left me desperate, my pulse was up to 160 and I couldn't sit down. I went to Joanna's workplace and asked her to check me in to the psych clinic. Instead, we went to my doctor, and a combination of drugs finally quieted me down.

Now I had a third front that I couldn't handle, one that was worse than the other two because it was internal. That fellow who was self-assured, self-confident, full of self-control and self-reliance found that he couldn't handle his own psyche and emotions. Any distressing thought brought huge waves of anxiety welling up. Just thinking of my three chronic conditions set off horrible feelings that I couldn't control. I became as dependent on Joanna as a 5-year-old child. I thought often of my dead father and my recently deceased sister.

I did something I never imagined myself doing—I went to a psychiatrist. Indeed, I begged my doctor to get me an appointment quickly. The psychiatrist listened to my story and told me I was depressed. He prescribed a new antidepressant and told me others would notice changes in the better for me before I would. The changes came, but slowly. By late fall I was feeling decent again, though I still had a bad back and asthma.

What to make of this experience of Lent in the summer? What to make of the Lord telling me that my former life would be required of me even when I thought I had it all under control? What to make of a proud man falling?

Well, the first thing to register is great gratitude to God for restoring me. My asthma is controlled well by medications, my back has improved so I can play winning tennis if I pick my opponents carefully, and my internal turbulence has passed. It's wonderful to be near normal again—something of a figurative resurrection. It is somewhat ambiguous, of course, because with the return of my mental health has come renewed pride and self-possession. I don't have the deep sense of connection with my loved ones that I had when I was so dependent on them. Nevertheless, I rejoice.

Second, the Lord taught me some humility. Here I was with so many things going for me that I had a nervous breakdown in the face of a case of asthma and a bad back. I now have a great deal of empathy for the mentally ill. I have a great deal of respect for poor people who don't have all my resources, yet they cope. Joanna works with lower middle-class women who have far more serious health problems than I; they are in horrendous economic situations and their family life is a mess, yet they are kind, centered, and joyful Christians. Ordinary beggars have more personal strength and will than I exhibited under far less stress.

Third, the Lord brought to naught the idolatrous image I had constructed for myself. He was powerfully teaching me about my mortality and preparing me for what will inevitably come, perhaps sooner, perhaps later. He was teaching me that I came from dust and to dust I will return. He taught me that I could not take my ease, expecting to control my future with my barns full. So perhaps I am more ready for the hardships of the future because I no longer have so many illusions about my ability to control it. Such a deeper sense of mortality brings a heightened sense of joy and gratitude for what comes from the Lord's hand day by day. Lent in summer also reminded me that this is no abiding city and that I need to cling to the promises of God in Christ for my surest future. When I receive the Eucharist, I receive the everlasting benefits of Christ that increasingly fill the emptying space of my receding mortal life.

Finally, and most profoundly, my Lent in summer taught me a new love for the church, the body of Christ on earth. Contrary to what many people experience, my time of depression did not bring me closer to God. My soul became cold and empty. I did my daily devotions but felt distant and disconnected from God, but of course it was not that God abandoned me. Rather, in my weakness, I had grown distant from God. I was not angry, just empty, flat. But I had a great desire to attend a men's spiritual formation group at our church. The group is made up of strong Christian men who care and pray for one another. I spilled my story, and they held me up, as did my wife, day after day. It was as if the faith of others pulled me through when I didn't have enough of my own. It was as if I had fallen out of the great stream of Christians as they follow Christ toward His cataclysmic battle with sin, death, and the devil. I was in danger of falling out or behind, but others reached out, grabbed me, and carried me along with the other marchers in the great Christian column. This experience helped me realize that God in Christ reaches out to us through faithful others, even when our faith is distressingly weak.

Indeed, through His Spirit He encourages others to help us respond.

All of us, no doubt, will experience our own Lents in some way. May the light of Christ illuminate your journey through your own Lent, even as it enables us to journey with Christ in His.

Amen.

Part 2

BASIC LUTHERAN ETHICS

LUTHERAN ETHICS

PERENNIAL THEMES
AND CONTEMPORARY CHALLENGES

INTRODUCTION

A living tradition, Alasdair MacIntyre writes, is "an historically extended, socially embodied argument, and an argument precisely in part about the goods which constitute that tradition. Within a tradition the pursuit of goods extends through generations, sometimes through many generations."[1] Lutheranism, if it is anything, is such a tradition. It is an ethos, a way of life shaped by a vision of God's activities and purposes. It is constituted and sustained by practices of many sorts: liturgical, religious, moral, and intellectual. One of these practices is ethics—the disciplined reflection on Christian moral life, Lutheranly construed. Lutheran ethics is critical and constructive reflection on Christian moral practice. As such, it is both descriptive and normative.[2]

Originally published in *The Promise of Lutheran Ethics* edited by Karen L. Bloomquist and John R. Stumme, copyright © 1998 Augsburg Fortress. Adapted and reprinted by permission.

My chief purpose in the following is to identify the basic themes of Lutheran ethics that are discernible within the larger tradition of Lutheran theological and ethical writing. This project will not be primarily historical in a technical sense nor will it be a survey of Lutheran writers and how they have employed these themes. Rather, I see this essay as a task of discernment, of recognizing and apprehending what is common and recurrent in Lutheran ethical reflection.[3]

My second purpose is to reflect critically about the points at which the modern world challenges the tradition of Lutheran ethical reflection. These challenges sometimes reveal the weaknesses and lacunae of Lutheran ethics but at other times disclose unrecognized strengths. The final section of the paper will identify such challenges.

I take up these tasks with some sense of urgency because I believe Lutheranism as a living tradition is at risk. In another generation or two the Lutheran Church itself may be merged into a generic amalgam of declining American Protestant groups. This may occur because of their inability to transmit particular Protestant traditions to new generations, especially in the face of the rampant individualism of postmodern American culture. Mergers may disguise for a historical moment the underlying decay of the traditions. In the coming century there may be little or no distinctive Lutheran ethos for ethicists to describe. Ethicists, however, may compound the problem by doing their share to dissolve the ethos. They may so strongly exercise various "hermeneutics of suspicion" on the moral and ethical tradition that has been handed down that there will be neither enough interest nor confidence in it to sustain it. So I pursue these tasks with the heightened awareness that the Lutheran tradition may be at risk.

I begin with themes in personal ethics, then move to social ethics. The distinction continues to be useful because there is an irreducible personal dimension to moral agency that cannot be exhausted by institutional analysis or action.

The Christian's Calling in the World

The central principle of Lutheran ethics is identical with its central theological principle: justification by grace through faith on account of Christ. As George Forell so succinctly put it:

> [Martin] Luther said that justification is the basis for all Christian ethics. There is no Christian ethics apart from Christian people; and only people justified by faith are Christian people. It was Luther who insisted that the person precedes the act, that ethics is always the ethics of people, and that one cannot have moral acts apart from moral people.[4]

Or to quote another master of Lutheran ethics, Einar Billing:

> Whoever knows Luther, knows that his various thoughts do not lie alongside each other, like pearls in a string, held together only by common authority or perchance by a line of logical argument, but that they all, as tightly as petals of a rosebud, adhere to a common center, and radiate out like the rays of the sun from one glowing core, namely, the gospel of the forgiveness of sins.[5]

Christian morality, then, is response to the Christian Gospel. God in Christ offers the grace and mercy that justifies us mortal and sinful beings. We need not climb up some ladder of increasing righteousness to make ourselves worthy before God. Such a path is fruitless because none can stand on their own before God's demand. Attempts to do so lead either to frustration or a destructive spiritual pride. Rather, we are justified before God on account of Christ. We become saints before God not on account of any extraordinary obedience or even faith that we might offer but because of the extraordinary grace of God in Christ. We are called by God to be His own in Christ.

Such a powerful event, however, has a history; it is not a point in time suspended above and beyond a prior and succeeding history. God has long dealings with Israel and the church; God has long dealings with us.

This is another way of saying that Lutheran ethics is not simply Christomonist. The Gospel is preceded by the Law, by the workings of God as Creator, Lawgiver, Sustainer, and Judge. The God of the Old Testament is active in world history—as well as in our own personal history—before we meet the Christ of the Gospel. In fact, God's activity on behalf of mankind after the fall typifies the eventual advent of Christ, the Word made flesh.

Our first parents were created in God's own image and met and walked with Him. Even after the fall, God promises to overcome conflict, despair, and death. Not only does He enter into a new, covenantal relationship with fallen humanity, renewing the shattered image, but He also allows us to work here on earth and enter into positive, reciprocal relationships with one another despite sin. We are given both an eternal and a temporal destiny. We are given a meaningful story, the gift of a new, hopeful context for our obedient lives, one that yearns first for the hope of conversion and then for the revealed joy of God's people. We are meant not only for covenantal existence here, based on the shedding of Christ's blood for all people, but also for an eternal fellowship with God Himself.

Moreover, the covenantal existence offered us is not something we each must construct *de novo*. It is already anticipated in the structures of life in which we are embedded. Lutherans have called such structures "orders of creation" or "mandates" (Dietrich Bonhoeffer)[6] or "natural orders" (Forell)[7] or "places of responsibility" (Benne).[8] God works through these structures to provide moral contexts within which we can live.

God gives these structures moral direction, using many means to sustain their moral character. The standards for them are derived at times directly from the Decalogue, sometimes from a rational appropriation of the moral law, and sometimes from human practical experience or engagement with the world. Externally, they are guided by positive law, but at deeper levels, that positive law is often shaped by moral reason. This moral reason is finally a reflection of the Law "written on the heart" (Romans 2:15) that God has placed in every human soul. Thus non-Christians also have God-given capacities to discern the moral ordering of our common life.

Modern Lutheran ethics have recognized that these "natural orders" are not static. God's "Law of Creation,"[9] to use Gustaf Wingren's phrase, is dynamic. Older structures are reshaped in accordance with God's will, which both Christians and non-Christians try to discern in their own ways. These structures are shaped not only by God, they also are subject to the individual and corporate sins of humans, who can bend them away from God's intentions. They are battlefields upon which both God and Satan contend. They are arenas of blessing, conflict, and judgment. God's hidden hand works through them in mysterious and unrecognized ways.

Discerning God's Law in these structures is thus a great challenge for Christian ethics. We are called to reject those guidelines and practices that are directly contrary to God's Word and to affirm and work toward those that more adequately represent the divine purposes. This task is fraught with ambiguity. This, however, does not excuse us from making clear judgments when possible and maintaining a humble uncertainty when necessary.

The Law of God not only orders our common life (its political use), but it also serves as a teacher that convinces us of our sin and drives us to the Gospel of grace and mercy. In Lutheran terms, this is the "theological" use of the Law.

Lutherans have a realistic estimate of our life under the Law in relation to other humans, as well as our life under the Law in relation to God. Both relationships lead inexorably to a crisis of conscience that opens the way for the Gospel. In our common life we are buffeted by claims and obligations—behind which is God's Law—that divest us of our proud self-sufficiency or complacency. We know we are up against a great demand. This demand often comes to us through other human beings, but the sensitive conscience also examines itself before God. In the court of God we know, as Luther confessed, that we are all beggars.

Driven by life under the Law, Christians then receive the Gospel in their repentant hearts, and this brings the forgiveness of sins and affirmation of the new creation in Christ Jesus. Thus we are back to the center of the Christian life: justification by grace through faith on account of Christ. From this glowing core of God's extravagant love in Christ we move outward and forward in the Christian life.

Faith fastens in trust to the God who has offered such grace in Christ. It allows the love of God in Christ to permeate the soul and to bend the will outward to the neighbor. Indeed, in the "happy exchange" with Christ, our faithful hearts receive the righteousness of Christ. Our faith becomes active in love. This love expresses itself in deeds that follow spontaneously from faith and no longer from the compulsion of the Law. Such love is creative and dynamic. It goes beyond the Law in its affirmation that God's goodness is more than just "not bad," though this love does not violate the Law, respecting the third, regulative use. It "grasps the kind of hand that need holds out," to use the words of Joseph Sittler.[10] It is a love shaped by the engendering deed of God's love in Christ. It is self-giving and neighbor-regarding.

This agape love that moves from God-in-Christ through the Christian is initiatory; it does not wait on formal signs of distress to grasp the hand that need holds out. It is disinterested; it does not demand a return before it acts. It is extravagant; it does not parcel its efforts out in a *quid pro quo*. It is universal; it does not observe the limits that human love sets around its own in-group. It is biased toward the lost, the last, and the least, much like parents who lavish love on the needy child even while loving all their children equally. It invites mutuality; it does not keep the other dependent. It risks forgiveness; it is not bound to a strict reciprocity.

This heightened sense of both divine and human agape seems to differentiate Lutheran ethics from others. Without affirming the exaggerated separation drawn by Anders Nygren between eros and agape,[11] Lutherans seem to have such a high estimate of human agape because they have such an acute sense of God's agape in Christ. Reinhold Niebuhr, in a backhanded compliment, confirmed that observation when he remarked that

Lutheran ethics are so unworldly because they have such a profound notion of agape love.[12]

This emphasis on the transcendent character of agape love leads Lutheran ethics to a paradoxical view of agape's relation to mutual loves. The denial and affirmation of these loves reflect their denial and affirmation in the cross of Christ. Agape love can never be domesticated into principles and rules, however important these are for the moral life.

The whole dynamic of faith that fastens to the Gospel and love that is activated by this faith is illustrated in Luther's well-known formulation of the Christian life in "Treatise on Christian Liberty": "A Christian is a perfectly free lord of all, subject to none. A Christian is a perfectly dutiful servant of all, subject to all."[13] The Christian is freed by the Gospel from all striving for salvation even as he or she is sent to love the neighbor. The Christian life is seen as the response of obedient and grateful love to the Gospel.

It is important to note here that Lutherans see the whole process of salvation, including the ensuing sanctification, as the work of the Holy Spirit in their lives.[14] There is no room for boasting. The whole of the Christian life is a work of the Spirit.

I now return to the "places of responsibility" in which all humans are located. It is in those places that we are called by God to exercise our obedient love to the neighbor in response to the Gospel. If we are called by God through the Gospel to be eternally His, we are also called by God to help the neighbor in and through the places of responsibility we have been given. We are given both an eternal and a temporal destiny by God.

Luther enumerated three "orders" to which the Christian is called: family, state, and church. This number reflects a medieval context that did not differentiate family and economy.[15] Later Lutheran ethics recognizes four orders: marriage and family, work, public life (citizenship and voluntary associations), and church.[16]

As mentioned above, these places of responsibility are guided and sanctioned by positive law, cultural expectations, and, finally, by moral claims that are sometimes in tension with both positive law and cultural expectations. These places are also ambiguous because they can be both gifts—covenantal structures—sustained by God and curses twisted by sin and evil. Lutheran ethics maintains that these are the places in which all humans are given the obligation to live responsible lives. Moreover, Christians are to see them as divinely given callings in which to exercise their particular gifts for the sake of the neighbor.

Lutheran ethics thereby affirms that faith not only fastens to Christ for salvation but also discerns a deeper meaning in the ordinary structures of life. They are, despite all contrary abuse, blessings of God to be accepted with gratitude and joy. Further, they are the places in which we discern our special missions in life, our callings. They provide roles for Christians to play in the drama that God is unfolding. They provide the location for Christians to play out their temporal destinies.

Yet these structures and their demands are very worldly. Some of the demands are clearly helpful, but some are highly ambiguous. Some occupations and roles are even "out of bounds" for Christians. Those that are legitimate according to the Law press certain demands on the Christian. For example, we are obligated to a specific family and a specific occupation with all the prescribed roles that these places of responsibility demand. These demands are the way the world under the Law must come to terms with both finitude and sin. They are the work of the hidden God but also the work of sinful human beings under the sway of Satan.

While beholden to their particular responsibilities, Christians do not simply live up to the worldly demands of the callings; they also go beyond them. This is the dynamic work of love. The agape love that flows through the Christian creates a lively tension with worldly demands. Some demands are simply accepted and done with a joyful heart. Others are stretched intensively and extensively. The radical force of agape love leads to a restlessness about the world as it is. It summons the Christian to widen and deepen the "reach" of covenantal existence.[17] It awakens the Christian to the call of Christ to love others as He has loved us.

In attempting to state concretely what this lively obedience might look like, Lutherans have often turned to the Decalogue. Following their mentor Luther, they exposit the Decalogue not only in its negative formulation but also in its indeterminately positive thrust.[18] The call of love therefore does not lead to antinomianism; there is structure and form to the Christian life. Love is the leaven and salt that enriches these structures and forms without violating them.

When Christians "stretch" the worldly expectations of their roles in their places of responsibility, they often run into difficulties and/or resistance. There can be an excruciating gap between what the world demands or allows and the summons of Christian love. In these instances the Christian is conformed to the crucified Christ.[19] As Luther said, if Christians take their callings seriously, they will not have to seek the cross; it will find them. Love does not simply triumph in this world. Worldly success is not a guaranteed product of the Christian life; bearing the cross is more likely.

The theology of the cross permeates Christian existence in the world. It disallows the kind of optimism that suggests Christians can build the kingdom of God by their energy and will or even that they can discern clearly and confidently what "God is doing in the world." Such confidence is more Reformed than Lutheran.[20] Yet Christian obedience makes a difference in the world. It sustains and renews as God wills. To the eyes of faith, agape love is the scarlet thread that holds together the fabric of covenantal existence; without it the world would indeed unravel.

The theology of the cross likewise prevents undue optimism about our own sanctification. Although the Spirit imputes to us and indwells in us the righteousness of Christ, the Old Adam in us never dies in this life. We are sinners and saints all the days of our life on earth. We regress as well as progress. The struggle goes on.

This struggle throws us back on the mercy of Christ, which is new every morning. We are reminded again and again that our status before God depends on His grace in Christ, not on our own works. We are driven back to the promises of our Baptism and to the Table of the Lord for sustenance for our daily lives. Our hope in the steadfastness of God's mercy enables us to move forward into the future, confident that the paralyzing obstacles of our sinful existence can be overcome by a power beyond us.

Taken as a whole, our lives in the Spirit can show growth. In one of his more surprising sayings, Luther remarks:

> This life is not righteous, but growth in righteousness; it is not health, but healing; not being, but becoming; not rest, but exercise; we are not yet what we shall be, but we are growing toward it; the process is not yet finished, but it is going on; this is not the end, but it is the road; all does not yet gleam in glory, but all is being purified.[21]

This exposition of Christian life applies to all callings whether they operate in the private or public spheres. The personal and social are inextricably related. Husbands and wives in marriage, teachers in school, politicians in office, and pastors in the church are all summoned by God to work out their callings in those places. In so doing they transform ordinary places of responsibility into Christian callings.

THE CHURCH'S CALLING IN PUBLIC LIFE

If the above applies to the individual Christian's calling in his or her places of responsibility, the following pertains to the social or institutional relationships. The church as an institution has a calling in a world of institutions. As a corporate body it is called to relate to the corporate structures of the world. The church is and has a social ethic.

Clearly the Lutheran tradition has a particular way of construing the relation of the church to public life. Some scholars, such as Ernst Troeltsch[22] and, following his lead, Reinhold Niebuhr,[23] have condemned that particular way as cynical and defeatist, leading to a pallid quietism. But such a posture has not been true of the Lutheran tradition in America, especially as it has developed in this century. Lutheranism in America, surrounded by a heavily Calvinist ethos and fed by the Luther research of the Scandinavians, has not been so passive. Yet because of mainly the-ological themes that have shaped its tradition, it has related to the public world differently than the Reformed and Catholic tradi-tions. A number of scholars have called for a stronger Lutheran voice in the ongoing discussion of religion's role in public life.[24]

I contend that Lutheran social ethics does not lead in a spe-cific ideological direction, if that is taken to mean a fairly detailed blueprint for public policy. Rather, Lutheran ethics provides a framework for doing social ethics or public theology. It elaborates a set of theological assumptions that stipulates how the church and public life ought to be related. It does so not only for the sake of politics and society but also for the sake of the church's fidelity to its own biblically warranted mission in the world. What is legally permitted in our society—the direct and aggressive inter-vention of the church in political affairs—may well not be good for the church and its mission. Undue entanglement in politics can be the ruination of the church.

The Lutheran ethical tradition does, however, set a general direction for public policy. It tends toward "Christian realism," a general tendency that can be refracted in a number of different policy directions. Lutherans of various political persuasions share commitment to this framework.[25]

Four main themes constitute the Lutheran ethical tradition as it applies to public life. They are: (1) a sharp distinction between salvation offered by God in Christ and all human efforts; (2) a focused and austere doctrine of the church and its mission that follows from the first theme; (3) the twofold rule of God through Law and Gospel; and (4) a paradoxical view of human nature and history.[26]

Salvation versus Human Effort

I have stated a distinction as a contradiction, but overstate-ment often has a point. Particularly in the political sphere, humans are prone to claim salvific significance for their efforts at social and/or political transformation. The twentieth century, per-haps the bloodiest of all centuries, has been crammed with these attempts. When the God-man Jesus Christ is refused as Savior, the man-god in many different guises rushes in.

The good news of the Gospel is that God saves us through His gift of grace in Christ alone. Our salvation is sheer gift. We need do nothing but receive the gift with a repentant heart. This Lutheran insistence on a radical doctrine of grace puts all human efforts into proper perspective. They deal with penultimate attempts to improve the human condition, with relative goods and bads, not with salvation. This means that politics is desacral-ized and relativized, as are education and therapy. Salvation is through Christ, not through human political schemes or educa-tional or psychological efforts. Lutherans might appropriately speak of liberation ethics but never of liberation theology in the sense that revolutionary praxis is synonymous with salvation. This understanding of the Gospel provides a critical shield against the constant attempts in American Christianity to give redemptive significance to movements of social transformation.

The world has had enough experience of revolutionary change to obviate any claims that political or social "transforma-tion" leads to anything remotely resembling human fulfillment. Such a verdict is supported by human observation and experi-ence. But for religious people to make those claims is especially baffling. The Lutheran vision cuts off such claims for the sake of the radicality and universality of the Gospel. The radicality of the Gospel insists that salvation is pure gift; we do not earn it. If we do not recognize that salvation is a pure gift of God, we dishonor God, who gave His Son in the unique and decisive saving act. When we claim an active part in the drama of salvation, we are implying that God's action in Christ is not good enough. Some-thing else, presumably our virtuous action, must be added.

The universality of the Gospel is compromised if we fail to distinguish sharply between God's saving act in Christ and all human efforts at improving the world. In any overt or covert claim for human effort as a constitutive part of our salvation there are always those on the right side of the struggle and those on the wrong. Some are saved and some are damned, not because of their faith or lack of faith in God's work in Christ but because they either are or are not participants in the group or process that claims to be bringing redemption. Their salvation is made dependent on which side they find themselves.

The picture is clear: The claims of the man-god always exclude; the Gospel, however, does not. All humans, regardless of their location along the world's fault lines, are equidistant from and equally near the grace of God in Christ.

The New Testament Gospel of the suffering God who abjured all worldly power and all worldly group identification rules out schemes that compromise the radicality and universality of the Gospel. The cross of Christ freed the Gospel from enmeshment in all human efforts to save the world. No one was with Christ on the cross to die for our sins. Or, viewed differently, everyone was with Christ on the cross but only as passive inhabitants of His righteous and suffering person.

When we are freed from the need to look for salvation in human schemes, our eyes should be clearer to make the very important distinctions between the relatively good and the relatively bad in the realm of human action. Liberated from the worry about our salvation, we can turn unobsessively to the task of building a better world, not by prideful claims of transformation but by determined yet humble attempts to take firm steps for the better.

The Purpose of the Church

If the most important event that ever happened in human history is the event of Christ, particularly His cross and resurrection, then the essential and unique mission of the church is its calling by God to proclaim the Gospel in Word and Sacrament. In the Lutheran vision, the Gospel of Christ is the church's treasure. The church is the earthen vessel whose sacred obligation it is to take the Gospel to every nook and cranny of the world. Its calling is to proclaim the Gospel and to gather a people around that Gospel, forming them through the Spirit into the body of Christ.

No other community has that calling; no other will promote the Gospel if the church fails in its task. So the church must take with utmost seriousness the terrible simplicity of its task. Of course it must be engaged in deeds of charity, and it must be concerned with justice. Of course it must involve itself in many other activities—financial, administrative, liturgical, and educational. Of course it must witness in the public sphere. But the church is not primarily a political actor, a social transformer, or an aggressive interest group. If it acts primarily as one of these, it is identified and treated as one more contentious worldly group. Furthermore, it loses its own integrity or reason for being.

The church must attend to its own core vision by proclaiming it and attempting to be faithful to it through its practices. (Stanley Hauerwas is at least partially correct when he argues that the church does not have a social ethic; it *is* a social ethic.[27]) The church cannot ensure that its Gospel vision will prevail in human hearts; only the Holy Spirit can capture those hearts for the Gospel.

At the very center of this core vision is the event of Jesus as the Christ. Surrounding it is the biblical and early church's witness to the events of Jesus' life, death, and resurrection. This apostolic witness is both a record and an interpretation of that revelatory event. It incorporates not only the "glowing core" of God's justification of sinners on account of Christ but also the key teaching without which the Gospel makes little or no sense. The Old Testament background, the doctrine of the Trinity, the eschatological tension between the Christ event and the coming kingdom, and the calling of the church and individual Christians to their mission in the world are all essential elements in this core vision. These are well summarized in the ecumenical creeds.

This core vision ought to be held with clarity and confidence by the church. Its main elements are stable through time, though they must be interpreted afresh for each new generation. This core makes up the great tradition that can be traced from the time of the apostles to the present day. Its main tenets are not negotiable if the Christian faith is to remain the Christian faith.

Closely related to this central religious core is the central moral vision of the Christian faith. The Decalogue, the calling of all Christians to faith active in love and justice, the preciousness of all created life redeemed by Christ, and the covenantal context of God's creation (which includes the special covenant of man and woman in marriage) constitute the moral core of the Christian vision. They, too, are constant through time, though they must be applied creatively to each new historical situation. It is difficult to imagine authentic Christian identity without them.

The next concentric circle away from this inner orb includes the more speculative theological reflections of the church, including its social teachings. This band represents the efforts of the church to apply its religious and moral vision to the dynamic world around it. These efforts entail significant steps in moving from the core vision to its application to specific problems. Each steps means an increasing chance for disagreement among Christians who hold their core vision in common. Theological reflection on society, the arts, science, and so on, and social teaching on economics, politics, and society are examples of this extension of Christian meaning. Ventures in this direction are important in the life of the church, but unanimity on them is highly unlikely. The church needs to allow a good deal of latitude for disagreement and plurality of opinions. These extensions should not conflict with the core vision itself.

Finally, there is a concentric circle that represents the church's posture on specific public policy issues. Such specific commitments on the part of the church should generally be quite infrequent. In special times with regard to special issues, the church may have to stand for or against particular policies. In normal times, however, it is important for the church not to commit to particular policies because there are many other agencies through which Christians can exert their influence. Further, there is much difference of opinion among intelligent Christians of goodwill on such specific policies.

It is essential that the church be able to distinguish these different circles or levels of discourse. It must hold their contents with differing degrees of authority and commitment. The central religious and moral core ought to be held with clarity, confidence, and steadfastness. It has the highest degree of authority and consensus in the church. The outer circles are much more susceptible to genuine and permissible disagreement. In moving toward the outer circles, the church has less and less warrant and knowledge for pronouncing or acting upon its judgments. (Again, there are exceptions. If a social practice is glaringly in opposition to the Christian religious and moral core, the church must speak and act, though there still would be discussion of *how* to do so.)

The American Lutheran tradition has been quite admirable in distinguishing these levels of authority. It has been a refreshing alternative to the American churches on both the left and the right that conflate the levels into one or collapse the periphery into the core. The liberal churches are often confused or permissive about the core but dogmatic about the periphery. Denial of the decisiveness and uniqueness of Jesus as the Christ creates little alarm while dissent on "inclusive language" can bring ostracism. Current secular ideologies play the functional equivalent of the core. No longer clear or confident about their central reason for being, such religious groups turn to secular sources for their identity.

Activist conservative churches are more likely to elevate their conservative political commitments to the level of dogma. They often engage in "straight-line" thinking. They hold their religious and political commitments with equal intensity and are thus as likely as their liberal compatriots to exclude persons from the "circle of faith" on the basis of their political persuasion. In either case, the integrity of the church and its mission is threatened along with the radicality and universality of the Gospel.

THE TWOFOLD RULE OF GOD

Perhaps the most difficult element in Lutheran social ethics, yet one of the most important, is the doctrine of the twofold rule of God, sometimes called the "two kingdoms" doctrine. This doctrine has also been the most vulnerable to distortion. Karl Barth was the first to call this Lutheran teaching "the two-kingdoms doctrine," and he was not paying a compliment to the Lutheran tradition. Rather, he was sharply criticizing those Lutherans in the 1930s who had used Lutheranism's doctrine of the twofold rule of God to justify Adolph Hitler and National Socialism.[28] Actually, Barth was criticizing the misuse of the teaching.

This teaching is misused when it is interpreted dualistically instead of being seen as a highly dialectical and paradoxical view of God's twofold rule. In a dualistic model, which is a Lutheran heresy, there are two completely separate spheres, one having to do with earthly society and the other having to do with the salvation of our souls. Moreover, this dualism is often spatial: The secular world and the world of the church are two separate realities. The secular world becomes autonomous, running according to its own principles and rules, and the Christian must simply submit to them. The church preaches the Gospel, which then affects only the inner souls of Christians and perhaps their intimate relationships. As one Lutheran jurist put it, the issues of public life "should remain untouched by the proclamation of the Gospel, completely untouched."[29]

Such a dualistic approach was used to argue that Christians as Christian had no grounds for resisting tyrannical governments, be they of Hitler, Joseph Stalin, Auguste Pinochet, or John Vorster. This led to the infamous political quietism that Lutherans have sometimes fostered. As with all heresies, this dualistic approach has an element of truth in it, but it is so magnified that it pushes out the other elements that make it a genuinely useful doctrine.

The doctrine of the twofold rule of God is more than useful, however. It is deeply biblical and Christian and not a Lutheran oddity. In Romans 5, Paul writes of the two aeons: the new era that Christ is bringing into the world and the old aeon that is under the rule of Law and sin. The same eschatological tension is present in other biblical sources. The new order of Christ is in tension with the old order, yet Christians must live in both. Jesus said we must give Caesar what is his and God what is God's (Matthew 22:21). There is a duality but not a dualism at the heart of the Christian vision. It cannot be flattened into one dimension. We are caught in two realities that must be taken seriously. Carl Braaten puts the essence of the doctrine succinctly:

> This doctrine of the two kingdoms marks out the iden-
> tity of the church within the global horizon of the poli-
> tics of God and the divine governance of the world. This
> doctrine draws a distinction between the two ways of
> God's working in the world, two strategies that God uses
> to deal with the powers of evil and the reality of sin, two
> approaches to human beings, to mobilize them for active
> cooperation in two distinctly different kinds of institu-
> tions. One is created as an instrument of governance
> seeking justice through the administration of law and
> the preservation of order, and the other as an instru-
> ment of the Gospel and its sacraments announcing and
> mediating an ultimate and everlasting salvation which
> only Christ can give in an act of unconditional love and
> personal sacrifice.[30]

This biblical and Christian perspective arose when the king-dom expected by the followers of Jesus did not come. The king-dom had come in Jesus—the preacher had become the preached—but the full realization of what was announced and experienced in the Christ event did not take place. Nevertheless, Christians believed that the world they were given to live in and to follow Christ in was not abandoned by God. The Old Testament witness to God's creating, sustaining, and judging activities was not discarded. Instead, it was affirmed in the face of heresies that tried to split the Creator from the Redeemer God.

Surely the God who in Jesus suffered on a cross and died for all and who rose again approaches humans differently in the Gospel than in their worldly life in society. There is a twofoldness in God's action in the world, a twofoldness that both generates and reflects a real tension in the individual and corporate lives of

Christians. All major Christian religious traditions recognize in some fashion this tension between Christ and the ongoing societal necessities of the world. They are aware that following Christ and living in the world is no easy task. Those who are unaware of that understand neither Christ nor the world.

Christian traditions, however, handle this tension in very different ways. H. Richard Niebuhr's *Christ and Culture* is a classic analysis of these differences. The "Christ against culture" (sectarian) tradition escapes the tension by withdrawing from the world. The classic "Christ above culture" (Roman Catholic) tradition aims to manage the tension by forging Christ and culture into a grand synthesis presided over by the church. The "Christ transforming culture" (Reformed) tradition seeks to convert the culture toward the will of God as it is discerned by the church and carried out by its members. The "Christ of culture" (liberal religion) tradition escapes the tension by absorbing Christ into the enlightened culture of the day.[31]

The "Christ and culture in paradox" (Lutheran) tradition handles the tension in a paradoxical way through its teaching on the twofold rule of God. It is not the tension of Christ and culture that is contentious but how that tension is handled. Of the five possible ways to manage it suggested by Niebuhr, the Lutheran way comes closest to living with an unresolved tension. The other traditions move more vigorously toward resolution, which can often be problematic and perhaps unbiblical.

In the Lutheran ethical view, Christians live in two realities at the same time. Each reality is under the governance of God but in sharply different ways. God governs the "kingdom of the left" with the Law and the "kingdom of the right" with the Gospel. God's aim in both modes of rule is the same—to overcome evil and recall the disobedient creation to Himself—but God uses different means in each "kingdom."

The twofold rule of God is closely related to a Lutheran understanding of Law and Gospel. If the Law and Gospel are not accorded their proper meaning and functions, either the Law is made into the Gospel or the Gospel made into the Law. In the former, the demands and operation of the Law are viewed as redemptive, which makes Christ unnecessary. In the latter, the extravagant love revealed in the Gospel becomes a guiding principle for ordering life in the rough and tumble of this world. In this case little account is taken of the power of sin and evil in the world, and society becomes vulnerable to the most willful agencies of evil. Such an approach dishonors God the Creator.

Both pitfalls are common in American Christianity. Human efforts are often made de facto substitutes for the liberating power of the Gospel (making the Law into the Gospel) and the radical love revealed in the Gospel is often used as a direct principle for commending public policy (making the Gospel into the Law). The former secularizes the Gospel while the latter sentimentalizes it.

While the two ways that God rules the world must be clearly distinguished (for sake of both the Gospel and the Law), they are not finally separated. God the Creator and God the Redeemer are not separate deities. Likewise, the two ways that God reigns are not separate spatially or existentially; they interact in creative ways. A tentative duality does not lead to a final dualism. There are three ways in which the twofold rule of God comes together creatively in this world.

The first way is in the calling of each Christian person as elaborated above. As faith, love, and hope are kindled by the Spirit in the hearts of Christians, they will practice those virtues within and through the worldly callings they have been given. These Spirit-driven virtues will affect the responsible roles Christians have as family members, workers, citizens, and church members. They will transform these worldly responsibilities into authentic Christian callings. God's creative love enters the world through the exercise of Christian vocation.

Christian virtue will be a leaven that works creatively on the hard demands of worldly life. It is the creative task of each Christian to find the fitting deed between an adventureless acceptance of the world as it is and an irresponsible desire to replace it with some utopian scheme. Insofar as that deed is truly fitting, it will cooperate with God's dynamic law of creation.

Second, in corresponding fashion, the church is a place where the twofold rule of God is conjoined. It is called to proclaim the whole Word of God—both Gospel and Law. The church's proper work, of course, is to prolaim the Gospel, but the church is also responsible for addressing the world according to God's Law. Because the church operates in society only with the power of the Word, the powers it claims are thoroughly in the realm of persuasion, not coercion.

The church is called to apply the dynamic Law of God to all the structures of social life. The radical love expressed in the Gospel is relevant, at least indirectly, to the affairs of the world, just as Christian virtues are relevant to the lives of individual Christians in their callings. These insights are to be applied vigorously and realistically, avoiding both cynicism and sentimentalism. The Gospel is relevant to the world's affairs in a paradoxical fashion. It constantly judges whatever is achieved in the world and is a constant lure to higher achievement. It is always "out in front," as is God's eschatological future, and cannot be captured or legislated in the present. The person who fully expressed this radical Gospel love was crucified; the Gospel ethic does not fit smoothly into the world.

Finally, it is in God's total action in the world that we confess the conjoining of the two ways He reigns. The actions of God the Creator and God the Redeemer cannot finally be separate. Yet in this world even the eyes of faith cannot perceive how this is so. Short of the eschaton, God's rule is of a twofold nature. We affirm this with humility and openness, for our human constructs cannot hold God hostage. Signs of God's ongoing redemption may indeed erupt spontaneously amid worldly affairs. Although they may not fully manifest the final kingdom of God, they may be anticipations of the eternal *shalom* for which the whole world strains. Yet they must be consistent with the only clear anticipation we have of that kingdom, Jesus as the Christ.[32]

The Paradox of Human Nature and History

"Whatever your heart fastens to, that is your god," said Luther. From the viewpoint of Lutheran theological ethics, humans are irretrievably committed to finding something other than God on which to fasten their hearts. This inescapable sin, however, is not so simple. We do not fasten to the unalluring and worthless things of the world but to what really tempts us. The highest temptation is devotion to ourselves. Obsessed with ourselves, we make ourselves the center of the universe. This crowds out everything else except what will feed the image of ourselves we have concocted. Whether our obsession be that of willful assertion or self-pitying negation, it mocks the divine command "to love the Lord your God with all your heart, mind and soul." We love ourselves or what gives us importance and immortality.

None are good. All human actions are tainted with the effect of our sin. Christians can never be completely free of the old Adam in this life. This Augustinian view of human nature extends to human action in society. Human sin is particularly magnified and unrestrained in the life and action of groups.

Yet humans are not dirt. Even in their fallen state they possess qualities of being created in the image of God. The created self longs for wholeness and completion, though it cannot heal or complete itself. The created self has capacities for moral reason, which Luther called "civil righteousness." Humans have capacities for justice.

Moreover, humans never lose their dignity in God's eyes. They are beloved for what God has made them to be in Christ, not what they have made of themselves. They are infinitely valuable because they have been given a destiny in their creation and have been redeemed by the work of Christ. They can refuse that destiny and that redemption, but they can never lose the "alien dignity" that creation and redemption bestow on them.

Humans find themselves in a paradoxical predicament. Created and redeemed by God, they are "exalted individuals."[33] They have a capacity for freedom, love, and justice. Yet they use their freedom to fasten to lesser things, creating a hell for themselves, other human beings, and the world around them. They are a paradox of good and evil, manufacturing idols of the good things they are given. And they cannot solve this predicament on their own.

This paradox of human nature creates the paradox of human history. "History cumulates, rather than solves, the essential problems of human existence," wrote Niebuhr.[34] The fulfillment and perfection of history are not ours to grasp; we cannot be gods in history. Great evil is done by those who try to complete history by their own powers.

Rather, it is up to God to bring history to an end (its *finis*) and to fulfill its purpose (its *telos*). God has given us an anticipation of the kingdom in Christ and will bring it to fullness in His own time and by His own will. We are in an interim time of struggle between Christ's first and second coming.

Given this scenario, we are freed from trying to manage history according to great schemes. Instead, we must strive for relative gains and wait on God. We must work for reform without cynicism's paralysis or idealism's false hope. The Lutheran vision leads to a nonutopian view of history that is not cynical. It expects neither too much nor too little of history.

The "Lutheran attitude" reflected in these four main themes provides a wholesome corrective to an American Christianity that is all too prone to identify promising human achievements as the salvation of God, to make the church into anything but the proclaimer of the Gospel, to apply directly the "Gospel ethic" to the power struggles of the world, and to hope for the intractabilities of individual and corporate sin to be completely overcome by some sanctified human effort.

Contemporary Challenges

The perennial themes I have elaborated provide Lutheranism with a coherent and persuasive account of Christian ethics in both its personal and social dimensions. As these themes engage the modern world, they meet challenges that demand serious reflection and, in some cases, reconstruction. By way of conclusion I examine three clusters of challenges: theological, ecclesiological, and epistemological. I will only sketch the outlines of what are enormous and complex challenges.

THEOLOGICAL

A persisting tendency in Lutheran ethics is to reduce the whole of ethical life to the motivation touched off by justification. Dazzled as they are by the wonder and profundity of God's justifying grace in Christ, Lutherans are tempted to think that the only really interesting ethical question is the motivational one. After being affirmed and reconciled in Christ, Christians are powerfully motivated to live the life of love.

The theological problem revealed here is a kind of a soteriological reductionism that downplays the role of the First and Third Persons of the Trinity. The ethical weakness that ensues is one of lack of ethical substance. The Gospel forgives and motivates but from what and to do what? Lutherans have shied away from contemporary explications of the Decalogue that would give Old Testament content to the ethical life. Love becomes both a permissive affirmation of any behavior and a rather amorphous serving of the neighbor. Without a richer notion of life in community (covenantal existence) that comes from our Jewish roots, Lutheran ethics does not really know what is "good for the neighbor."[35] We tend to beg the question. Likewise, without a richer doctrine of creation, we do not know what is "good for the creation." A more fulsome theological explication of the First Article will aid in giving more content to an ecological ethic.[36]

We Lutherans also tend to have an undeveloped doctrine of the Spirit in the Christian life on the other side of justification. We seem to be uninterested in the holiness or righteousness that is given to us in the Spirit. Recent Finnish Luther research has argued that Luther had a strong notion of the actual living Christ being infused by the Spirit into the Christian, leading to some notion of divinization. Such a line of argument has ethical implications. Perhaps more can be said about such "sanctification" than Lutherans have been willing to say. Certainly there is a powerful challenge to say more about the nature of the Christian life, whether shaped by the Decalogue and/or the Spirit.

Like other mainstream Protestants, Lutherans have relied on the general culture to do their work for them. The general Protestant Ethic had established notions of marriage and sexual ethics, the calling, and humane values of justice and civility. But that established culture has been fractured by the new world that surrounds us. Lutherans need a more specific notion of the Christian life if they are to respond to this chaotic world. They cannot do that by relying solely on justification. Lutheran ethics will have to be more trinitarian.

ECCLESIOLOGICAL

Lutherans are debating whether the church is a constitutive dimension of the Gospel. Traditionally the Word is proclaimed from "outside us" and "over against the church." While this emphasis on the transcendence of the Word over all institutional forms is salutary in many ways, it also leads to an undeveloped notion of the church.

Thus Lutherans have been weak in developing a notion of the church as "a community of character." We have left that to our sectarian and Catholic comrades. But we need to get serious about this issue. Can Lutherans talk about the church as a living tradition that forms moral virtues, or does such talk threaten the spontaneous love that flows "unmotivated" from justification? What is the relation between agape and virtue? Are they antithetical? If they are, can Lutheranism ever talk persuasively about Christian virtue?[37]

Further, can Lutheran ethics really talk about a decision-making process without questioning the "ecstatic" notion of motivation with which they have operated for so long? Will such attention to weighing relative goods and bads clash with the spontaneity of love with which we have been enamored? Will we be able to give ethical dignity to anguished decisions? How does a community of faith sustain and support such ethical necessities?[38]

This ecclesiological underdevelopment also relates to social ethics. Does Lutheranism have any received body of social teachings? I have argued above that Lutheranism provides an important framework for social ethics and that it leads toward a form of "Christian realism." But can we be more specific about this "Christian realism"?

It has often been remarked that Lutheran social teachings are thin compared with Catholic social doctrine. We simply don't have much of an inheritance. A good deal of this has to do with confusion about authority within the Lutheran churches. The sixteenth-century confessions have little authoritative social doctrine. Our contemporary Lutheran churches claim little authority for their social teaching. Indeed, with each new church merger, what little authority achieved in the past is jettisoned as the church tries again to re-invent social doctrine. Even when it is able to make social statements, it is unclear how much authority such documents indeed carry.[39] This confusion about the authority of Lutheran social teaching simply reflects the larger problem of authority for the Lutheran churches.

A more robust trinitarian ethic as well as a more developed ecclesiology may together help to address this problem of authority. Further, such an approach may strengthen the motivation for Christians in the body of Christ to become a "people," a counter-culture that implants in its members a comprehensive vision of life out of which they live their whole lives.[40]

EPISTEMOLOGICAL

This challenge emerges globally with the severe questioning directed at Enlightenment claims for autonomous reason, reason with a capital *R*. The Enlightenment project lifted up universal, autonomous reason as the way to Goodness, Truth, and Beauty. But as Western people have become more and more aware of the historical conditionedness of all epistemological claims, such an elevated notion of reason has been dramatically diminished. Indeed, autonomous reason claims less and less substantive meaning for itself and has become more and more procedural in character. The earlier claims of autonomous reason have also been challenged by the masters of suspicion—Sigmund Freud, Karl Marx, and Friedrich Nietzsche—and by their intellectual descendants—feminists and multiculturalists.

This dethroning of reason has interesting consequences for Lutheran ethics, which have always had a high regard for reason when it comes to ascertaining the secular values of truth and justice. Luther had a good deal of confidence in practical moral reason. Immanuel Kant took him one further and made reason the only trustworthy source of moral guidance. But were the guiding norms attributed to moral reason more an unrecognized vestige of the surrounding Christian culture than the products of that reason itself? Can reason play such a constructive role in the Lutheran ethics of the future? Or are the historicist postliberals right in their claim that reason is simply an instrument that operates within traditions?

But reason has not been the only target of the various forms of the "hermeneutic of suspicion." The Lutheran tradition itself has become an object of critical scrutiny, as have other religious traditions. Feminists, liberationists, and multiculturalists have all discerned the biases of the "oppressor" in the theological and ethical formulations of these traditions. How far do these suspicions reach? Into the institutional forms that are the external accoutrements of the tradition? Into the traditional social and moral teachings of the church? Into the core itself? How far can these suspicions be taken before the tradition itself is either dissolved or divided? Can those who bear the suspicions also be constructive? Is there a *yes* to go with the *no*? Or are we left with a limp *maybe*, an attitude upon which it is difficult to preserve or renew a tradition?

I end where I began. Lutheran ethics needs a Lutheran ethos upon which to reflect. A Lutheran ethos needs a living tradition to form it. A living Lutheran tradition needs the Holy Spirit to keep it living. The promise of Lutheran ethics depends on how the above challenges are met, but it depends far more on whether the Spirit continues to bless the Lutheran Church with life and power.

NOTES

1. Alasdair MacIntyre, *After Virtue* (South Bend, Ind.: University of Notre Dame Press, 1981), 207.

2. This definition of ethics identifies ethics as a second-order intellectual practice. It implies that ethics (the theoretical activity) has a moral ethos (the practical, lived dimension of moral existence) upon which to reflect. Its major emphasis is reflection on a way of life, though it also takes up specific issues in light of this way of life. This manner of defining ethics is distinguished from more rationalist and deductive ways of construing ethics. They are located in a living tradition. Further, it is important to note that the perennial themes that I will be delineating emerge from an American Lutheran ethos, though there would be much overlap with the themes from other Lutheran communities around the world. But there are Lutheran communities both in the United States and in the world that approach moral existence from a different angle than will be represented in this essay.

3. I have used "Lutheran tradition" in a way that needs clarification. The themes I will elaborate are drawn from what I consider to be the "dominant" or "normative" ethics of the major Lutheran churches of the United States. These ethics drew on the classic traditions of European Lutheranism but refracted them through an American context much affected by other Christian traditions and by our peculiar American experience. These North American traditions contained and contain many "minority voices" within them. One could catalogue the particular perspectives of smaller American Lutheran churches—the American Evangelical Lutheran Church, the Suomi Synod, etc.—as well as strong voices of individual theologians who did not easily fit the classical mode—those of Joseph Sittler and A. D. Mattson come to mind. In recent times "minority voices" also include African American and feminist perspectives. But I have chosen not to delve into these minority perspectives in this essay, partly because of space and partly because of my understanding of my task, which is to elucidate the dominant themes carried officially by the major Lutheran church bodies of North America. These bodies include the predecessor bodies of the Evangelical Lutheran Church in America, as well as the ELCA itself. Indeed, the crucial ELCA document "The Church in Society:

A Lutheran Perspective" (1989) clearly manifests many of the
themes that I will identify in this essay.

4. George Forell, *Faith Active in Love* (Minneapolis: Augsburg, 1954),
84.

5. Einar Billing, *Our Calling*, trans. Conrad Bergendoff (Rock Island,
Ill.: Augustana Book Concern, 1951), 7.

6. Dietrich Bonhoeffer, *Ethics*, trans. N. H. Smith, ed. Eberhard
Bethge (New York: Macmillan, 1955), 73ff.

7. Forell, *Faith Active in Love*, 112ff.

8. Robert Benne, *Ordinary Saints: An Introduction to the Christian
Life* (Minneapolis: Fortress, 1988), 69ff.

9. Gustaf Wingren, *Creation and Law* (London: Oliver & Boyd, 1961).

10. Joseph Sittler, *The Structure of Christian Ethics* (Baton Rouge:
Louisiana State University Press, 1958), 76.

11. Anders Nygren, *Agape and Eros* (London: SPCK, 1932).

12. Reinhold Niebuhr, *The Nature and Destiny of Man* (New York:
Scribner's Sons, 1941), 1:220. Niebuhr was reflecting on what he
termed "Lutheran quietism." He notes that Lutheranism has both a
profound estimation of human sinfulness and divine grace. Both,
he asserts, fit together. The miserable condition of humans must
be addressed by a radical divine grace. This grace he compares to a
peak that is so high and glorious that it makes foothills (the relative distinctions so important to political judgments and responsibilities) seem flat and undifferentiated. Thus, he claims, Lutherans
tend to bask in the wonder of grace and ignore political responsibilities. Niebuhr contrasts this with what he calls the "more superficial" doctrines of sin and grace of British and American Protestant Christianity, which, ironically lead to more activism in the
political sphere.

13. John Dillenberger, ed., *Martin Luther* (New York: Anchor Books,
1961), 53.

14. Forell, *Faith Active in Love*, 86.

15. Forell, *Faith Active in Love*, 122ff.

16. Bonhoeffer, *Ethics*, 73; and Benne, *Ordinary Saints*, 69.

17. I realize this construal of the work of love seems to give it a "liberal" or "progressive" bias. But that is not necessarily the case.
When the structures of "covenantal existence" are being damaged
by permissiveness or lack of realism about human motives and
behavior, love may in fact adapt more "conservative" strategies to
help the neighbor. The main point is that love is always asking the

question: Which of my actions will bring good to the neighbor? The answer to that question does not always lead toward more "liberal" or "open" attitudes and actions.

18. Luther expositied the Decalogue in both the Small and Large Catechisms as a guide to the Christian life. George Forell, in his durable *Ethics of Decision* (Philadelphia: Fortress, 1955), follows a similar path.

19. Bonhoeffer is particularly instructive in elaborating this notion of "conformation" with Christ. The Christian is conformed to Christ incarnate, crucified, and resurrected. See Bonhoeffer, *Ethics*, 17ff.

20. Billing is particularly interesting on this point. He argues that the Lutheran idea of the calling is concretely focused on daily duties. We live out our callings with the hope that they will contribute to God's reign. "We can never foresee the results of our acts, least of all when the goal is the Kingdom of God. To maintain that our feeble deeds do serve this infinite goal is and remains a matter of faith. Our day's work lies ahead of us. It seems small and inconsequential. But God who gave it to us must also know its value, so go to it!" (*Our Calling*, 26).

21. Luther, "Defense and Explanation of All the Articles (1521)," LW 32:24.

22. Ernst Troeltsch, *The Social Teaching of the Christian Churches* (New York: Harper Torchbooks, 1960), 2:569–76.

23. Niebuhr, *Nature and Destiny of Man*, 1:184–98.

24. Foremost among them is Mark Noll, "The Lutheran Difference," *First Things* (February 1992): 31–40.

25. The social ethics of the Lutheran Church in America, as articulated in its social statements, tended in a mildly left-of-center political direction, though it is interesting that its "Peace and Politics" statement was the only mainstream church statement that morally legitimated a deterrence-based nuclear ethic. William Lazareth, George Forell, and Richard Niebanck, whose theological counsel was formative in those documents, were political liberals. Right-of-center social ethics are more difficult to find in official Lutheran statements but are well represented in the writings of individual Lutherans such as Meilaender, Neuhaus (before his conversion to Catholicism), Nuechterlein, and Benne.

26. These four themes are drawn from my reading of Lutheran social statements, from the suggestions made by a large number of Lutherans who were asked to enumerate key Lutheran themes by the ELCA Division for Church in Society, and from the American Lutheran ethical writing of Forell and Lazareth in particular. All

these, it seems, have been shaped by the dynamic portrayal of Lutheran social ethics manifested in Scandinavian writers such as Aulén, Billing, and Wingren and German writers such as Bonhoeffer and Thielicke.

27. Stanley Hauerwas, *The Peaceable Kingdom* (South Bend, Ind.: Notre Dame University Press, 1983), 99ff.

28. As claimed by Carl Braaten, *Principles of Lutheran Theology* (Philadelphia: Fortress, 1983), 124.

29. Braaten, *Principles of Lutheran Theology*, 124.

30. Braaten, *Principles of Lutheran Theology*, 135.

31. H. Richard Niebuhr, *Christ and Culture* (New York: Harper & Brothers, 1956).

32. I offer these preceding paragraphs as counterevidence to the criticism made by some scholars that my presentation of Lutheran theology leads to undue social conservatism. I believe I have argued in this entire essay that worldly institutions and practices are under constant judgment by both the Law and the Gospel. Both Law and Gospel prod Christians not to conform to the world as it is but to work incessantly for a better one. Therefore I cannot see how the theology I elaborated has intrinsically conservative implications. It is more likely that we disagree on how we *employ* these basic theological themes than on the themes themselves. Our argument may be one less in principle than in application. The employment of theological principles will be affected by one's political and philosophical orientation, as well as one's situation in life, and I certainly admit to differences among Lutheran writers.

33. The concepts of "exalted individual" and "destiny" are developed by Glenn Tinder, *The Political Meaning of Christianity* (Baton Rouge: Louisiana State University Press, 1989), 19ff. Tinder's key categories are modern articulations of Reformation ideas.

34. Niebuhr, *Nature and Destiny of Man*, 2:318.

35. This weakness is being addressed in this volume by Reinhard Hütter, whose essay on the commandments in the Christian life is a salutary step forward. See "The Twofold Center of Lutheran Ethics," in *The Promise of Lutheran Ethics*, ed. Karen L. Bloomquiest and John R. Stumme (Minneapolis: Augsburg Fortress, 1998).

36. Larry Rasmussen has dealt constructively with this issue in *Earth Community, Earth Ethics* (Maryknoll: Orbis, 1996). Gilbert Meilaender, another leading Lutheran ethicist, has employed a rich

understanding of a theology of creation in *Bio-Ethics: A Primer for Christians* (Grand Rapids: Eerdmans, 1996).

37. Among Lutheran ethicists, Martha Stortz develops a strong link between religious practice and moral formation. In doing so, she goes around Lutheranism to Luther himself, who evidently saw certain Christian practices as contributing to moral virtue. See also the important article by David Yeago, "The Promise of God and the Desires of our Hearts," *Lutheran Forum* (Pentecost 1996): 21–30.

38. It is pleasing to note that Lutherans have grappled with the challenge of ethical decision-making. See James Childs, *Faith, Formation, and Decision* (Minneapolis: Fortress, 1991), and Paul Jersild, *Making Moral Decisions* (Minneapolis: Fortress, 1990).

39. James Childs engages the problem of moral authority in his book mentioned in n38.

40. A number of Lutherans are writing on the relation of ecclesiology to ethics. Among the most important are Reinhard Hütter, "Ecclesial Ethics, The Church's Vocation and Paraclesis," *Pro Ecclesia* (Fall 1993): 433–52; "The Church as Public: Dogma, Practice, and the Holy Spirit," *Pro Ecclesia* (Summer 1994): 334–61; and David Yeago, "Messiah's People: The Culture of the Church in the Midst of the Nations," *Pro Ecclesia* (Spring 1997): 146–71.

THE PARADOXICAL VISION

A LUTHERAN NUDGE FOR PUBLIC THEOLOGY

The world is awash with the dynamic and sometimes dangerous interactions of organized religion with its surrounding
society. This worldwide phenomenon should not be of great surprise to informed observers of religion because it is obvious that
the great religions have comprehensive visions of life that have
public, not only private, relevance. Those religions are currently
expressing their visions, some of them with increasing vehemence.

All this "revolting religion," as one of my students once put
it to describe the Reformation, is still very much with us, much to
the surprise of those partisans of Enlightenment secularism who
have had so much influence among Western elites. The Enlightenment project expected religion to be privatized, marginalized,
and finally made to wither away as a publicly relevant enterprise.
Reason and science would bring forth a progressive world thank-
fully sanitized of religion. This bias has led to a peculiar blindness
on the part of that elite to the power and influence of religion,
even when it is confronted by rising tides of Islamic revival.

Originally published in *Pro Ecclesia*, vol. IV, no. 2 (Spring 1995).
Amended and reprinted with permission.

Obviously, this expected disappearance of religion as a publicly relevant undertaking has not happened. Humans are meaning-seeking creatures who will in one way or another search for transcendent truths and values that can guide private and public life. If classic religions do not provide such meanings, psuedo-religions such as Nazism or Marxism will step into the vacuum. The question is not, then, *whether* religion will affect public life. The more appropriate questions are: What *kind* of religion will it be, and *how* will it effect public life?

WHAT KIND?

In America, Christianity will continue to be the most dominant religious tradition. More than 85 percent of Americans consider themselves to be Christian. Christianity simply has no serious religious rivals. More specifically, Reformed Protestantism and Roman Catholicism will provide the main themes for religious involvement in American public life. Mark Noll, the distinguished evangelical historian of American religion at Wheaton College, has argued that the "dominant pattern of political involvement in America has always been one of direct, aggressive action modeled on Reformed theories of life in the world."[1] Americans, he says, "have moved in a straight line from personal belief to social reform, from private experience to political activity."[2] This approach has been characterized by great confidence in discerning the will of God for public, institutional life. On the right it has meant direct biblical blueprints for what God wants in the world. On the left it has meant "reading God's agenda in the world." Both right and left enthusiastically view their activities as cooperating with God in building His kingdom on earth, which is to be the salvation of all.

This form of "constructive Christianity," to use H. Richard Niebuhr's phrase, has had enormous effects on American public life, many of which have been positive. Generating great movements for social reform, planting and nurturing myriads of institutions, and shaping the general public culture of America are cases in point. However, there are liabilities, which show up dramatically when the deeper religious roots of the Reformed spirit are eroded. Then, bereft of humility before divine transcendence, human arrogance with all its fallibilities and follies becomes overbearing, if not downright dangerous.

What remains of this "constructive" attitude when the great Reformed theological themes are gone is the following: a crusading spirit to remake the world according to its vision; strong confidence and clarity about what is to be done; a secular version of redemption in which what is possible for the individual soul is applied to public life; and a certain kind of totalistic hope for *full* transformation of human life and society.

The Reformed posture in its religious mode is now being carried more by Southern Baptists and other religious conservatives than by the old-line churches. They, however, are required to share public space with the Catholic voices that have become stronger and more frequent. Indeed, expressions of Catholic public theology may well have superseded Protestant ones in terms of public audibility and visibility. Catholics, too, however, have a long history of exhibiting many of the same characteristics that Noll identified among the Reformed. *Direct*, *aggressive*, and *confident* are adjectives that apply as well to Catholic interventions. Further, the Catholic bishops have been able to speak with more authority and clarity than their Protestant compatriots in recent years, which has in turn encouraged more and vigorous interventions.

Noll, in the article already cited, calls for a stronger Lutheran voice in the interplay of religion and public life. Like Andre Siegfried before him, Noll calls for a nudge in the Lutheran direction.[3] Noll then gives a few hints as to what that voice might sound like. In the following I will elaborate more systematic reflections on what this Lutheran nudge might look like.

THE LUTHERAN CONTRIBUTION

Lutheranism, as noted by Noll, has a particular way of relating the church to the public order. However, this "Lutheran attitude" does not lead in a specific ideological direction, if that is taken to mean a rather detailed blueprint for public policy. Rather, the paradoxical vision provides a *framework* for public theology. It elaborates a set of theological assumptions that stipulate how organized religion and politics ought to be related, not so much for the sake of politics and society but primarily for the sake of the church. What is legally permitted—the direct and aggressive intervention of the church in political affairs—may well not be good for the church and its mission. Undue entanglement in politics can be the ruination of the church.

Further, the paradoxical vision sets a general direction for public policy rather than a specific set of policy injunctions. It tends toward what has been called "Christian realism," though that general tendency can be refracted into a number of different policy directions. There are both left-wing and right-wing Lutherans who share commitment to this framework.[4]

Four main themes constitute the paradoxical vision as it applies to public life. They are: a sharp distinction between salvation offered by God in Christ and all human efforts; a focused and austere doctrine of the church that follows from the first theme; the twofold rule of God through Law and Gospel; and a paradoxical view of human nature and history.[5]

SALVATION VERSUS HUMAN EFFORT

I have stated what is meant to be a distinction as something of a contradiction, but overstatement often has a point. Humans, particularly in the political sphere, are prone to claim salvific significance for their efforts at social and/or political transformation. The twentieth century has been crammed with those bloodstained attempts. When the God-man Jesus Christ is refused as Savior, the man-god in many different guises is given full sway.

The good news of the Gospel is that God saves us through His gift of grace in Christ. He has chosen to reconcile us to Himself by sending His Son, by breaking through to us from His side, as it were, and not insisting that we climb some ladder of achievement through our own efforts. We *trust* God to save us in Christ; we do not earn our salvation nor even add something to what He has offered. It is sheer gift.

This insistence on a strong doctrine of grace puts all human efforts in proper perspective. They deal with penultimate improvements in the human condition, with relative goods and bads, not with salvation. This means that politics is desacralized and relativized. Salvation is through Christ, not through human political schemes nor through psychological or religious efforts. Following from this, we might appropriately speak of liberation ethics but never of liberation theology, if that is taken to mean that revolutionary praxis is the same thing as salvation. Such a judgment provides a critical shield against the constant attempts in American Christianity to give redemptive significance to ecological, psychological, spiritualist (New Age), feminist, and now multicultural movements.

One would think that the world has had enough experience of revolutionary change to obviate any claims that political and social "transformation" lead to anything remotely resembling human fulfillment. Ordinary human observation and experience arrive at such a negative verdict. But for religious people to make such claims is even more baffling.

Such sacralizing claims are ruled out by the paradoxical vision. We are obviously not capable of our own salvation. The paradoxical vision, however, aims at cutting off such claims for even more profound reasons than their lack of empirical validity. It does so for the sake of the Gospel, for its radicality and universality. The radicality of the Gospel insists that salvation is a pure gift; we do not earn it. If we do not recognize that, we dishonor God who gave His Son in the unique and decisive saving act. When we claim a part in the drama of salvation, we at the same time insist that God's action in Christ is not good enough. Something else, presumably our virtuous action, must be added.

Furthermore, the universality of the Gospel is compromised if we fail to make a sharp distinction between God's saving act in Christ and all human efforts at improving the world. In any overt or covert claim for human effort as a constitutive part in our own salvation, there are always those who are on the right side of the struggle and those on the wrong side. Some are saved and some are damned, not because of their faith or lack of faith in God's work in Christ but because they either are or are not participants in the group or process that claims to be bringing redemption. Their salvation is dependent on which side of earthly fault lines they find themselves.

The picture is clear; the claims of the man-god always exclude. However, the Gospel does not. All humans, regardless of their location along the world's fault lines, are equidistant and equally near the grace of God in Christ.

The New Testament Gospel of the suffering God who abjured all worldly power and all worldly group identifications simply rules out those schemes that compromise the radicality and universality of the Gospel. The cross of Christ freed the Gospel from enmeshment in all human efforts to save the world. No one was with Christ on the cross to die for our sins. Or viewed differently, everyone was with Christ on the cross, but only as passive inhabitants of His righteous and suffering person.

When we are freed from the need to look for salvation in human schemes, our eyes should be clearer to make the important distinctions among the relatively good and the relatively bad in the realm of human action. Liberated from the worry about our salvation, we can turn unobsessively to the human task of building a better world, not by prideful claims of transformation but by determined yet humble attempts to take small steps for the better.

THE PURPOSE OF THE CHURCH

If the most important event that ever happened in human history is the drawing near to each of us in Christ, then the essential and unique mission of the church from the point of view of the paradoxical vision is its calling by God to proclaim that Gospel in Word and Sacrament. The Gospel of Christ is its treasure; the church is the earthen vessel whose sacred obligation it is to take the Gospel to every nook and cranny of the world. Its calling is to proclaim the Gospel and to gather a people around that Gospel, forming them through the Spirit into the body of Christ.

No other institution has that calling; no other institution will promote the Gospel if the church fails in its task. So churches must take with utmost seriousness the terrible simplicity of their task. Of course they must be engaged in deeds of charity and they must be concerned with justice. Of course they must involve themselves in financial, administrative, and educational activities. Of course they must witness in the public sphere. But the church is not primarily a political actor, a social transformer, or an aggressive interest group. If it acts primarily as one of these, it is identified and treated as one more contentious worldly group. What's more, it loses its own integrity, its own reason for being.

Presently we are witnessing the sorry sight of many churches losing confidence and zeal for their essential and unique calling. They no longer believe their Gospel message is of utmost importance. They marginalize it in their own activities and institutions. How else can one account for the lack of any real margin of difference between church and secular schools, colleges, hospitals, and homes for the elderly? How else can one account for the disastrous drop in home and foreign missionary activity on the part of so many languishing church bodies?

THE TWOFOLD RULE OF GOD

The paradoxical vision holds that God rules the world in two distinct ways—through Law and Gospel. The Law is the instrument of God to sustain and order the world. After the fall, God did not abandon the world. He continues to sustain it through the Law, which is all the energies and actions of God that restrain, guide, and shape the world. Because the Law must deal with human sin, it has a hard edge to it. Indeed, God often wields the Law of judgment against nations and empires, bringing them to naught. But the Law also builds up human life, working through many agencies to create a more humane and just world.

The Law is summarized in the Ten Commandments and carried by the moral teachings of the church, but it is also discerned by human reason and experience amid the dynamics of life. The Bible contains many signposts for recognizing the operation of God's Law in the world, but it has no blueprint for the complexities of modern economic, political, or social life. Humans have to work out anew what God demands in every generation. Secular people, because they also have the gift of reason and the benefit of experience, can contribute to this ongoing discernment of the Law, though they may not call it God's Law. Christians are obligated not only to cooperate with secular people in discerning and doing good works of the Law but also to imagine and initiate programs that extend human justice.

The Law of God is not salvific. All the efforts that God and humans make in the horizontal realm of the Law may lead to human betterment, but they do not save. Rather, God has chosen a particular route to reconcile humans to Himself. That route is Christ. God has reached out to call a disobedient and lost humanity to Himself through the cross and resurrection of Jesus Christ. This is pure gift; in the realm of salvation, humans are completely receptive. Their faith in the saving act of Christ will be acted out in deeds of love, but those deeds of love are the result of faith in God's work in Christ, not a substitute for it.

Christians exist at the juncture of the two ways that God reigns and must live creatively between the horizontal pressures of the Law and the call of the Gospel. However, they must be careful not to confuse the two, that is, to act according to Law when they are in the realm of the Gospel or to act according to Gospel when they are in the realm of the Law. They are to observe a tentative, though not a final, dualism.

MAKING THE LAW INTO THE GOSPEL

This confusion is a favorite for those, mentioned above, who are tempted to claim salvific effect for human effort. They mistake some ameliorative, but always ambiguous, project for the

Gospel itself. There are many negative effects of this mistake, the first being a dishonoring of God's will to save through His Son, the Christ. But others follow. Human efforts that are invested with salvific import are often dangerous. Reinhold Niebuhr, for example, pointed out the perils of both hard and soft utopianism.[6]

In the "hard" category, the awful legacies of Nazi and Marxist revolutions are a case in point. When humans claim to bring heaven to earth by force, they bring hell instead. A fascinating aspect of hard utopianism is its endorsement by so many respectable intellectuals.[7] One can only make sense of this by reminding oneself that the longing for salvation has not departed from the minds and spirits of even secularized intellectuals; it is merely displaced into utopian schemes whose claims, in retrospect, seem utterly incredible.

Softer varieties of utopianism abound. The secular world is prone to view an expansion of scientific knowledge as salvific. Or education in a broader sense will save us. Or health and well-being will, or schemes of self-esteem, or new spiritual techniques. But all, because they are infected with human self-interest, are ambiguous at best. They are not able to reconcile us to God. Yet depleted religious traditions often grasp at this soft utopianism, and sometimes even at the harder variety, when they lose their confidence in the Gospel. Not only the world mistakes the Law for the Gospel; churches themselves do too.

MAKING THE GOSPEL INTO THE LAW

Reinhold Niebuhr, though he did not put the issue in the concepts I am using, was a formidable opponent of this confusion. He believed that liberal Christianity had taken the radical love of the Gospel and turned that "impossible possible" into an ethical norm that could then become a "simple possibility in history."[8] Indeed, his whole career as a public theologian could be understood as a protest against the sentimentality inherent in the liberal tendency to make the Gospel into the Law. From the early *Moral Man and Immoral Society* to the late *Structure of Nations and Empires,* Niebuhr demonstrated the folly of applying the ethic of *agapé* love directly to the struggles for power in the world.[9] Doing so, he argued, led to political irresponsibility. In international affairs it led to pacifist tendencies, and in domestic affairs it issued in blindness toward the necessity of countervailing power.

Niebuhr's arguments are essentially Lutheran in character. Although expressed in different language, they are anchored in the paradoxical vision's insight into the dialectical relationship between the radical love of God in Christ and the realistic pursuit of earthly justice, between Gospel and Law. Indeed, I believe Niebuhr to be the greatest practitioner of two-kingdoms thinking in modern religious history. Many of his great contributions to the development of Christian realism are drawn from the paradoxical vision, though he would no doubt resist being claimed for the "Lutheran attitude."

Niebuhr's warnings have gone unheeded in much of American Christianity. The mainline churches rushed headlong toward sentimentalism in foreign policy debates. They demanded "nuclear freezes" even amid Soviet arms buildups. They believed that forgiving love and "turning the other cheek" were Christian responses to power politics. In domestic affairs, they commend compassion without accountability.

All this is not to say that Christian love has no relevance to public life. Rather, it operates as both motivation and ideal in the Christian life, which creatively integrates the twofold reign of God. But expressing *agapé* love is no simple matter; it is indirectly related to the norms that govern political and economic life. As Niebuhr has it, *agapé* love judges all lesser efforts, serves as a goad to higher achievement, helps discriminate among options, and is a source for repentance and humility.[10] Further, such love can never be triumphant in history nor can it be totally defeated. It is instructive to remember that the one person who did live fully out of *agapé* love ended up on a cross, crucified by the best and brightest of the time.

THE PARADOX OF HUMAN NATURE AND HISTORY

"Whatever your heart fastens to, that is your god," said Luther. From the paradoxical vision's perspective, humans are irretrievably committed to finding something other than God to which to fasten their hearts. This analysis of inescapable sin, however, is not so simple. We do not fasten to the unalluring and worthless things of the world. On the contrary, we fasten to the things that really tempt. Highest among our temptations is devotion to ourselves. We are obsessed with ourselves and make ourselves the center of the universe. Our attention to ourselves crowds out everything else except those things we want to feed the image of ourselves we have concocted. This obsession may be one of willful assertion or self-pitying negation, but in either case it makes a mockery of the divine command "to love the Lord your God with all you heart, mind, and soul." We love ourselves or those things that can lend ourselves some semblance of importance and immortality.

Thus none are good. All human actions are tainted with the effect of our sin, even those performed by Christians. We can never be completely free of the old Adam in this life. This Augustinian view of human nature extends to human action in society. Human sin is particularly magnified and unrestrained in the life and action of groups. It is especially expressed in collective situations.

Yet humans are not dirt. Even in their fallen state they possess qualities of their creation in the image of God. There is an essential self that longs for wholeness and completion, though it cannot heal or complete itself. This essential self has capacity for moral reason, for what Luther called "civil righteousness." Humans have capacity for justice.

Moreover, humans never lose their dignity in God's eyes. They are beloved for what God has made them to be, not what they have made of themselves. They are infinitely valuable because they have been given a destiny in their creation and have been redeemed by the work of Christ. They can refuse that destiny and that redemption, but they can never lose the "alien dignity" that their creation and redemption bestows on them.

Humans find themselves in a paradoxical predicament. Created and redeemed by God, they are exalted individuals. They have a capacity for freedom, love, and justice. Yet they use their freedom to fasten to lesser things, creating a hell for themselves, their fellow human beings, and the world around them. They are a paradox of good and evil, manufacturing idols of the good things they are given. And they cannot solve this predicament on their own.

Thus the paradox of human nature creates the paradox of human history. "History cumulates, rather than solves, the essential problems of human history," wrote Niebuhr.[11] The fulfillment and perfection of history are not ours to grasp; we cannot be gods in history. Indeed, as we have mentioned, great evil is done by those who try to complete history by their own powers.

Rather, it is up to God to bring history to an end (its *finis*) and to fulfill its purpose (its *telos*). God has given us an anticipation of the kingdom in Christ and will bring it to fullness in His own time and by His will. We are in an interim time of struggle between Christ's first and second coming.

Given that scenario, we are freed from trying to manage history according to great schemes. Rather, we must strive for relative gains and wait on God. We must work for reform without cynicism's paralysis or idealism's false hope. Thus the paradoxical vision leads to a nonutopian view of history that is not cynical. It expects neither too much of history nor too little.

The "Lutheran attitude" reflected in these four main themes provides a wholesome nudge to an American Christianity that is all too prone to identify promising human achievements as the salvation of God, to make the church into anything but the proclaimer of the Gospel, to apply directly the "Gospel ethic" to the power struggles of the world, and to hope for the intractabilities of individual and corporate human sin to be overcome by some sanctified human effort.

FURTHER IMPLICATIONS

The paradoxical vision also moves toward indirect ways of connecting the church to the public world. The second theme particularly calls the church to the task of nourishing and sustaining the callings of lay Christians as they move from the church into the world. If the church is really the church it will effect an internal "revolution of the heart" among its laity that will indeed affect the world. The church will form the hearts and minds of laity who will then enter all the complex interstices of the public world that are unreachable by the direct efforts of the church.

Indeed, I suspect that the most effective public theology of the next century will be done by laypeople who have been formed powerfully in the church and are able to connect Christian formation with the learning and activity of secular callings. Christian legislators have far more political impact than either church statements or advocacy centers. Christian professors in universities have more effect in shaping the "normal sciences of the day" than the resource materials cranked out by church and society bureaucracies. Christian doctors will have more voice in shaping a humane medicine than theological ethicists in seminaries.

Christian laypersons, however, will need help and encouragement in connecting their Christian convictions to their public lives. The church must spend far more time in playing another indirect role, that of a mediating institution. Not only must it form the hearts and minds of its laity, it must help laity connect the social teachings of the church with their public lives by providing contexts in which those connections can be self-consciously made. The Lay Academies of Europe have been models in this regard, though they seem now to be succumbing to the temptation of the activist American churches: They are increasingly letting the society know "where they stand." But if the church is to take seriously its role to mediate its tradition to the challenges of the modern world through the lives its laity, it will have to give more attention to that task and resist the temptation to pronounce and act on everything in sight.

Moreover, the church must also show more courage and resolution with regard to its related institutions. If it cannot insist that its vision make a margin of difference in the life of its schools, colleges, homes, camps, and hospitals, it really has little business trying to shape and transform the larger public world. The church must begin shaping a "counter society" in its own institutions. Such integrity and courage will be much more persuasive to the broader society than any amount of lecturing.

These indirect ways of connecting the church to public life do not preclude the more direct ways. There will still be room for judicious and authoritative social statements, pastoral letters, and papal encyclicals. There will even be room for direct action, for "advocacy," for "socially responsible investing," for boycotts, for community organizing, for partisan campaigns, and for other sorts of semicoercive modes of action. But each of these instances strains the unity and catholicity of the church by precipitating disagreements on issues rarely central to its main task. A wise church will hesitate to engage in direct action.

The paradoxical vision leads to a different way of construing the public role of religion than does the Reformed or the Catholic. Its themes serve as guardians of the radicality and universality of the Gospel, of a proper understanding of the church's task, and of the two ways that God reigns. Churches ignore these themes at their great peril.

NOTES

1. Mark Noll, "The Lutheran Difference," *First Things* (February 1992): 31–40.

2. Noll, "Lutheran Difference," 37.

3. Andre Siegfried, *America Comes of Age: A French Analysis* (New York: Knopf, 1927).

4. The public theology of the Lutheran Church in America, as articulated by its social statements, tended in a left-of-center political direction. William Lazareth, George Forell, and Richard Niebanck, whose theological counsel was formative in those documents, were and are political liberals. Right-of-center public theology is more difficult to find in official Lutheran statements, but it is well repre-

sented in the writings of individual Lutherans, Richard Neuhaus and this writer among them. But in all these examples, public theology is framed by the paradoxical vision.

5. These themes are drawn from my reading of recent interpretations of the paradoxical vision, which is indebted more to Scandinavian and American scholarship on Luther and Lutheranism than to German. These are, in my opinion, more dynamic and open than the German and are more influenced by the strengths of other Christian traditions, especially the Reformed. My main sources are: Gustaf Wingren, *Luther on Vocation* (Philadelphia: Muhlenberg, 1957), and *Creation and Law* (London: Oliver & Boyd, 1961); Einar Billing, *Our Calling* (Rock Island, Ill.: Augustana Book Concern, 1951); Gustaf Aulén, *Church, Law and Society* (New York: Scribner's, 1948); George Forell, *Faith Active in Love* (Minneapolis: Augsburg, 1954); and William Lazareth, *Luther and the Christian Home: An Application of the Social Ethics of the Reformation* (Philadelphia: Muhlenberg, 1960).

6. See Niebuhr's discussion of both types of utopianism in *Reinhold Niebuhr on Politics*, ed. Harry R. Davis and Robert C. Good (New York: Charles Scribner's Sons, 1960), 12–36.

7. It remains to be seen whether intellectuals on the left will be held accountable for their flirtations with the Marxist-Leninist regimes and movements of the last fifty years. Intellectuals who showed any affinity with fascism are constantly being exposed for their errors. Heidegger's intellectual respectability has been solely challenged. Recently even Mircea Eliade, who tried to stay clear of politics for the last thirty years of his life, has been scrutinized for his earlier lapses. But thus far, few intellectuals who sympathized with Marxist-Leninism are being called to account. Indeed, they seem to wear their past enthusiasms as proud, even if faded, garlands of moral authenticity rather than as shameful reminders of their complicity with regimes at least as destructive as the fascist ones we rightfully condemn.

8. Reinhold Niebuhr, *An Interpretation of Christian Ethics* (New York: Seabury Press, 1979), 103ff.

9. Reinhold Niebuhr, *Moral Man and Immoral Society* (New York: Scribner's, 1960), and *The Structure of Nations and Empires* (New York: Scribner's, 1959).

10. Niebuhr, *Interpretation of Christian Ethics*, 62ff.

11. Reinhold Niebuhr, *The Nature and Destiny of Man* (New York: Scribner's, 1949), 2:318.

ORDINARY SAINTS

SIGNS OF THE CHRISTIAN LIFE

I don't know anyone who has religious values." I often receive this response when I ask students to write a paper describing people they know who model religious values. The assignment is for a course called Values and the Responsible Life, which is a segment of the general education program at Roanoke College, Salem, Virginia. Other responses are just as disconcerting:

- "Religious values are different for every person."

- "My dad was brought up religious but isn't any longer, so I'll describe his moral values."

- "I don't know anyone who goes to church a lot."

- More interesting but just as troubling: "Religious stories have a moral purpose—it doesn't matter what the stories are as long as they lead to a moral life."

Some of our students don't have religious people close at hand whom they can describe. But the majority of our students are from mainstream Christian homes. A significant minority come from evangelical or fundamentalist homes. Even those who claim a religious upbringing have difficulty discerning religious values in others. They lack the spectacles for seeing signs of the Christian life.

What should these students be looking for? In general, I'm expecting students to be able to discern how Christian convictions affect ordinary life. Unfortunately, one of the problems the students have is that they are looking for extraordinary examples of faith and life—the Mother Teresas or Billy Grahams. When they don't see the heroics, they think there is nothing there. They miss the Christian values in the lives of the ordinary saints who surround them.

That phrase—ordinary saints—seems contradictory but is in fact a helpful key to understanding the Christian life. It points accurately to the biblical idea of a saint, which was rediscovered in the Reformation by Martin Luther and John Calvin. Saints are ordinary people of faith.

SIGNS OF CHRISTIAN LIFE

Saints are ordinary in two ways. First, they are saints because of their faith in the amazing grace of God, not because of their heroic faith or deeds. They are righteous before God not because they have earned it but because of Christ, who exchanges with us His righteousness for our sin. Luther called this "the happy exchange," which is celebrated in so many of our Lutheran hymns. Our personal faith may be ordinary, even weak, but God's promises in Christ are not. God's grace holds us fast, even in our weakness.

We are ordinary saints in another significant way. We are called to respond to God's grace in Christ by lives of thankful obedience in very ordinary places of responsibility. We normally are not called to spring free of the obligations of ordinary life. We need not wander about, looking for places to invent a Christian life. Instead, we are given places to work out obedient lives—marriage and family life, work, public life as citizens and volunteers, and church. In these places, the marks of ordinary saints are faith, love, and hope. They become practical in the lives of everday believers.

FAITH

The vertical dimension of faith—our confidence in the justifying grace of God in Christ—is accompanied by horizontal effects. The Spirit of God enables our faith to become practical. It affects the way we live in the world. It does this by giving a deeper meaning to our ordinary lives and by leading us toward our own mission within everyday life.

Tennis great Arthur Ashe, when asked if he did not angrily question God "why me?" when confronted with the miserable reality of AIDS, said something memorable and Christian. He said, "Well, when I stood at Wimbledon holding the championship trophy, I didn't then ask 'Why me?' but I should have." Ashe knew that his own talents and many of the opportunities of his life were not his own but were given to him. He recognized the unmerited blessings of life that flow from God's hand.

As Christians, we look on the gifts of family, spouse, country, church, nature, as well as the mysterious gift of life itself, with joy and gratitude. The Christian embraces these gifts with thankfulness. All facets of life have a deeper meaning to the Christian: They are unearned gifts of God. Christians exhibit a deep-down sense of joyful appreciation for what the Creator has bestowed upon them and all fellow creatures. The same love that sent Christ also created the world and all therein.

Practical faith, however, is not merely passive gratitude. God's gift also becomes our task and opportunity. Faith in God means that our lives have worldly significance and purpose. We are to use our talents and freedom to discern and pursue God's intentions for us in the world. We have a part to play in God's story. In other words, a Christian has a calling, or better, a series of callings. Each of our ordinary places of responsibility can become callings for the Christian.

The great reformers—Luther and Calvin—emphasized that work in the world, even the most humble kind, has religious and moral significance because it helps the neighbor and pleases God. Such work, moved with the intentions of God, preserves and enriches the world. Further, the reformers affirmed that we have callings as parents, citizens, friends, students, and workers.

There is the fine scene in *Chariots of Fire* when the young sprinter headed for the Olympics is confronted by his pious sister. She tries to get him to give up the "frivolous" activity of competitive running and get to the mission field in China where he can engage in the serious work of saving souls. Yes, he tells his sister, in due time I will take up that task, but right now "God has given me the gift of speed and when I run I can feel his pleasure." In short, Eric Liddell had a calling.

Practical faith in God means confidence that we have purposeful callings in our daily existence. Our calling, as the Christian writer Frederick Buechner has put it, is where "our deep gladness meets the world's deep need." Today we are aware that God may present us with a succession of callings and that the opportunities for faithful service end only with life itself.

LOVE

If practical Christian faith enables us to discern deeper levels of meaning in our ordinary lives, Christian love is the dynamic element that bends our intentions and actions outward toward the neighbor. Christians are called to reflect the amazing love of God in their relations with others. Of course, that is easier said than done because our sin, and the world's sin, makes our ordinary lives full of self-interest and conflict. We remember that the one life lived fully out of extravagant love—what Christians call *agape*—ended in crucifixion.

We are caught between the demands of worldly responsibility and the call of God to love with the kind of love He showed for us in Christ. But that is precisely the situation in which mature Christians are to take responsible risks. Not willing simply to accept the world as it comes to them, Christians are called to be its salt and leaven.

An art teacher in a large urban school tells the story of a believable predicament. She had a student who almost ruined her class in the preceding year. She flunked him because he hadn't handed in any work during the entire year and had created havoc in the classroom. He asked to take the course again; she said no. But during the course of the year, he asked her if he could study in her office because his study hall was so noisy. She took a responsible risk and allowed him to study there. As time went on, he asked to do errands for her. She assigned him some, and he performed them well. The relationship bloomed, and she began tutoring him in other subjects. At the end of the year, he surprised her by bequeathing her his undying friendship in his senior class will.

This little story is instructive. The teacher did not sentimentally lower her standards. But at the same time she did not just leave the student as she found him. She took a risk in taking him into her office. Out of Christian love she bestowed upon him a measure of dignity and worth. She acted imaginatively and courageously within the creative tension between worldly duty and Christian love. Hers was a "tough love."

In such an example, which can be duplicated by the thousands among the ordinary saints of God, the Spirit works through Christian love to heal and restore the world. Through this service to all, the world is moved a bit closer toward the intentions of God. As Christians participate in this work of love and justice, they often experience suffering. As Luther noted, Christians need not seek the cross in their callings; the cross will find them if the unique lure of Christian love is taken seriously. This "stretching," this "responsible risk," will be painful. But it will be an echo of that love which was stretched on a cross twenty centuries ago.

Hope

But so what? Like the teacher's efforts, our little deeds of love seem so insignificant in the larger scope of things. We and our deeds will soon be forgotten—a trip to any churchyard presses home that fact. Further, even our good deeds are contaminated by our own self-interest, and their effects often turn out to be different than we intended. From a worldly point of view, the Christian life seems so futile.

After all these years away from my hometown in Nebraska, I still receive the town paper. I read the obituaries carefully because I know so many of those who are now dying. They were young people when I was growing up. But one entry particularly caught my eye. It was that of an elderly nun who had spent her whole life working in a local home for the aged. From the time of her arrival as a novice to the time of her death as an elderly woman, she had cared for old people—dressed, cleaned, conversed with, and nursed those who were soon headed for the grave. What's more, by the time she died as an old woman, she had no relatives left. She was buried in the paupers' cemetery next to some of those she had served earlier. What a foolish and wasted life! No travel, sex, family, bright lights, or acclaim. From the world's point of view, she had thrown her life away. Ah, but from a hopeful Christian view, her life shines in glory. She had a deep sense of the meaning of life, a firm calling, and had reflected the love of Christ for many years toward some of the most lowly and lonely of God's creatures.

Christian hope means that such a life of discipleship is not lost. She, and we, are given a destiny in our creation and redemption. She was called to play her part in the spiritual drama authored by God. She did so faithfully. Her worldly life and deeds are valued by God at a level the world does not know. They are used by God in this life and are prized eternally. Their significance, hidden to the world, is guaranteed by God.

Moreover, our earthly destinies are not the end. Christian hope means that those who fasten their hearts on the promises of God in Christ are destined to participate in the eternal life of God. Following Christ, the Conqueror and King, the firstborn of the dead, we are carried through the terrors of sin, death, and the devil to the right hand of God Himself. There, with all the saved, we are destined to serve God and enjoy Him forever.

This hope has great practical consequences. We can live the lives of ordinary saints without grasping for earthly security or success and without the despair that comes when we haven't attained them. Our hope gives us the proper detachment from those worldly gods and allows us to live our lives and die our deaths in serenity and peace.

So there is faith, love, and hope. They do indeed become practical in the lives of ordinary saints. They make a difference in the way Christians live their lives. They are visible signs.

RADICAL ORTHODOXY

THE NEO-AUGUSTINIAN TEMPTATION

There is a rising strand of Christian social thought inspired by a fresh reading of Augustine's *City of God*. It now goes under the name "radical Orthodoxy." Those involved are prolific, erudite, and, for the most part, quite young. Their intellectual seniors include George Lindbeck and Stanley Hauerwas, both of whom helped to bring ecclesiology back into Christian ethics. But the young ones have taken off from there. Names such as John Milbank and David Yeago in theology, Reinhard Hütter in ethics, and Richard Hays and N. T. Wright, biblical scholars upon whom the others draw heavily, are representative of this increasingly visible trend.

The movement, if it is cohesive enough to be called that, is committed to the construction of an independent and distinct churchly culture based upon the full narrative of Israel and the church as it has been carried through the ages by the Great Tradition. Theologically, the neo-Augustinians are anti-foundationalists who believe that a religious tradition such as Christianity is

Originally published in *First Things*, 81 (March 1998).
Amended and reprinted with permission.

a cultural-linguistic system that cannot and should not be compromised by any standards not its own. They learned that from Lindbeck.

Biblically, radical Orthodoxy argues that the early Christianity depicted in the Pauline letters was a churchly "public" or culture of its own, flourishing alongside but radically distinct from the Roman, Jewish, and Hellenistic cultures of the time. "Paul already regards the church as a new public order in the midst of the nations with its own distinctive culture," argues David Yeago.[1] Christians who entered such a culture were "dying to the world" in the sense that they were entering a new ecclesial world.

Ethically, radical Orthodoxy contends that the practices of this distinct, living tradition form the Christian virtues that sustain such an ecclesial world. The church's worship, preaching, teaching, and communal life shape the virtues that maintain the practices of marriage and family life, charity, hospitality, governance, art, and thought that provide a real alternative to the dying world about us. The church essentially needs no sources other than its own for the ethical task. Milbank asserts that the church produces its own "ecclesial society," with its attendant ontology, social theory, ethics, and economics.[2]

Ecclesiology, that formerly stuffy branch of systematic theology, takes on urgency in the writings of the neo-Augustinians. The church is a constitutive dimension of the Gospel, manifesting a comprehensive new life. It is the body of Christ in a direct and literal way. It is a people in continuity with the people of Israel. It needs to live truly from its own sources and forget about worldly relevance. "The Church is a public in its own right," says Hütter.[3] "The world," when it is pressed hard, is simply another religious vision of life that is a poison when ingested uncritically by the church.

II.

The neo-Augustinians are sharply polemical. Above all, they are contemptuous of the "modern settlement," to use Yeago's term,[4] in which secular, liberal society with its procedural rules of justice has succeeded in marginalizing the religious vision. The modern settlement has insisted on a "naked public square" in which religion is sentenced to the private sphere of life. Meanwhile, modernity's own "scientific" way of understanding life is dogmatized as the only public meaning available. Rather than being "objective" or "scientific," secular social theories are, Milbank argues, "concealed theologies or anti-theologies."[5] In this "settlement," Christian belief then becomes a weekend hobby in no real competition with the serious ways of understanding life in this world—sociology, psychology, economics, and political science.

A second object of the disdain of the neo-Augustinians is the religious individualism—both sophisticated and kitsch—that has accepted the modern settlement. The sophisticated are the highly educated "new class" that Ernst Troeltsch typified many years ago as "mystics" who wouldn't be caught dead identifying themselves with a specific tradition or belonging to a real church. The kitsch-devotees are the practitioners of the popular religion that searches for contact with the "divine spark" in each individual. This is the gnostic element ingrained in so much American religion. It has, these critics say, little moral seriousness and no people-forming capacities.

Almost as objectionable are the desiccated religious bodies that have accepted the modern settlement, albeit unconsciously. Mainstream church bodies have tacitly bought the argument that politics and therapy are more important than Christian faith; therefore, they allow their theologies to become handmaidens of ideology or psychology. They give sacred legitimation to secular knowledge and action and thereby become "relevant." (Several of the neo-Augustinians have made the surprising charge that the theology of Reinhold Niebuhr is best understood as a religious legitimation of liberal democracy.) These mainstream bodies, though they think they are involved in "transformation," are more likely being acculturated more deeply into the modern settlement. According to Hütter, such attempts ironically "deepen the Church's irrelevance and undermine its public (political) nature by submitting and reconditioning the church according to the saeculum's understanding of itself as the ultimate and normative public."[6]

Other churches—represented by the church-growth movement—tacitly accept the notion that the religious needs and wants registered in the open market should be the guiding signals for religious practice. They become "relevant" in another way. But, as with the mainstream, they are no longer drinking from their own wells. In the church-growth world, according to Hütter, "religion itself increasingly becomes another commodity regulated by market forces."[7]

The radical Orthodox project sounds like a new sectarianism, but it is far from that. Its proponents believe in culture—Christian culture. They are not inimical to the arts, music, politics, economic life, education. But these cultural activities, they insist, will have to be renewed—if not entirely rebuilt—on Christian assumptions. Culture under the modern settlement is depleting its inheritance from the Christian past and is gradually descending into perversion and chaos. A new culture must arise from the church.

The neo-Augustinians are also catholic—even if they are Lutherans, Methodists, or Presbyterians. They transcend modern Christian divisions by retrieving a premodern Christian consensus. They have a "high" Christology, sacramentology, and ecclesiology and are committed to maintaining strong continuity with the great catholic tradition. They emphasize catholic substance over Protestant principle.

III.

There is much that is attractive and compelling in this movement. Its confidence in and clarity about orthodox Christianity is highly persuasive. It is refreshing to encounter serious thinkers who argue unabashedly that the Christian vision is true and trustworthy and that it matters ultimately.

This neo-Augustinian outlook is particularly tempting in moments when one is convinced that the current culture of the

West is unraveling. Modernity's commitment to individual rights and procedural justice seems to have no way of affirming substantive moral notions about how we should live together in community. Indeed, "rights talk" is being used as a sledgehammer to destroy the inherited moral substance of our common life. The Protestant culture that provided the social glue for most of American history is in shambles and shows scant prospect of being revived or renewed. What little remains of the Protestant Establishment indicates no commitment to such traditional Judeo-Christian notions as the sanctity of life at its beginning and end; marriage as a lifelong covenant of fidelity between a man and a woman; intrinsic, nonutilitarian moral norms; or grateful acceptance of given forms of life.

As one watches the moral norms that make for decency and restraint slowly erode, it is tempting to declare a pox on our national house and opt out of the struggle for a common culture. It would be pleasant to lose oneself in an ecclesial culture that affirms orthodox Christianity and is eagerly building a parallel culture, one built on the rock instead of the endlessly shifting sands of modernity. In such circumstances, one could quit the perpetual struggle with those in both church and society who seem to have wholeheartedly bought into the modern settlement. Who wants always to appear reactionary or nostalgic?

This new vision offers the prospect of creating a genuine "people," not merely a collection of political or psychological activists or, worse, religious consumers. It aims at incorporating full persons into a full ecclesial culture that can overcome the terrible fragmentation of modern life into semi-autonomous spheres of existence. One would have a coherent and cohesive "world" to live in alongside the dying world around it. Wasn't this in fact what the early church provided at the beginning of the common era?

IV.

Ah, but wait. As attractive as this radical Orthodox vision is, it finally is more a temptation than a real option. The main reason for this response is theological. If God is indeed the creator and sustainer of the larger world of economics, politics, and culture, then we as Christians are called to witness there. Our salvation is not in that witness, but our obedience is. Although we know that such a contemporary culture is debased, we also know that it is not beyond redemption. Indeed, reminding ourselves of the illusions of perfectionism, we might even grant that, relatively speaking, it is not all that bad. In any case, modernity's norms of procedural justice and individual rights offer openings for Christian witness.

From this theological perspective, it is better to side with those who are willing to struggle for a decent, common culture—though success is by no means assured. The right-to-life groups, the Christian Coalition, Bread for the World, the American Family Association, and many others make a worthwhile difference in the struggle for America's soul. And these religious groups have secular allies. The "principled pluralism" suggested by Os Guinness that aims at an overlapping consensus is not without prospects of success in the lively world of American politics. There is still much that is good—given and sustained by the Creator—in our common life outside the church.

We need also to remind ourselves how suffocating and stultifying it can be to inhabit an exclusively ecclesial reality. The ecclesial realities that have historically been constructed have often been as oppressive as their secular counterparts. When the neo-Augustinians write glowingly about ecclesial life, one wonders what church they are talking about. Even the strongest churches I have known could be characterized more aptly as bands of forgiven sinners than as shining knights in the kingdom of God. Indeed, when one thinks of real, existing ecclesial publics, one thinks most immediately of the mega-churches that do in fact create a parallel culture for their members. Yet whatever the mega-churches' contributions to Christian life and mission in our contemporary world, they do not seem to measure up to what the neo-Augustinians have in mind. One wonders what church could measure up.

There is much to be cherished in the neo-Augustinian vision. We do need to become more of a people shaped by a richer and more comprehensive ecclesiology. We do need to center on the Grand Narrative of the Great Tradition. We do need to march to the beat of a drum other than the world's. But at the same time, we need to witness in and struggle for that world. That is our calling. That is the church's calling.

NOTES

1. David Yeago, "Messiah's People: The Culture of the Church in the Midst of the Nations," *Pro Ecclesia* (Spring 1997): 152.

2. John Milbank, *Theology and Social Theory: Beyond Secular Reason* (Oxford: Basil Blackwell, 1990), 422.

3. Richard Hütter, "The Church as Public: Dogma, Practice, and the Holy Spirit," *Pro Ecclesia* (Summer 1994): 352.

4. Yeago, "Messiah's People," 148.

5. Milbank, *Theology and Social Theory*, 15.

6. Hütter, "Church as Public," 349.

7. Hütter, "Church as Public," 336.

THE LAKE WOBEGON FACTOR

NO PUBLIC VISIBILITY, PLEASE—
WE'RE LUTHERAN

I.

That great proponent of social Gospel activism, Walter Rauschenbusch, made this exasperated assessment of early twentieth-cen-
tury Lutheranism: "Thus far Lutheranism has buried its ten talents in a tablecloth of dogmatic theory and kept its people from
that share in the social awakening which is their duty and right."[1]

It seems that things have not changed much. More recently,
many heavy-hitting theologians have criticized the alleged "quietism" in Lutheran theological ethics. Among the critics are Reinhold and Richard Niebuhr, Paul Tillich, and Karl Barth. Contemporary Lutheran theologians have spent a good deal of time and
energy defending Lutheran ethics from such charges. As a
Lutheran, you cannot easily escape the "weak on social ethics"
designation. Indeed, when I criticized the undue enthusiasm for

Originally published in *The Cresset* (Reformation 1997).
Amended and reprinted with permission.

American democratic capitalism of several of my ethicist colleagues, they retorted that it must be a difficult thing to try to live up to that slightly oxymoronic calling—Lutheran ethicist.

Sociological studies have indicated that Lutherans, members of perhaps the largest European heritage group in North America (the German-Americans), are underrepresented in high political office. Lutherans can't claim a president, though a much smaller German sect, the River Brethren of Kansas, brought forth Dwight Eisenhower.

When one looks at the highly visible elite sectors of American life, one is tempted to come to the conclusion that Lutheranism simply doesn't produce "winners." Perhaps there are some anonymous Lutherans occupying lofty positions, but by and large the positions at the highest level of politics, media, business, and education seem rather unpopulated by identifiable Lutherans. We simply don't seem to incubate the kind of people who show up on the cover of *Time* or *Newsweek*.

Although I will qualify this judgment shortly, it seems that Lutherans are not the public hero type. A number of reasons for this fact have been put forth. One is that our strong ethnic traditions have kept us isolated from the mainstream. Even our heroes—who perhaps could have "made" it in the larger world— remained within the friendly confines of their ethnoreligious cultures. Another reason is that our leaders and theologians have been rather in-grown and church-centered. They do not seek a wider public visibility. A third reason is that the Lutheran theological tradition itself leads toward a grateful acceptance or tolerance of what is given. Lutherans do not rock the boat with public social criticism or activism. Closely related to this religious quietism is a cynical view of politics and public life in general that is attributed to Lutheran theology: The authorities are ordained by God and must be obeyed, but that doesn't mean we have to like them. For the most part the authorities have the thankless but necessary job of providing barriers to sin. Finally, there is a genuine humility and diffidence in the Lutheran ethos that shuns attention or ostentation, let alone glory. How many Lutherans have bumper stickers on their cars? I would submit not as many as Baptists or Methodists.

Does this mean that our permanent destiny is that depicted by Garrison Keillor in his Lake Wobegon stories? Does Lutheranism shape the ordinary people of small-town and rural, and now suburban, America in such a way that they remain invisible Everyman and Everywoman? Or, if they rise above that level of ordinariness, do they soon lose their souls or their Lutheranism?

II.

Now I will begin my counterattack. Lutheranism in America *has* produced a significant number of the visible elite, and many of them publicly identify themselves with the Lutheran ethos. In the following I will submit a number of candidates in this category, though I hasten to add that my list is limited by my own knowledge and *Sitz im Leben*. Certainly others might come up with many more possibilities, which suggests that we Lutherans should take up a more systematic account of our "elite laity," to use a phrase of the late Mark Gibbs. In the following I will list only those of roughly contemporary times; a broader historical survey would turn up many more individuals.

Interestingly enough, the most visible Lutheran elite seem to be clustered among the intelligentsia. This is not so odd when one considers the intellectual nature of the Lutheran tradition. "How dare you not know what can be known!" roared Martin Luther. The intellectual attitude has a long history among us. Among our kin, it tends to be preferred over politics.

No doubt one of our most famous contemporary intellectuals is Martin Marty. A fellow townsman from that abode of smart Germans—West Point, Nebraska—Marty is one of the most recognizable names among public intellectuals. (Others who have been connected with West Point are the Bohlmann brothers, Fred Niedner, Oswald Hoffman [from Snyder, a suburb of West Point], and yours truly.) Marty's intellectual work and commentaries on historical and contemporary religious life in the United

States are constantly sought by the elite and popular centers of American culture.

Although more known in elite than in popular centers, Jaroslav Pelikan is certainly as formidable a public intellectual as Marty. Pelikan has occupied a number of prestigious academic positions in two of America's great universities, and his scholarly work is greatly respected and widely known among the highly educated.

Peter Berger, a sociologist of religion and economic culture, has played an important part in insisting on the irreducibility of religious conviction and activity amid a secularizing intellectual culture. He has also played an important role in the critique of American religion in its manifold forms.

Kenneth Thompson is a major scholarly figure in the field of international relations. He writes important works and administers the Miller Center of Public Affairs at the University of Virginia. Jean Bethke Elshtain is increasingly visible as a public intellectual.

In theology, national figures include George Lindbeck, George Forell, Carl Braaten, and Robert Jenson, though we have others of like quality whose voices are more limited to Lutheran circles.

We have a number of high-level Lutheran educational administrators, perhaps the most visible among them the retired chancellor of the University of Minnesota, Nils Hasselmo.

Among the "harder to categorize" is Richard Neuhaus, who, in his earlier Lutheran incarnation, was a highly visible public theologian. Indeed, in the field of religion and public life it is difficult to name a more influential figure in American life. Neuhaus's ventures into social activism, organization founding, writing, and editing have earned him a place among the American elite.

Lutherans have produced a number of notable contemporary writers, foremost among them John Updike. While no longer a member of a Lutheran congregation, Updike was nurtured in a Pennsylvania Lutheran culture that appears repeatedly in his literary work. He expresses a number of Lutheran themes, among them the paradoxical character of human nature and history. Walter Wangerin is an increasingly celebrated writer whose work is shaped by the Lutheran perspective. Garrison Keillor, now a Lutheran but always an accurate evoker of Lutheran ways, has gone a long way to make the Lutheran ethos winsomely familiar among radio listeners across the country.

Although Lutherans are underrepresented among the country's political elite, we lay claim to the former Chief Justice of the Supreme Court, the late William Rehnquist. Ernest Hollings and Paul Simon have been well-known Lutheran senators. Edwin Meese was a major figure in the Reagan administration. The Chaplain to the Senate was James Ford, who held the position for many years. Other senators and representatives come from states with large Lutheran populations, and those populations also frequently elect Lutheran governors, the most visible among the current crop being Arne Carlson of Minnesota.

The military, including its chaplaincies, has had its share of Lutheran leaders, but the names of those Lutherans have not been highly visible to the general public.

Lutherans have "made a name" for themselves as leaders in the voluntary sector. Charles Lutz has published a book entitled *Loving Neighbors Far and Near* in which he recognizes Lutheran leaders such as Arthur Simon and David Beckmann. The former founded Bread for the World while the latter, after important positions with the World Bank, is currently executive director of Bread for the World.

Although certainly not household names, there are major leaders in the business world who are Lutheran in a serious way. William Diehl, himself a well-known writer on lay ministry, has profiled some of those leaders in *In Search of Faithfulness*.

III.

Garrison Keillor depicts the Lutheran folk of Lake Wobegon as ordinary farmers, teachers, pastors, storekeepers, wives, husbands, mayors, bankers, n'er-do-wells, and other assorted types. They work out their Christian lives in ordinary places but sometimes have extraordinary insights into mortality, sin, grace, and duty. Keillor is on to something.

I have argued in another book (*Ordinary Saints: An Introduction to the Christian Life*) that Lutherans, as well as other Christians, are "ordinary saints." They are ordinary in two basic ways. They are regarded as saints (holy) before God, not because of their extraordinary deeds or even unshakeable faith but because of the extraordinary grace of God in Christ that holds them fast even in their weakest moments. Lutherans believe they are justified by grace through faith on account of Christ, not by their deeds. They are also ordinary saints in their relation to their fellow human beings. They live out their faith, love, and hope in ordinary places of responsibility that God has given them. They accept their "given" locations with gratitude, and their faith becomes active in love and justice in those places.

Thus Lutherans are not only receptive in terms of grace, but they also show a similar posture in the categories of time and space. They receive with gratitude the "places" they have been given. In these places they express a marked "dailyness" that is often unrecognized by a world that celebrates the unusual and dramatic. It is in the ordinary times of work, play, love, and worship that the Christian life is lived.

Add together these three elements—justification by grace, locatedness, and dailyness—and you do not have the formula for world-beaters in the public sphere. Glory and power are not Lutheran concepts; bearing the cross is. Further, Lutherans do not worry overmuch about their election and signs of the same. They are less likely to think they are glorifying God in their callings than humbly helping their neighbor. They shun the schemes of works-righteousness so heavy in some forms of Protestantism. They don't even make the "decisions for Christ" that some of our more Pelagian brothers and sisters are wont to make.

Indeed, the Lutheran tradition may tend to make its adherents foot soldiers of the Lord rather than His generals or colonels. Certainly, they may have a few of those elite and perhaps a few more sergeants and lieutenants. But Lutheran piety is fitter for humbler things. Lutherans take seriously the paradoxical nature of life on earth.

But not to worry. Lutherans will get their measure of heroes and luminaries. Some will step forward in times of crisis. There have been a goodly number, and there will be others. But in this era of an unraveling civil society, the real heroes might well be those who exercise and maintain their public and private commitments in less auspicious ways. The most helpful engagement with the public world might be through faithful husbands and wives, mothers and fathers, workers and teachers, doctors and lawyers, volunteers, pastors, and laity. Without the healthy "small platoons" that these Christians sustain, there won't be any public life worthy of the name anyway.

NOTES
1.   Walter Rauschenbusch, *Christianizing the Social Order* (New York: Macmillan, 1912), 125.

LIVING THE WHOLLY CHRISTIAN LIFE

Too many of us are "partial Christians." Our Christian convictions apply only to a small part of our life—and that portion is shrinking. It will continue to shrink unless we regain a comprehensive vision of life that helps us reunite what modern life breaks apart.

Voices I hear in my personal and professional life reveal that the modern world is tearing us apart. Listen.

- "My Sunday life has nothing to do with my life in the rough and tumble of law," said the young lawyer, scrambling to establish her practice.

- "My work as a scientist is separate from my life as a Christian," asserted a professor at a college at which I was lecturing.

- "The therapist told me to go ahead and have an affair to get the attention of my husband," a Christian friend shakily told me.

- "I make my investments totally with regard to the profit-making capacity of the firm, not with regard to what it makes or how it acts," offered another Christian friend.

- "I judge television programs strictly according to their entertainment value," said a member of a nearby congregation.

- "Religion and politics have to be kept separate," remarked an older acquaintance.

- "Religious convictions should have nothing to do with our hiring policies as a college," asserted one of my colleagues.

- "Our Lutheran social agency cannot allow religious convictions to directly enter into our treatment of the disturbed young people we are dealing with," declared an executive acquaintance of mine.

- "We need to market this senior-citizen facility as a comfortable and attractive nonsectarian enterprise," argued a consultant hired by a Lutheran facility.

DIVIDED LIVES AND SOULS

As the above quotes from personal and institutional life suggest, our modern world breaks us apart. And it does so in two ways. First, it separates our lives into independent sectors that are governed by the principles developed in and by those sectors. Education is education, politics is politics, economic life is economic life, and each is understood and governed by independent ways of knowing and acting. Even private life is often understood according to the principles of psychology and sociology.

Western history has been the long story of each sector of life declaring its independence from the control and presence of religion. Admittedly there is much good that has occurred because of this secularization process. Knowledge and efficiency has definitely increased in each of these sectors. But this process also has had its costs: Our lives are no longer whole. We are often forced to become partial Christians.

But our modern world breaks us apart in a second way. It separates us from the heights and depths of our lives. Because it has had such enormous success manipulating natural forces, science is expected to understand and provide guidance for each area of life. Thus our lives are reduced to a series of causes and effects that science can describe and predict. This seems to leave little room for human freedom, let alone for the mystery of God's presence and action.

Thus our lives in business, education, and politics become increasingly this-worldly, flattened into one dimension. Even our personal lives are understood in purely one-dimensional terms. Sex is understood as physical functioning. Relationships become little more than need fulfillment as described by psychology and sociology. Even dying and grief are reduced to five stages, wringing the mysterious depth out of the experience.

PARTIAL CHRISTIANS

These two processes dividing life into independent spheres and draining our experience of transcendence can never be totally successful. Humans seek wholeness even as they seek the mysterious "something more" their spirits demand. So religion continues to prosper.

In the modern world, much religion is highly individualistic. People concoct their own brands. Our church traditions continue to survive, however. People want the church and its perspective when births, marriages, and deaths occur and when they want their children to have strong moral values.

But often people do not live wholly Christian lives. Their Christian convictions only apply to small areas of their lives. Their god is a "god of the gaps." God fills in the meanings for those parts of life that are not accounted for by economics, psychology, and sociology—or Ann Landers. Indeed, our churches are inhabited by many of these folks. They are partial Christians not because they are unmotivated but because their Christianity applies only to small parts of their lives. They are succumbing to the compartmentalized, secularized world.

The most impressive churches I know recognize how people have been affected, and they are busily constructing a counterattack. They know that Christians have to be whole people, living out a comprehensive vision of life that gives meaning and guidance to all they do. These churches also know that Christians need depth and transcendence in their lives. They need to be in touch with God—the Ground, Origin, and Aim of our lives.

To Transform Our Lives

Only the Holy Spirit can enable us to live wholly and in God's presence. But we can work to make things open for the workings of the Spirit in our individual and churchly lives.

Practically, alert congregations concentrate on Christian education, especially for adults. Partial Christians need a holistic Christian vision of life to live wholly. One way to do this is to anchor people in the biblical vision of life. The Bible reveals God as living and moving through all of life and history. This God who is active in all areas of human life also demands and elicits human response in all those areas.

Another way to impart a whole view of life is disciplined theological study. Theologians have thought through the faith comprehensively. They have sketched out how God relates to our complete lives. To study a popular theological writer such as C. S. Lewis or a more technical theologian such as Reinhold Niebuhr will make clear to serious seekers that the Christian meaning system applies to all of life, not to a few gaps left over after the world has done its job. Serious churches must be in the business of helping members develop a comprehensive vision of life.

Many Christians need help to relate the biblical or theological vision of life to the "independent" sectors in which they spend most of their waking time. Thus churches who truly understand their task have courses that help laypeople make the connections between Sunday and Monday. After all, these connections do not come automatically.

Finally, churches must help Christians plumb the heights and depths of their lives in a world increasingly flattened into one dimension. It is essential that churches offer worship services that are a "foretaste of the feast to come." They must do all they can to provide a worship life that includes the transcendent. Fine music, liturgical excellence, robust singing, and beautiful sights, sounds, and even smells are essential to such worship.

Worshipful and frequent celebration of the Eucharist provides connection with the living Christ, a connection that adds depth and richness to the spiritual lives of participants. As eucharistic practice becomes central to the lives of individual Christians and of whole congregations, they begin to perceive all of life as sacramental. God is discerned more and more in the ordinary.

Personal devotional practices are also crucial. Laypeople often need help and direction in establishing disciplined Bible reading, prayer, contemplation, Sabbath observation, devotions, discussion. These activities enable laypeople to recover the spiritual heights and depths of their lives. These dimensions are already touched in the moments of birth, marriage, Baptism, and death, but Christian lives are not whole until sacramentality is extended to common life too. This does not mean that Christians live in spiritual ecstasy all the time, but it does mean that lives are touched by the Spirit more plentifully than merely in the gaps, as important as those might be.

Christians need to live their lives wholly. May the Spirit bring that wholeness into our individual and churchly lives.

Part 3

Politics

RELIGION AND POLITICS

HOT AND COOL CONNECTIONS

The modern world is awash with examples of lively interactions between religion and politics. Sometimes it is politics or law affecting religion. The Supreme Court allows school vouchers that may be used at religious schools, rules that anti-abortion activists cannot be prosecuted with antiracketeering legislation, and endorses access to public school rooms for religious organizations. Yet the FBI attacks the Branch Davidians in Waco, and the Justice Department pursues a local fundamentalist church that pays heads of household more than nonheads of household because St. Paul says so. In addition, a circuit court strikes down as unconstitutional the requirement that school children recite the Pledge of Allegiance, which contains the phrase "under God." In reaction to this, the Senate votes 99–0 in favor of the pledge being recited in all American public schools, though a higher court nullifies the earlier judgment. All these are examples of the public sphere affecting religion.

Originally published in *The Cresset* (Lent 1996).
Amended and reprinted with permission.

But religion also affects politics. Internationally, we have militant Muslims agitating for Islamic republics. Christians and Muslims fight for political power in Africa. Osama bin Laden calls all Muslims to holy war against the "crusaders." Indeed, Samuel Huntingdon writes in his *Clash of Civilizations* that the conflicts of the twenty-first century will feature clashes of religio-cultural civilizations, not the ideological clashes that consumed the twentieth century. Stories are now unfolding that point out the importance of the papal role in the fall of Communism and the Lutheran role in assuring a peaceful transition from Communism to democracy in East Germany. Above all, churches and ecumenical agencies wade in with strong opinions about the justice or injustice of the war with Iraq. Dramatic examples all.

The American scene is just as interesting. The issue of abortion simply won't go away, thanks to the passion of religiously based protest groups. In state after state these groups are succeeding in getting legislatures to enact more restrictions on access to abortion. Religious groups advocate for and against legislation that would legitimate the blessing of homosexual unions. Organizations such as the American Family Association tenaciously challenge the television and film industries to clean up their acts. Mainstream Protestant denominations continue their advocacy efforts in national and state legislatures as they have for many years. But, above all, there is the rise of evangelical and fundamentalist Christians as political actors. Now representing 25–30 percent of the American population, their votes and organizations are forces to be reckoned with at all levels of American politics.

The effectiveness of the so-called Religious Right has raised the hackles and fears of secularists and liberal Christians alike, though it is difficult to see how the involvement of the Religious Right is any different in principle from what liberal Christians have been doing for many years. At any rate, religion is taking on a vigorous new role in American political debate and action.

This profusion of "revolting religion," as a student of mine once described the Reformation, comes as a surprise to many of the elite centers of Western culture. After all, one of the expectations of the more militant edge of the Enlightenment was that religion would be increasingly relegated to the private sphere, where it could not become a public nuisance or worse. That more militant Enlightenment party thought that reason, science, and technology would lead us away from the oppression of kings and the obfuscations of priests toward a world of eternal progress. Marxism was but a nasty variant on this Enlightenment belief.

Religion, irrational and therefore dangerous in their view, would gradually disappear among the educated classes and would no longer play a role in education, politics, law, medicine, or any other public endeavor. As the history of the West has unfolded, these desired outcomes were partially realized. The secularist hopes seemed to have become more plausible.

Wishing, however, did not make it so. Indeed, the ideological blinkers worn by secularists prevented them from even seeing the emerging role of Islam on the world stage. Islam as a publicly relevant religious movement was and is real. Secular intellectuals are only now catching on to the perennial relevance of religion to politics. Whether they like it or not, it is a fact.

No religion worth its salt lacks a public dimension. Great religions are comprehensive visions of life. Their themes are relevant for all of life, not just for the private sphere. Theistic religions affirm that God is the God of all life, not just of the inner recesses of the heart. Belief in God's universal law will have public repercussions for any society with a critical mass of serious believers. This is just as true of the United States or Slovakia as it is of Iran or India. The religious impulse for public relevance is irrepressible. Indeed, after long years of marginalizing the public relevance of religion, the West is now finding that religion is asserting its public face.

So the question is not *whether* organized religion will affect politics but *how* it will do so. Moreover, there are great stakes involved for both church and society in the manner in which this "how" is addressed and acted upon. Some kinds of interactions are dangerous for both church and society. Indeed, I will argue below that the greatest dangers with regard to this issue in this country regard the church, not the society. Christian churches have more to lose than their societies if they do not attend carefully to how they involve themselves in the political order.

In the following I will move through the two basic ways that the church affects politics—indirect and direct. Those two break into further subdivisions that I will explicate briefly. (Those who wish a more detailed elaboration of this topic might consult my book, *The Paradoxical Vision: A Public Theology for the Twenty-first Century* [Minneapolis: Fortress, 1995].)

By "indirect" I mean that the church as an institution does not become directly involved in political life. What political effect it does have comes through its laity who are involved in the political world. "Indirect" ways of connecting the church to politics are characterized further as unintentional or intentional. Let's look at the indirect and unintentional mode first.

THE ETHICS OF CHARACTER

The indirect and unintentional mode means that the church simply affects the deepest inward orientation of persons—their character—through its preaching, teaching, worship, and discipline. When the church is really the church, it has a profound effect on the formation of the outlook and character of its participants. In fact, when the church does indeed bring forth a "revolution of the heart and mind" of its members, it does have a powerful and deep-running effect on its surrounding society. It is arguable that this is the most powerful way a religious tradition affects public life. And it certainly is the least controversial.

There have been many historical studies of this mode. Max Weber, in *The Protestant Ethic and the Spirit of Capitalism*, and A. D. Lindsay, in *Essentials of Democracy*, showed how the church, without conscious intent, had a powerful affect on economic and political life respectively. Weber argued that capitalism could not have emerged without the "this worldly asceticism" of Calvinism, while Lindsay contended that the development of democracy in

England would have been impossible without the dissenting communions that practiced democracy within their churches.

In a similar vein, Glenn Tinder, in *The Political Meaning of Christianity*, argues that Christianity, through its millions of laypeople, has provided the spiritual center of democratic politics with its belief in the "exalted individual." We also have many contemporary examples of Christian laypeople who have been formed powerfully in their churches and who then act out their belief in the specialness of each human person in their public political life. As voters or leaders (consider former Illinois Senator Paul Simon or former U.S. Supreme Court Chief Justice William Rehnquist), they insist on just and humane policies.

Interestingly, The Lutheran Church—Missouri Synod has rarely moved beyond this indirect and unintentional mode. Yet it has been a powerful former of persons and has much indirect effect on public life through laity who have been shaped by its ethos. A surprising number of Missouri Synod laypersons and clergy have entered formal political or associational life.

This mode of connecting religion and politics has much to recommend it. It keeps the church from becoming politicized, it respects the works and gifts of the laity, and it focuses the church on its primary mission of proclamation. While many, if not most, members would like to stop with this level of church-political connection, it is to my mind insufficient. First, the church as church is entrusted with the whole Word of God for the world; it must articulate Law and Gospel to the world, not just to individuals. Second, members often fail to connect their faith and their daily life in the public world. Third, the task of formation is not being done so well these days. The laity's character is not shaped so decisively by the church as we all would like. We cannot simply rely on unintentional influence.

THE ETHICS OF CONSCIENCE

So we need a more intentional way of connecting the church with political life. We need an ethics of conscience to build on the ethics of character. This more intentional way aims at awakening the conscience of the laity by bringing the laity into a lively conversation with the social teachings of the church. Like the first indirect way, the institutional church does not become a direct actor, but unlike it, the church does try intentionally to connect the teachings of the church with the public life of the laity by stimulating their conscience.

The Evangelical Academies of Germany are excellent examples of what I mean. The academies were formed after World War II to guard against any future takeover of the public world by demonic powers, which had happened so disastrously under the Nazis. The academies brought together theologians and ethicists of the church for conversation with laity in specific callings. They also brought together diverse parties within large institutions who had natural conflicts of interest, for example, union and management. The idea was to provide a grace-full context for working out connections between Christian values and worldly challenges. In the mutual conversations that ensued, all parties became more aware of the teachings of the Christian moral tradition, the issues involved in contemporary challenges, and how the two related.

This sort of heightened moral deliberation can and does go on within our churches, but it needs much more disciplined attention than it currently receives. This "ethics of conscience" approach needs to be carried on at all levels of the churches' life if laity are to be equipped to make connections between their Sunday and Monday lives. This is not a simple task, of course, for many reasons. Many laypeople don't want their consciences stimulated when they come to church. Others invest their own social and political opinions with undue religious weight, making civil conversation well-nigh impossible. Many local congregations lack materials and talent to pull off such moral deliberation.

Nevertheless, it seems to me that this is a place for the church to direct far more attention than it has in terms of materials and training. This indirect and intentional approach really aims at equipping the saints for their lives of service in the world.

If done well, it promises far more than the more unintentional approaches to religion and politics.

There are several other indirect but intentional subcategories that I will mention only in passing. One involves the capacity of the church to awaken the consciences of the laity, then encourage them to form independent voluntary associations of their own or to join other associations that have already been formed. One thinks here of voluntary associations such as Bread for the World or Right to Life. These independent voluntary associations are numerous, for example, Lutheran Peace Fellowship, Cry for Renewal, Catholic Worker, and literally hundreds associated with the numerous denominations.

These organizations allow Christian people to band together to express an agenda that is so controversial or outright political that the churches themselves cannot properly handle it. They continue to be important conduits of Christian political witness, even as they provide significant voices for democratic political life. (In this regard, it is difficult to understand why so many secular and Christian liberals seem to regard the Religious Right's efforts as somehow an illegitimate religious incursion into political life. One can certainly criticize the Religious Right's stance on the issues, as well as its implicit claim that its stance is "Christian," but as a political force, it is a perfectly legitimate expression of a Christian voice in political affairs, just as, say, the National Council of Churches is another legitimate voice.)

Another indirect and intentional way the church can affect the public order is through its church-related institutions. If the church really has the courage to embody its vision and values in the institutional life of its related colleges, social service agencies, senior citizen homes, etc., it will make a strong public witness. Such "social pioneering," as H. R. Niebuhr termed it, has been and is one of the most effective ways of influencing public life. Institutional incarnations of religious values demonstrate the connections between church and world in a particularly persuasive way.

THE CHURCH AS CORPORATE CONSCIENCE

If the church were to take these indirect modes of connecting religion and politics seriously, it would have its plate full. And there would be less energy and time left for the direct ways of relating religion and politics. However, there are theological and ecclesiological reasons for more direct approaches to religion and politics. Theologically, the church is entrusted with the Word of God in both Law and Gospel; it is called to address them both to the world, not just to its own congregants. God's moral and religious claims are on the whole world, not just Christians. Ecclesiologically, the church is more than its dispersed laity. As an institution it, too, is the body of Christ; it is called to act corporately, not only individually.

Thus we have a warrant for direct and intentional approaches to the world. The best examples of these are papal encyclicals, bishops' letters, and church social statements. In such instruments the church not only addresses its laity but also tries to influence public policy. There are scores of statements now on American policy toward Iraq, most of them poorly done. In truth, Catholics have been far more successful along these lines than Protestants. Although every mainstream Protestant communion tries mightily to make an impact on the world with its statements, they are for the most part ignored by both its laity and the world.

There are reasons for this disparity. First, Catholics speak with moral weight because of the size of their communion and because the pope has retained a measure of moral authority. Second, Catholics speak relatively infrequently on carefully chosen topics. This gives them time to craft statements carefully and to take seriously the input and feedback they invite. Third, Catholics seem to argue from their own unique moral tradition. This gives them a certain immunity from the world's ideological divides and lends them an integrity that is increasingly scarce in our fractured public world. Fourth, they carefully distinguish among levels of authority. Affirmations of core convictions that all Catholics should hold are distinguished from public policy options about which Catholics of goodwill and intelligence can disagree. Room is made for both consensus and disensus.

It should be noted that historically one of the most effective means of public witness has been a prophetic *no* to certain political or social practices. The Confessing Church's direct refusal to capitulate to Nazi demands on the church is a case in point, as was the Norwegian church's resistance to Nazism. The pope's denunciation of abortion as part of the "culture of death" is another. Often, when social practices move toward the demonic, a vigorous proscription rather than a presumptuous prescription is called for.

Despite all, the church must act as the conscience of the body of Christ. It should do so wisely, sparingly, and authentically. When it does so, direct and intentional influence is a legitimate and effective way the church connects with the political sphere.

THE CHURCH WITH POWER

Some of the dramatic examples of the church's involvement with politics that I listed at the beginning of this essay demonstrate this direct approach to the political sphere. Under this mode the church moves beyond persuasion to more coercive types of involvement. It uses its institutional power—money, staff, troops—to sway public policy according to its will. This approach is the most controversial and debatable way of connecting religion and politics. It is controversial because it commits the institution, the body of Christ, to partisan public policies about which the membership often has no consensus. It is debatable because it commits the church to the use of power, the "earthly sword," a practice against which the reformers protested. God has given the church the power of the Word, they argued, not worldly power, and when the church becomes too involved in political power, it loses its integrity as the body of Christ. It lends its sacred symbols to worldly projects.

Protestant churches participate in "soft" forms of direct power when they operate advocacy offices in national and state legislatures, when they use their pension and investments to induce businesses to follow policies the church endorses, and when church bodies commit money and leadership to "conflict-oriented" community organizations. The controversy surrounding each of these activities bears witness to their borderline legitimacy.

A wise church, I believe, will use such means only when there are no other options for the church or the society. The church, for example, must inescapably invest its money, so it should do so on the basis of its own values. But it should do so within rather wide parameters; it should proscribe or support business practices only at the obvious extremes. It should not be overly aggressive and intrusive with regard to the vast majority of enterprises in the murky middle. With regard to society, the church may responsibly act directly if there are no other organizations to do so because they are absent or have been suppressed. The Polish Catholic Church's support of Solidarity is a case in point. The Catholic Church's withdrawal of support for Ferdinand Marcos in the Philippines is another. In both cases the church withdrew from direct political action when other options became available in the society.

CONCLUSION

It is clear that there are a number of options for connecting religion and politics. I have outlined several of these options and have commented on their legitimacy. I believe the Lutheran tradition strongly prefers the more indirect connections, though it leaves room for judicious use of the direct. We would do well, I think, to focus more attention on the indirect and intentional ways to make a public impact. The laity in the world and in church-related institutions are the foot soldiers in the battle for a humane and justly ordered world. The church should heed its calling by preparing them more fully.

RELIGIOUS FAITH
AND POLITICAL OFFICE

AN ILLICIT CONNECTION?

The religious expressiveness of vice-presidential nominee Senator Joseph Lieberman has caused quite a stir. It seems to have been the stick that broke the camel's back. After all, at least three out of the four candidates for president and vice president have talked openly of their faith and how it relates to their politics. Dick Cheney seems to be the only reticent one of the four when it comes to expressing his faith in public. Certainly President Clinton has not been bashful about his faith. Indeed, commentator Mark Silk has suggested that Clinton has been the most religion-friendly president since Eisenhower and perhaps of all time.

But Lieberman's openness and assertiveness about how his religious practices and convictions affect his political life seem to have stimulated a major discussion. In general, conservatives have welcomed this, with some provisos. A recent issue of *The Weekly Standard* was entitled "Faith Talk." Although its editors lamented

Originally published in *The Cresset* (Reformation 2000).
Amended and reprinted with permission.

the religiosity and self-righteousness involved in some such expressions, they welcomed the more overt role for religion in public life. The editors of the evangelical Web site *Religion Today* appreciated Lieberman's public religious articulations but worried that they are a strategy to revive a "religious left."

However, most liberals and secularists among the elite were less than welcoming of Lieberman's public professions. The Anti-Defamation League, the American Civil Liberties Union, and Americans United for Separation of Church and State called upon him to cease and desist, worrying that appeals along religious lines violate the American ideal. Our local newspaper, *The Roanoke News*, applauded the cautions that those organizations raised, while at the same time it appreciated Lieberman's elaboration of the sources of the personal values that might affect his decision-making. But the same newspaper chastised him for "substituting noble motive for reasoned argument as the justification for the positions he takes," as if religion has nothing to add but motive to policy formation. The liberal columnist Robert Reno was contemptuous of Lieberman's "oozed religiosity." He raised the alarm that "stuffing more religion into politics" will lead inevitably to sectarian conflict and bloodletting.

Most of the public conversation about religion in political life has been pretty muddled and confused, some of it downright wrongheaded. The interaction between religion and politics—and politics and religion, for that matter—is a complex phenomenon upon which I would like to shed some light. I have written extensively on this issue in my book *The Paradoxical Vision: A Public Theology for the Twenty-first Century*.

This current conversation gives me a chance to focus on one particular facet of a highly complicated subject matter. That focal point is on the ways in which public political figures connect their religious convictions to their political life. Further, we can reflect on some of the standards for better or worse ways of connecting faith and politics on the part of public officeholders.

I.

First, let us clear up some confusion. The case of Lieberman—of an individual political figure connecting his faith with his office—easily can be distinguished from church-state issues. Unfortunately, the "separation of church and state" phrase is such an omnipresent mantra that it is used in all-purpose ways, even to stricturing an individual such as Lieberman. Church-state separation refers to institutions and their relations. Although there is good reason for keeping those two institutions separate (no established church, for instance), there is no constitutional or practical way to keep individuals—even public officeholders—from exercising their religious beliefs as a basis for their political actions. It is totally misplaced to wheel out the slogan of church-state separation to try to silence individual believers.

Indeed, the issue of political officials connecting their faith and their work is a subspecies of the general subject of religion and politics. Religion and politics constitutes a much larger field of interest, including church-state relations. But the field of religion and politics also includes inquiry into the religiously informed voting patterns of believers, the programs and actions of the thousands of nonchurch yet religious voluntary associations, and of course how public figures connect their faith and work. All these actions examined in such studies are actions that are constitutionally protected. Further, they would be impossible to bar from use because they issue from deeply held but often private convictions that would be impossible to identify or limit. Religion and politics as a field of interest also includes the ways that politics—including the judiciary—affect religious life not only in its institutional but also in its individual dimensions.

So religion and politics will interact, even the religion and politics of political figures. Certainly the connection of religion and politics by political figures has been evident throughout the ages. Plato's philosopher king was essentially a religiously inspired ruler. The Christian prince of the Middle Ages was expected to protect Christian convictions and practices. The founders of our country certainly expressed religious convictions in our founding documents. One does not have to look far to detect the underlying Judeo-Christian belief in the sanctity of the individual person in our nation's guarantees of "inalienable rights." The political philosopher Glenn Tinder has located the "exalted individual" as the spiritual center of Western politics, adhered to and expressed by many political exemplars of our tradition.

Robert Bellah, in his study of American civil religion, showed how every newly elected president feels compelled to rely on "God-talk" to legitimate, bless, sometimes criticize, and often inspire the nation to higher achievements of justice. Sometimes the inaugural addresses are boilerplate, but at other times they embody profound religious insights for the nation and its trajectory. Who cannot admire the deep religious wisdom in the inaugural addresses of Washington, Lincoln, and many other thoughtful presidents? Obviously these are positive cases of officeholders expressing their religious convictions in public.

II.

So the question is not so much whether the religion of officeholders will interact with their politics but how it will do so. We should add the qualifier that the officeholder has to be serious about his or her religion, as Lieberman seems to be. There are indeed officeholders who either are not seriously religious or hold their religious convictions in a completely different realm than their political activities. Such seems to have been the case with John F. Kennedy, who assured those who were worried about his Catholic upbringing that his faith would make no difference whatsoever to his political actions as a prospective president. No doubt many other political figures make no connection between their faith—if they have any—and their politics. However, for those who take their religion seriously, there can be no separation of their faith and politics, though there certainly ought to be a distinction.

The great religious traditions—Judaism, Christianity, Islam, and Hinduism—provide comprehensive visions of life. For the dominant traditions in America—Judaism and Christianity—God is the God of all, not just the private places of one's own heart. God is a God of history. The biblical narrative, and the reflection upon it in both Judaism and Christianity, provides wisdom about the origin and destiny of the world, about the character of history and its unfolding, about human nature and its predicament, about human salvation, about our callings as human beings, and about human moral conduct in the world. Each item of religious wisdom has political implications, though it may well be indirect and varied. A whole vision of human flourishing in the world is borne by these traditions.

These traditions involve far more than just motivation, though they do involve that. Secularists are willing to allow for religious motivation, but they would like those so motivated to be quiet about it. Further, they allow no real content—religious and moral principles growing out of those traditions—to become operative in political life because they have bought the secularist argument that religion is irrational and arbitrary. Therefore the content of religion ought to remain private. If it doesn't, as Reno argued, it will lead to irrational and irreconcilable conflicts.

But such a judgment simply cannot hold. Without the religious and moral content of the Jewish and Christian traditions, there would have been no Declaration of Independence, Revolutionary War, U.S. Constitution, abolition movement, prohibition movement, civil rights movement, and no current lively debate over abortion, euthanasia, sex education, foreign policy, and the employment of faith-based organizations to get the work of our society done. It is true that sometimes the religious and moral content for these items was filtered through the language of the Enlightenment or some other less overtly religious ideology, but nevertheless the fundamental notions come from the religious traditions.

There is little doubt, then, that public officeholders who are seriously religious will connect their faith and their politics.

Lieberman's religious expressiveness is not at all extraordinary. However, that said, there remains the question of what are the better or worse ways of making the connection. There are ample cases of poor or even worrisome connections.

III.

The first kind of bad connection could be termed the *instrumental*. By this I mean that religious concepts or practices are simply used to sanctify or legitimate the public official's own ambition or ideology. Religious principles are not given an integrity of their own; they are simply used for the politician's own purposes, be those purposes personal or ideological. In some extreme cases, dangerous demagogues use religion to enhance their own power. When an ex-Communist such as Milosevic in Serbia wraps himself in the symbols of Orthodoxy to maintain and extend his own power, we have a demagogic use of religion.

The instrumentalizing of religious principles and practices are not always so extreme. Religious conservatives and liberals have long used verses from the Bible to proof-text favorite policies that have no necessary connection to those verses. Conservatives have used biblical imagery of evil to legitimate anticommunism. Liberals have used biblical passages to reinforce their preferred welfare policies. President Clinton has used the practices of confession and absolution to defend himself amid his various skirmishes. Instead of keeping such practices private where their authenticity would be much more credible, he stages public events that promote his own political welfare.

The temptations of instrumentalizing religion for political purposes are manifold. As political figures use religion, it is quite likely that their motives run the continuum from worthy to base, with most in between. But the crass instrumentalization of religion is evident enough in the modern world to warrant the call for reticence in the use of religion. Those who have protested Lieberman's eager use of religion have a point. Religion can easily be corrupted by reducing it to an instrument for other purposes.

Another hazard for political figures using religion in their political activities is what could be called the *direct line* use. By this I mean that a simple, direct line is drawn from a religious principle to a particular policy. Our local newspaper rightly criticized Lieberman for such a misstep. Citing the commandment to honor one's father and mother, Lieberman invoked that injunction to support the Democrats' proposal to add a prescription drug benefit to Medicare. A simple line was drawn from one to the other when in fact the movement from one to the other was far from simple or direct. Liebermann was rightly criticized for such a simplistic use of a religious precept.

IV.

A far more persuasive use of religious principles is indirect. Most usable religious principles are of a high level of generality. "Love thy neighbor." "Do justice and mercy." "All humans are created in the image of God." "Thou shalt not steal." They provide basic moral presumptions of a high level of generality. They rarely issue forth directly and simply into specific policies. There are many steps to negotiate as one moves from those high level, general principles to specific policies. Persons with the same core beliefs, persons of goodwill and intelligence, part ways as they negotiate the many steps from the religious principle to the concrete policy. That is why many Christian persons with the same core religious and moral beliefs can disagree on specific policies. Sincere Christians inhabit both sides of the political divide on most issues. That fact does not mean that their religious convictions are irrelevant; it simply means that they move from general principle to specific policies along different trajectories. It also might mean that they order their principles along a different scale of priority.

One might think of the movement from core religious and moral principles to specific policy as one of traversing a number of concentric circles. At the center stand the core biblical principles. But those core principles, general as they are, must be given more specificity by intermediate guidance principles. Does doing justice, for example, mean affirmative action or equality of opportunity? When one begins to answer that question, one draws upon different philosophical conceptions of justice, on one's assessment of human nature, on the role of disincentives and incentives in public policy, and a host of other considerations, including the question of feasibility. The best arguments start from solid religious premises and persuasively move through a number of subarguments to concrete public policy. There certainly are better and worse kinds of arguments, though we naturally judge those arguments through partisan eyes.

There is little doubt that seriously religious political figures not only are motivated to do good in politics but also at their best operate from fundamental—though general—religious principles. As those principles move toward concrete policy, though, they necessarily include many other sorts of judgments that are not biblical or even religious. Contrary to some secularist objections, though, there is no reason why the full argument—from religious premise to specific policy—should not be made public. Religious political figures have as much right to articulate publicly the basis of their political judgments as do secular figures. It's just that there has to be a certain amount of sophistication and humility about the complexity of the argument.

Let me add several provisos here. My emphasis on indirectness does not mean that all policies deserve respect as they move from the general to the specific. Some indeed represent inferior movements that must be ruled out. One cannot, for example, begin with the principle of the sacredness of each individual before God and wind up with a racist policy. One cannot hold the commandment against killing and blithely take life at its beginning and ending. So not "everything goes" in this indirect approach. The religious principles themselves rule out certain policies.

Another proviso. This emphasis on indirectness does not rule out a direct and prophetic response to certain obvious evils on the basis of rather simple biblical principles. When the Nazis declared many sorts of people to be subhuman and proceeded to treat them that way, there was little need on the part of courageous religious and political figures to go through complex and indirect arguments. A simple and resounding *no* was the best response. Biblical principles demanded such simplicity. Certain obvious goods and evils should elicit simple but passionate responses on the part of seriously religious political figures. However, most policies do not exhibit such clear qualities of good and evil.

A robust connection between the political actor's religious faith and his or her public actions is certainly not an illicit one. But as in the case of most profound issues, the exercise of religion in politics by the political actor is a complex one that needs careful consideration. Perhaps these reflections might add a bit to such consideration.

Faith-Based Organizations as Instruments of Public Policy

When newly elected President George W. Bush made clear his intention to make tax dollars available to faith-based organizations (including churches), the usual suspects stepped forward. The ubiquitous Barry Lynn of Americans United for Separation of Church and State complained that "Bush is proposing an unprecedented program of tax support for religion, involving literally billions in public resources. His plan for social services would essentially merge church and state into a single bureaucracy that would dispense religion alongside assistance to the needy."[1] On the other side are those who saw no danger to church or state in this new Office of Faith-based Action. Louis Sheldon of the Traditional Values Coalition argued that "there are basic services provided by faith-based institutions which can be delivered free of any constitutional concerns."[2]

Originally published in *The Cresset* (Easter 2001).
Amended and reprinted with permission.

This is, of course, true if the services offered have no sort of religious teaching or practice connected with them. But aren't serious religious organizations going to offer services with religious meanings deeply involved in them? Such a point is made by Elizabeth Strother, an editorial writer for our local newspaper, *The Roanoke Times*. She detects that many, though certainly not all, services offered by religious organizations are freighted with religious meanings and practices. In those cases, "the mission and the message are one," she writes. "It's not faith-based. It's faith."[3] This observation leads her to turn against the new Bush initiative because it will break through the "thin wall of separation" our revered Thomas Jefferson supposedly erected.

Except for the fevered exaggerations of Lynn, perhaps all the points made above are true. But where does that leave us? A bit muddled, I believe. It would help if we could sort out what we mean by faith-based organizations, their motives, their activities, and their effects. It seems that faith-based organizations include churches (St. Andrew by the gas station), as well as the independent or semi-independent organizations (Catholic Charities, Lutheran Social Services) associated with them. It also includes organizations formed by religious people that are completely freestanding (Prison Fellowship). All of these examples provide faith-based services.

But now things get interesting. What is it about faith-based organizations that poses constitutional or political problems in funding them? If we do a bit of Aristotelian analysis, we can break their work into some useful categories—motive (why they do what they do), manner (how they do it), action (the program itself), and results (effects on the persons involved in the services). These categories can shine light on the problems before us.

I.

Let's start with *motive*. Most faith-based organizations began with 100 percent of their staff members of the sponsoring tradition. Lutheran orphanages, for example, were staffed almost wholly by

Lutherans. These Lutherans were presumed to be motivated by the love of God and love of neighbor. Although staffs are now much more pluralistic, it is a rare faith-based agency that does not claim that its motive is love of neighbor, one of the great religious commandments. Even the more secularized of these religious organizations try to seek out persons who have a genuine commitment to help those in their care. Most are not reluctant to use the rhetoric of obeying and pleasing God by serving the needy, at least to their church constituency. What they say to government funding agencies is another matter. (It is interesting that government or secular agencies might well want these highly motivated folk, but they would be unable to recognize publicly the motives of many of their staff. Many schools of social work want these sorts of people but will not or cannot recognize their motives.)

Certainly the public rehearsal of their religious motivation should not disbar faith-based organizations from receiving federal funds. Many secular organizations are staffed by persons with religious motivations. Why should they be funded and those who profess their motivations be disbarred from government funds? To disbar faith-based organizations is to show hostility, not neutrality, toward religion.

II.

Let's move on to the *how* or the *way* that faith-based agencies offer their services. If there are sufficient numbers of highly motivated religious persons in a faith-based agency, there should be a difference in the *way* or *manner* that services are offered. For one thing, such agencies will tend to be more efficient. They can tap into energy that will get more bang for the buck. Many church-connected organizations make precisely that point. They spend less on administration than their public counterparts. They provide services with less bureaucracy. Religious schools generally exemplify these characteristics. Their ratio of teachers to administrators is much better than that of public schools.

Faith-based agencies staffed by highly motivated religious people will tend to treat their clients or patients with more respect, perhaps even love. Further, they are more likely to be attentive to the whole person—including the emotional and spiritual dimensions of the persons served. These characteristics deal with the *way* or *manner* organizations proceed to offer services. What these organizations offer may be the same service or good that secular agencies offer, but it may be done better, with more efficiency and respect. For example, Lutheran Social Services offers low-cost, government-subsidized housing for the elderly poor in many areas of the country. The elderly of modest means are often drawn to such housing because the religious agency provides it with more efficiency, respect, and care.

It would be difficult to see the constitutional problem involved here. What the religious agency is offering is a "secular" service or good that nonreligious organizations also offer. Perhaps the religious agency can add another dimension to it because of highly motivated and loving persons employed by the agency. Why should faith-based organizations involved in "secular" services of this type be barred from government funds? (I certainly think that some secular agencies may do as well with equally highly motivated people, but perhaps general tendencies might favor the faith-based organizations.)

The answer to my question is: Those sorts of "secular" services supplied by faith-based agencies are not barred from government funding. There are already numerous examples of this kind of arrangement between local, state, and federal governments and faith-based organizations. This arrangement has been going on for many years without much notice. Catholic Charities and Lutheran Social Services would have to slash their staffs dramatically if government funding were withdrawn. Many services to needy persons would have to be shifted to secular agencies. Hundreds of church-related colleges offer liberal arts education to students who may well be at least partially and indirectly subsidized by the state or national government. If government aid to these kinds of faith-based services is what President Bush means in his new initiative, it is nothing new or path-breaking. Only obsessional separationists such as Lynn would and do object. Only highly independent faith-based organizations refuse government support. But the new initiative may extend support to groups that have not been supported before—local church food pantries and emergency services, for example. That, it seems to me, would be all to the good.

This is not to suggest that even this kind of public subsidy is without dangers, though I believe the danger is to the faith-based agency, not to the government or civil rights. Government funding inevitably includes regulation. Primarily this has meant regulations prohibiting discrimination on the basis of religion. Such implementation can quickly dilute the identity and ethos of the faith-based organization, if, for example, those organizations are required to employ people without faith. Or organizations may be required not to discriminate for people of the particular faith tradition that sponsors the organizations. Such regulation may also force faith-based organizations to hire people whose practices violate the moral principles of their faith, witness the pressure put on Catholic social service organizations to hire open homosexuals.

This latter problem, of course, is the source of much controversy in Congress. Rick Santorum, the proponent of the legislative initiative, withdrew his proviso that allowed faith-based organizations to discriminate religiously and morally. He did this to save the basic legislation in the face of serious opposition. This, it seems to me, is a grave problem. Local churches could be faced with antidiscrimination obligations that would vitiate their identities. Social service agencies would have to give up discrimination for members of their sponsoring traditions.

Further, access to government troughs also vitiates the will of faith-based agencies and their contributors to raise or give away their own money. If big-pockets government supports the work, why should individual donors do so, especially if there are many worthy projects that are not government supported? The professionalization made possible and necessary by large sums of government money also discourages the use of volunteers in the workings of the agencies. Amateur doers of good deeds are no longer needed or wanted. Such professionalization and specialization also hasten the secularization of the agency.

This arrangement has already secularized many religious organizations even as it has made many services available to a large number of people. That secularization is partly the fault of the governments involved but perhaps even more the fault of the agencies. Too many lost confidence in their own particular gifts and obligations as faith-based organizations. The fault is equally divided because both government and agency have not allowed what the agency does as service to be imbued with religious meanings and practices. Nor have they allowed the agencies to discriminate for members of their religious tradition. Those faith-based organizations have been only too willing to secularize for the money the state offers. In due time many lose whatever distinctiveness they had. It is a dangerous business to accept money from the government. It takes courage and shrewdness to receive government money without losing one's soul. It can be done, but I believe it is relatively rare.

III.

Let's now move from the motivation for and manner of the faith-based agency's services to the *what* of their services. This is the heart of the matter. To use our housing example, a serious faith-based organization would not only provide housing efficiently and respectfully to the elderly poor by highly motivated and loving persons, it would provide a chaplaincy and religious programming for them. It would provide them because it believes that the spiritual dimension of the lives of the elderly poor is just as important, probably more important, than the material conditions in which they live. To use another well-known example, Prison Fellowship does not just offer secular services with efficiency and care, it intends to convert prisoners to the Christian faith and way of life. The Christian vision shapes *what* the agency is offering. The *what* is pervaded by Christian meaning and practice. As Strother argued above: "The mission and the message are one."

Why, indeed, shouldn't *what* the faith-based agency offers be so pervaded? After all, Christianity, like all the world's great religions, bears an account of human meaning and flourishing that is comprehensive and central. It should indeed shape what good or service is being offered. Christians believe that receiving the Gospel and living a Christian life in response to it is essential for full human flourishing. Why wouldn't Christian faith-based organizations shape their offerings according to this vision?

Sadly, because government insisted that the *what* be nonreligious, many faith-based organizations secularized themselves by importing secular models of understanding and practice into their work. Christian homes for children moved from bringing up the children in the Christian life to using group homes driven by the models of behavioral psychology. Christian social services gave up pastoral care approaches for those of social work. Christian colleges gave up Christian humanism for Enlightenment models of teaching, learning, and research. And it is not as if these imports are neutral; most of them are pervaded by a different, if not contrasting, view of the world. There are some examples of resistance to this self-secularization, but the larger story has been dismal. The dangers of government regulation and of religious capitulation are herewith only noted; we could go into painful stories of how Christians gave up their approach for the secular.

Now, if President Bush means in his new initiative that *what* the faith-based organization offers can be pervaded by religious meanings and practices, then we are in a new ball game. Serious religious agencies—those whose efforts are yet permeated by Christian understandings and practices—should participate in this initiative only if this provision is enacted. They should be able to offer services shaped and pervaded by the religious account that their faith affirms. If they are not allowed to do this, they are on the way to self-secularization and their unique gifts will be lost. The service will be secularized; it will lose its religious punch. But if this stronger version of cooperation is what is meant by

President Bush, aren't we indeed "establishing" religious-based organizations, about which poor Barry Lynn constantly inveighs?

This is doubtful, if there are a variety of religious and non-religious organizations vying for government support. The government is only giving a fair shake to religious groups, not establishing them. It may not give them preferential treatment.

IV.

This stronger version will be given even stronger support if we add another analytical category—*results*. Isn't the government primarily interested in the *results* of the efforts of social service agencies—secular and religious alike? In efforts at rehabilitation, it wants criminals to reform their lives and become trustworthy citizens. Doesn't Prison Fellowship do that? With regard to housing for the elderly poor, doesn't the government want good housing and whole person care for its clients? Doesn't a full-blown Christian housing ministry do that? With regard to higher education, doesn't the government want well and broadly educated citizens who have the motivation toward service? Don't robust Christian or Jewish colleges do that? If *effects* are the focus of government policy, it would seem wise to include faith-based organizations, even if *what* they are doing is pervaded with religious meaning and practice. The *what* should perhaps be subservient to *results*. The legality of this point of view was argued years ago by Philip Kurland as part of the larger argument for government support for "mediating institutions" put forward by Peter Berger and Richard Neuhaus in their book *To Empower People*.

After supporting this strong version of cooperation between faith-based agencies and government, I end with a few caveats. Government must not intervene in what the faith-based religious organizations are doing. That is the road to secularization of those organizations; it would be better for them not to take government money. Many serious Christian organizations do not take government money for precisely this reason; they won't be able to permeate their service with Christian meanings and practices. Nor would they be able to hire only Christians of their persuasion.

Further, government should contribute only a share of the income of faith-based organizations so the organizations do not become lazy in cultivating a base of private supporters. Government should make sure there are alternatives to faith-based organizations so people are not coerced into religious practices against their will.

Moreover, government will have to scrutinize the results of the work of faith-based organizations, as well as secular ones. It will have to develop a sharp set of criteria so the results of the work of all organizations receiving support will be effective and comport with the general ideals and values of the American tradition. Young people going through a family service agency cannot come out the other end as racists or antidemocrats. Such criteria will address the "kook factor," I think. The Nation of Islam or David Koresh or extremist Muslim groups would be disallowed on these civic grounds. But if they do come out as good persons and citizens, what matter to the government if they became such through Christian or Jewish or Muslim or humanist formation and nurture?

V.

I am not so naïve as to believe that this stronger version of the initiative will see the light of day. If it would win legislatively, it would no doubt be struck down by the courts. It is only what should happen. If Santorum is willing to relinquish the nondiscriminatory proviso for faith-based organizations, this stronger version has virtually no chance of being enacted when this legislation is brought up again. In light of this fact, I would only advise those already beholden to government support to try to retain what Christian vestiges they have left in their overall efforts to supply basically "secular" services. They will perhaps receive more government support in the years ahead. But with that will come further temptations to give up even those vestiges.

I would welcome government support for the churches' ventures in food pantries, meal programs, emergency services, economic support, housing, etc. That sort of support seems to me the real promise of the program. But the churches should beware. If they get into paid staff in any of these ventures, they may be subject to antidiscrimination laws. And they may be encouraged to give up the volunteer nature of their programs if money is available for paid staff. That would be a shame, I think.

Those faith-based agencies whose work—what they are offering—is permeated by Christian understandings and practices should avoid the new initiative because it will be a plague for them. Government support will introduce a destructive virus into the center of their efforts. They may receive money, but they will give up their soul. Serious Christian operations of this sort prefer tax breaks for donors along the lines of the Charitable Choice Legislation or they prefer vouchers that would allow their clients to make free choices. In either approach, these Christian agencies can keep government intrusion at arm's length and thus protect their own specific identity and mission.

VI.

There is little in Lutheran theology that discourages this sort of interaction between church and state, even the stronger version outlined above. As William Lazareth put it well for the Lutheran Church in America, Lutherans believe in "institutional separation but functional interaction." The faith-based initiative does not violate this principle, as long as neither institution is compromised by the interaction. The grand tradition of Lutheran social care can be aided by this initiative. Churches and their agencies can be used for the civic good. If the legislation is crafted properly, perhaps faith-based organizations can receive government support to offer "secular services" without compromise, though they should remain wary. However, if Lutheran agencies offer services that are shaped by their religious convictions, they should steer clear of direct government support. It will rob them of their soul.

NOTES

1. www.au.org. Accessed August 17, 2001.
2. traditionalvalues.org. Accessed August 2001.
3. *The Roanoke Times* (February 5, 2001).

THE PERSISTENCE
OF CIVIL RELIGION

A judge in San Francisco has ruled that saying the Pledge of Allegiance in our schools is unconstitutional. A firestorm has ensued, with the whole Congress rising up in indignation that such a crazy ruling should be made. The president denounced the decision. There seems little chance the ruling will stand. Although the most brazen, this ruling is only the most recent skirmish about the role of God-language in our public life. There have been many others.

In recent days, for example, we have witnessed a successful—for the moment—legal challenge by two cadets to the Virginia Military Institute's practice of saying a nonsectarian grace before some meals at the school. Naturally the ACLU joined in protest of this "establishment of religion."

But the San Francisco judge, the ACLU, and others who want to sanitize all public space of religious symbols and language are bound to be frustrated. What is called "civil religion" has been

Originally published in *Journal of Lutheran Ethics*, vol. 2, no. 11 (November 2002). Available online at www.elca.org/jle. Amended and reprinted with permission.

present and active in the public sphere since the beginning of the Republic, and there is little chance that it will disappear despite the relentless efforts of activist judges and the ACLU. It is present in all the major events in American civic life and rushes in with special power in times of national crisis. In the 9/11 crisis, it was expressed in schools, Congress, the rhetoric of many leaders, the media, and especially in the civic piety of the people.

Even some of those who are sympathetic with the sanitizers' general program participated in the civil religion in post-9/11 times. Our local paper, *The Roanoke Times*, for example, ran full-page ads in several issues with the banner headline: "God Bless America." Indeed, the song of that name, with its overt religious language, has almost replaced the official national anthem as America's favorite hymn of unity.

Written in 1938 by Irving Berlin, a Jewish immigrant from Siberia, the song is a near perfect expression of America's civil religion. It strikes notes common to both the Jewish and Christian traditions—God's blessing and guidance. Moreover, one might expect American Muslims to share in such a civil religious expression, if "God" can be a worthy substitute for "Allah" for them. The civil religion carefully avoids allusions to specific elements of Jewish or Christian faith that depart from the civil religion's common ground.

American civil religion is the common denominator of a religious country under the First Amendment. When there is no established church or religion yet there is a great deal of religious vitality in the country, civil religion is an inevitable result. A religious people want a transcendent dimension to the great moments of national life, and civil religion is the vehicle for that. Military institutes desire moments of transcendence in the preparation of future soldiers. One might add that the pressure for that transcendent dimension in elementary and secondary education is also the result of a religious people seeking the blessing and guidance of God for the nation and for their children's lives. The Pledge of Allegiance is one such practice in the life of our schools.

It has been so from the beginning of our country. Part of American civil religion stems from the Deism of some of the founders, who rejected many specifics of Jewish and Christian religion for a presumed rational basis for religion. But civil religion's genius is that serious Jewish and Christian believers can use it for their public religious aspirations. And they have. Among the great practitioners of civil religion have been presidents who articulate their vision for the nation in their inaugural addresses. Many of these expressions are boilerplate, but some of them rise to grand heights. Abraham Lincoln's second inaugural address is perhaps the grandest and most profound of them all. What makes it so great is that Lincoln discerns both God's blessing and judgment in the cataclysmic movement of history in his time. His address is also ethically serious because it makes moral demands on the nation to complete its unfinished tasks.

Civil religion can be trivial or even dangerous if it is used merely to give a religious gloss to national ambition. But if there is a serious effort to connect America with both divine blessing and guidance, as the Pledge of Allegiance and "God Bless America" do, civil religion can be noble and necessary. And it won't go away.

Lutherans, therefore, should have a nuanced posture toward American civil religion. All religious aspirations—such as those implicit in civil religion—that arise in the left-hand kingdom are not necessarily evil. The point, as Philip Hefner and I argued many years ago in *Defining America*, is to keep civil religion healthy by emphasizing its critical edge along with its affirming edge. Civil religion will be used mostly to bless and affirm what the nation does. Sometimes that is good. However, it is particularly important for Christians to insist that civil religion also call America to live up to its best ideals—liberty and justice for all. Martin Luther King Jr. was an especially powerful wielder of that dimension of civil religion. He did not shrink from drawing upon its ideals.

Civil religion has nothing to do with salvation. Indeed, it becomes a false and idolatrous religion if it is inflated to that role.

But as a dimension of our life under the Law, it has important functions—for both good and evil—in our common life. It helps define who we are as a people. So the ACLU and the judge are right. Civil religion is a kind of "established religion," but it is a justified one that was intended and practiced by our founders, not an unconstitutional one. Christians should try to make sure it is used properly.

CAN LIBERALISM
BE TOTALITARIAN?

In the mid-1970s, officials from the Office of Equal Opportunity encouraged a bus driver to bring suit against Roanoke's Shenandoah Baptist Church and its school for paying "heads of households" more than nonheads. It was not a case of gender discrimination because if a woman were the head of a household, she received higher pay also. The church and school are of a fundamentalist Christian persuasion and thought they were following the New Testament literally when they set up such a pay scale. But the Feds saw it differently and engaged in an eleven-year litigation with the church and school to bring it to "justice." Finally, after thousands of dollars paid out by the fundamentalists to counter the near inexhaustible resources of the Justice Department, they wearily decided to settle for a three hundred thousand dollar fine!

One could scarcely believe that such a thing could happen in our country. But it did. A local congregation that thought it was doing the Lord's will was forced by the Justice Department to conform to liberal notions of justice. There are many examples of this

Originally published in *The Cresset* (Reformation 2001).
Amended and reprinted with permission.

liberal overreach. The Boy Scouts came within one vote of the Supreme Court from losing their freedom to select their leadership according to their own criteria. The Salvation Army was forced to pull out of San Francisco because it will not bow to local nondiscrimination laws that would force it to employ persons whose actions violate the group's moral convictions. Colleges and universities that accept, even indirectly, any kind of federal money have to submit to quotalike gender equity requirements in their athletic programs, among other things. Larger schools employ full-time "compliance" officers to make sure they follow the federal formulae. Any essentially private organization that interfaces with the public can be forced to alter its membership requirements. The long arm of liberal justice even reaches into family life and prescribes what kind of parental punishment of children is allowed. I fear that this interventionism will soon be applied to religious organizations, making them comply with the "just policies" that secular liberalism has legislated.

Abroad, the European Union is fast prescribing bureaucratic guidelines for all sorts of private life, extending from stringent laws that are running small butcher shops out of business to laws prescribing the exact size of condoms. As in the United States, liberal intervention into private economic life has prepared us for intervention into military and associational life, even family life.

I.

These liberal interventions seem to follow from three contested— and, in my view, faulty—principles of justice. First, liberalism holds to a doctrine of individual rights that can be used as a razor against any private organization or tradition. That doctrine came into play against Shenandoah Baptist. The individual's right to equal pay for equal work trumped the privately held notion that those financially responsible for families should receive more pay. It also came into play against the Boy Scouts. The individual right to be an atheist and to practice homosexual relations was held by a number of lower courts to preempt the Boy Scouts long-held requirements that members believe in God and uphold traditional sexual ethics. These rights might also be exercised against faith-based organizations that provide social services in the new initiatives being proposed by President Bush.

A second principle is that of equality of results. The older notion of equality of opportunity has gradually been displaced by the modern liberal notion of equality of results. It is not enough to make the race for social goods fair and equal, it is now necessary to fix the results of the race. This generally means that the composition of any enterprise, private or public, should reflect the composition of the surrounding membership or population. This scarcely veiled system of group rights, strangely at odds with the liberal doctrine of individual rights, means that "excluded" groups must be represented in a mathematically proportionate manner in whatever enterprise to which this principle is applied. This doctrine is at work in the Title IX laws that are applied to college and university athletic programs. It has also sustained the "set aside" programs in business as well as university admissions quotas, both of which are now under fire by the courts.

The third principle that has invaded the private sphere is that of unlimited accountability. By that I mean that accountability for actions has been diminished by those immediately involved in them and extended exponentially to all those remotely or indirectly involved in those actions. Applied in the economic sphere, this has meant class-action suits against many firms—pharmaceutical, medical, tobacco, automobile—that have sometimes resulted in the bankruptcy or near-bankruptcy of those firms. In the sphere of society, it has meant litigation against persons whose responsibility for a harmful action is remote, to say the least. A bishop friend of mine was subject to litigation in four different cases of sexual harassment that had occurred in local parishes before he was bishop! Many professionals live in fear of the consequences of this kind of unlimited accountability.

II.

The concrete examples listed above—generated by those three principles—illustrate a disturbing tendency of modern liberal regimes to impose their definitions of justice on the private sphere. It hearkens to the distinction that Hannah Arendt made between tyrannical and totalitarian regimes. Tyrannical regimes try to control the public life of a nation while totalitarian regimes try to destroy independent associational life and replace it with their own instruments of education and mobilization. She argued in her *Origins of Totalitarianism* that Nazi and Marxist-Leninist regimes offer clear illustrations of this phenomenon.

I am certainly not arguing that the United States or the European countries are falling into totalitarianism, but I am suggesting that their liberalism is exhibiting a growing tendency to intervene in private associational life and thereby destroy the freedoms essential to pluralist democracy. Several major theorists have noticed this tendency. John Gray, in *The Two Faces of Liberalism*, contrasts two kinds of liberalism, each with its own notion of tolerance. The first kind, Gray argues, assumes that there is one ideal of "the right" and that all reasonable persons will reach this conclusion, which then is ensconced in law. Once a consensus among the reasonable is reached, that notion of right can and ought to be imposed universally. Tolerance is offered only in those areas in which the right has not yet been decided. This vision was elaborated by Locke and Kant, says Gray. The second kind, associated with thinkers such as Hume and Hobbes, has less confidence in reason and people who claim to be reasonable. It is a "multiple-ideal" philosophy that tolerates many notions of the right and good in private life—among the parts, as it were—while holding to only a few procedural notions for the whole.

A concern similar to Gray's is articulated by Nancy Rosenblum in *Membership and Morals*. Rosenblum is worried that groups without the kind of "morals" favored by the liberal establishment will not only be denied membership in society but actually be persecuted. She ponders hard cases such as the Branch

Davidians led by David Koresh and the many militia groups that have popped up in our society. Most of these groups hold notions that are repugnant to an "enlightened liberalism." Yet, she believes, a liberal society ought to be tolerant of these groups as long as they don't directly harm others. She opts for a genuine pluralist liberalism, not the monist type that seems to be creeping into our current life. What is individual freedom without social freedom?

III.

This monist—or totalitarian?—liberalism justifies the overreach that disturbs me. But a thoroughgoing pluralism seems to move toward libertarian notions of politics and society, with little concern for a common good. However, if I had to choose between them, I'd go for the latter. People who have too much confidence in their own rational principles of what is right are all too easily tempted to interfere in the civic liberties of others who may appear "irrational" and, therefore, unjust. Such an insight was articulated memorably in William Buckley's remark that he would rather be governed by the first hundred names in the Boston telephone directory than by the Harvard faculty.

However, I don't think the only choices we have are an interventionist liberalism on the one hand or a libertarian liberalism on the other. It seems to me that we can avoid either by opting for a principled pluralism in which all parties—private and public alike—are invited into a thoroughly democratic conversation in which we try to find the overlapping consensus that can provide a substantive ethic for the common good. Thus though the freedom of the private sphere is amply honored, a principled pluralism also has the promise of constructing a public philosophy for the whole that exhibits many shared meanings and values.

A Christian Realist Approach to the Events of 9/11

I'm a loving person, but I have a job to do," said President Bush. His statement reminds one of the famous distinctions Luther made when he wrote about the Christian's calling. He said that if an individual Christian went into the forest and was beset by robbers, he might well not resist and even offer the robbers more than they demanded. However, if a Christian who was a sheriff went into the forest and was beset by robbers, it was his duty to arrest the robbers, using deadly force if necessary.

The sheriff inhabited an office with a set of duties, just as the president does. And the ethic of the personal realm—especially the Christian ethic of love—does not apply directly to the duties he has as president. Other principles have to guide him, principles that are more worldly, that allow for the use of power and force in realizing them. In doing his job, the president must follow the principles of the just-war tradition. America has been grievously wronged in terrorist attacks. There may be many just

Originally published in *Journal of Lutheran Ethics*, vol. 1, no. 9 (September 2001). Available online at www.elca.org/jle. Amended and reprinted with permission.

claims against America among Arab and Palestinian people, but no grievance, no matter how serious, can morally justify the direct attack on noncombatants by a group that is not legitimately constituted and that has no aim to restore a just peace.

These just-war principles allow for just retribution against our enemies and for vigorous defense of our people. However, our response to the horrible acts of September 11 must be deliberate, proportionate, and carefully directed against the perpetrators, not innocent noncombatants. As has been suggested by several statesmen, it is time to make a concerted effort to pursue and disarm or destroy *all* terrorist groups that have the international capacity to threaten our countries. The success of the terrorists of September 11 will give great encouragement to all terrorist groups. Now is the time to make preemptive, defensive moves against them. Failing that, we may well be facing far larger catastrophes precipitated by biological or chemical attacks, which may take far less ingenuity and resources than those used on September 11.

This Christian realism seems far more persuasive than the sentimentality that is exhibited by so many religious individuals and groups who commend the ethic of the Sermon on the Mount for guidance in this situation. The ethic of love, forgiveness, and nonviolence is proposed as the proper religious path to follow. But that is a confusion of what individual Christians might do and what the government must do. If the government does not act with firm retributive and defensive action, who will protect the sheep from the wolves? On the other hand, Christian realism is just as sharply distinguished from the blind bellicosity that would attack all Muslims or would obliterate whole countries. Such a crusade ethic is just as far from sober Christian ethics as sentimentalism.

Sentimentalism in Christian ethics is aided and abetted by the therapeutic culture in which we Americans are immersed. The therapeutic impulses of our culture lead us to equate our own feelings of shock and grief with those of persons who are directly affected by the horrible events of September 11. There are no doubt good reasons to counsel young children and those who have been seriously wounded psychologically by the disaster. But too often we focus on our therapeutic needs to be comforted rather than on those who need and deserve comfort much more than we. We should be less focused on ourselves and more on those with truly gargantuan needs.

There is an important role for religious communities in this difficult time. They are to place this tragedy into a transcendent dimension that offers solace and hope to all, pray for the injured and the families of the dead, pray for wise policies on the part of our leaders, help bind the wounds of the injured and offer support to their families, reflect critically on the role of our nation in the world, remind ourselves and others that even our enemies are creatures of God, and try to hold our nation accountable to the principles of a just war.

Beware of the Foreign Policy Opinions of Religious Professionals

Whenever mainstream Protestant religious intellectuals and church leaders—let's call them religious professionals—reach near unanimity on questions of political policy, especially foreign policy, it is time to be suspicious. They seem to have reached near unanimity in opposing American policy toward Iraq.

Now, it is axiomatic that on foreign policy questions those religious professionals are nearly always wrong. Their track record bears this out—their opposition to American entry into World War II against Germany and Japan before Pearl Harbor, near unanimous support of the nuclear freeze during the Cold War, endorsement of moral equivalency theories between Soviet socialism and the Western democracies, hostility toward Reagan's vigorous pressure on the Soviet Union, sympathy for Marxist-Leninist insurgencies in Central and Latin America, support for African

Originally published in *Journal of Lutheran Ethics*, vol. 2, no. 9 (September 2002). Available online at www.elca.org/jle. Amended and reprinted with permission.

socialism, antipathy toward antimissile defense systems, insistence on complete divestment of American economic assets from South Africa, and now resistance to American efforts to topple Saddam Hussein.

It's not that these folks have bad motives or goals. I admire them for their passion for peace. However, there are three weaknesses that usually bend their opinions in the wrong direction. They usually have too benign an assessment of the "opposition," be it the Soviet Union, the Sandinistas, socialist utopians, or now Saddam Hussein. The second weakness is that they shrink from employing realistic instruments of power—military power and the threat and use of it. They plead for persuasion and diplomacy, if not for love. They forget the important Lutheran teaching on the two ways that God reigns in the world—through love under the Gospel but through power under the Law. (Even our Lutheran bishop of the Evangelical Lutheran Church in America seems oblivious to that teaching.) The underlying problem seems to be that which Reinhold Niebuhr identified several generations ago— sentimentality. The religious professionals simply are incapable of a realistic assessment of evil in the world, as well as the harsh means necessary to deal with it. The third problem is that mainstream Protestants since the '60s have an inordinate dose of skepticism about America. One could even call it a "blame America first" syndrome. After having shaped the culture of America for centuries, these Protestants have decided that they don't like what they've brought forth. They've stood in an adversarial relation to America and its purposes for some time now.

To be honest, I have had reservations about our aggressive policy toward Iraq, but the unanimous opinions of religious professionals and a recent symposium at our college have dissolved many of those reservations. On successive evenings Roanoke College hosted Benazir Bhutto, Dennis Ross, and Stephen Cohen. (Bhutto is former prime minister of Pakistan, Ross was for twelve years the main American negotiator in the Middle East, and Cohen is the pioneer of Track Two behind-the-scenes diplomacy.) All three gave qualified support for vigorous action against the

Iraqi regime. All thought the fall of Saddam could do great good for the Middle East. Let me list some of their specific points, as well as some of their reservations.

None of our speakers denied that Saddam was seeking weapons of mass destruction and that if he had them he would be a major threat to the whole region, if not to the world. It is important to find out how far along he is with them and destroy them before they can be used. We cannot afford to be complacent in this matter. A preemptive strike, such as that of Israel on Iraq's nuclear reactor some years ago, would be justified, once we are reasonably certain of the existence of such nuclear or biological weapons.

In the meantime, Ross and Cohen found great benefit in the "saber rattling" the United States has done toward Iraq. That has resulted in a frantic scurry of the Arab states to insist that Saddam accept inspectors, who will not only try to find Saddam's weapons but to destroy them. Ross mentioned that the saber rattling alarmed those Arab states who thought they might be next in America's push against the "evil axis." They gathered quickly and drew up plans for the inspectors to return. Would that have happened without the saber rattling? Unlikely. And now we can afford to wait to see what happens with those inspectors.

Failing a successful inspection and disarmament, Ross suggested that a quick victory in Iraq would have positive short- and long-term effects in Iraq and the Middle East. It would rid Iraq of what he called "one of the last Stalinist regimes in the world," one which has used terror repeatedly against its own people, engaged in horrendous wars that have resulted in a massive loss of Iraqi lives, has refused to abide by United Nations sanctions and thereby has sentenced many of its subjects to starvation, has supported terrorism around the world, and has designs to dominate the Middle East with weapons of mass destruction. Iraqis would be elated were they rid of Saddam and his murderous regime. The fall of Saddam would dramatically strengthen reform elements in all the Arab and Islamic countries. Moreover, if we gave proper attention to building up Iraq after the fall of Saddam, Iraq could indeed be a model of a prosperous and moderate Islamic country.

It has oil, water, rich soil, an educated middle class, and few problems of overpopulation. It could be the beginning of a Middle East recovery.

The speakers had reservations about our emerging policy. Bhutto insisted that we consult widely with the United Nations and with allies. Ross and Cohen worried about the consequences of not quickly finding and capturing (or killing) Saddam or of not achieving a swift victory. The people of Iraq have been so brutalized that they will not risk resistance or independent action until they are certain Saddam and his murderous regime are really gone. A prolonged struggle would add fuel to the hard-liners' fire in all the Muslim countries. Both Ross and Cohen insisted that we give serious thought and planning to building up post-Saddam Iraq. We cannot walk away; we should work with Iraq like we did with the Germans and Japanese after World War II.

With those provisos, however, there seemed to be affirmation of current American policy. At the conclusion of a lively question and answer period with Ross and Cohen, one of my colleagues said, "Listening to them almost makes me a hawk." Well, my inclination was already in that direction and our guests confirmed that inclination. Later in our conference we will hear Edward Said, who will offer a sharply opposing viewpoint, but I think he will not convince me. Nor will the religious professionals—including our ELCA bishop. Paraphrasing Luther, I would rather follow the advice of bright laypeople whose vocation is international politics than that of religious leaders who have neither direct engagement nor accountability for the consequences of their opinions.

Part 4

ECONOMICS

LESS ENTHUSIASM, PLEASE, I'M LUTHERAN

A RESPONSE TO THE STACKHOUSE-MCCANN POSTCOMMUNIST MANIFESTO

I am tempted to endorse wholeheartedly the manifesto presented by Max L. Stackhouse and Dennis McCann. After all, they confirm the argument I made in *The Ethic of Democratic Capitalism— A Moral Reassessment* (1981) that the combination of political democracy and market economic arrangements is not only morally defensible but perhaps the best among possible options. Both men were then open to my argument when others were reluctant to be seen in public with such a benighted fellow.

Further, they had the courage on other issues to swim against the stream of conventional wisdom of the guild of Christian social ethicists. But, more important, they have done two things: 1) they have added their influential voices to the worthy purpose of calling Christian ethicists to turn their constructive attention toward the moral and practical *possibilities* inherent in varieties of democratic capitalism rather than diverting their efforts to the unrelenting and exaggerated criticism that has been so characteristic of the past; and 2) they have lent strong support for a renewed *public* relevance of Christian religious and moral claims for the evolving system of democratic capitalism in the face of a world that has marginalized and privatized those claims. These are important contributions.

But, alas, I cannot give three cheers for the particular form of their proposal. In brief, I think they need a dash of Lutheran diffidence to dampen an unseemly enthusiasm. They need a little more exposure to the Norwegian Lutherans of Lake Wobegon. There are two basic fronts on which their enthusiasm needs to be qualified.

First, they confuse the central Christian message of salvation with political and economic practice, in this case capitalist practice. In so doing they make the same mistake that Christian socialists and liberationists often have made, that is, thinking that human efforts at economic and political transformation are in some sense salvatory. The authors claim that if our generation does not respond to the challenge (the constructive engagement with capitalism they commend), we "betray the gospel." Further, that "working to serve people's needs in the marketplace may be a holy vocation in and for the salvation of the world." Or that "enhancing the capacity for capitalization . . . is . . . a new name for mission." The embodied principles of truth, justice, and love in public life will "enhance the salvation of both souls and civilizations."

These examples may simply be attributed to the careless exuberance of manifestos. But I think not. They represent a tendency to qualify the radicality and universality of the Gospel by conflating a desirable human practice with salvation. On the contrary, the Gospel announces God's action in Jesus Christ to save and redeem us. When we are brought by the Holy Spirit to open our repentant hearts to this news, we *receive* it. Salvation is not our work. Even holy vocations do not save. Civilizations as a whole are not saved by the Gospel; they have scarcely any capacity to repent, let alone to receive the Good News. We do not betray the Gospel when our parishes do not foster a constructive engagement with the marketplace. The church's uniquely God-given mission is to communicate the Gospel, not encourage capitalization, as worthy as that might be.

The manifesto's tendency to collapse redemption into a particular kind of creative action leads to an inclination to rule others out of the reach of redeeming grace. Earlier it was we proponents of democratic capitalism who were beyond the pale of God's redemption because we supported an unjust system (witness the anathemas of the *The Road to Damascus* document written by "Third World Christians"). Now it is the socialists or other radicals who believe that capitalism is of the devil who are charged with betraying the Gospel or denying God's rule in the world.

Both approaches undercut the universality of the Gospel. All repentant sinners have the possibility of being grasped by divine grace, not only those with correct political and economic opinions. Those who receive grace may change their political and economic opinions or they may not, but in any case there will continue to be a wide range of opinion among those who call themselves Christian. Not everything goes, but there must be room in the Christian fold for my rock-ribbed Republican father as well as the misguided leftists who wrote *The Road to Damascus*.

The second point at which their enthusiasm needs to be diminished concerns their particular formulation of public theology. It simply claims too much. Theology and communities of faith transcend political economy, they say, and "provide the model for the common life." "Interests not guided by theology and channeled by covenanted communities of faith march through the world like armies in the night." "Any account, including a Marxist one, of why things are the way they are that does not speak of theology and ecclesiology errs." Public theology will construct a "cosmopolitan social ethic" in which "democracy, human rights and a mixed economy are acknowledged as universal necessities."

I too hope for a time when Christian theology and ethics will have more public relevance than they presently have. But Stackhouse and McCann think theology and ecclesiology will be on the front line of the public discussion and sometimes in their enthusiasm seem to claim a dominant role for them that is a bit embarrassing. And presumably it will be theologians and ethicists who will be pressing the project forward. Maybe even pastors and priests.

I would propose a different model of relevance. First, where theologians and ethicists are doing the talking, their publicly significant insights will have to be modulated by a language more universally available than their own professional argot. Their language will be a public philosophy informed by theology and ethics. Reinhold Niebuhr's capacity to speak in the language of such a religiously informed public philosophy made him the last real public theologian we have had in America. Further, as was demonstrated by Niebuhr, that kind of public philosophy will be made up of many notions that are not supplied by theology and ecclesiology. They simply will not provide *the* model.

Moreover, it is my hunch that the most effective public theology will be carried forward by laity who are more expert in their fields than theologians and ethicists will ever be. These laypeople will be informed by theologians but will filter their religious notions through the conceptual apparatus of their own fields. The laity have come of age; they are on the front lines of public theology.

There are exciting signs of this development. Glenn Tinder and Charles Taylor in political philosophy, Robert Bellah in sociology, and a host of topflight Christian philosophers are making a public impact in ways that professional theologians simply can't. This development is also occurring in economics, but we don't yet have a major Christian economist in whose thought Christian claims are clearly evident. If we had, there may have been a different list of priorities for economic action than that proposed by Stackhouse and McCann.

In summary, I strongly affirm the manifesto's basic intentions: to give up the blinding hatred of capitalism enough so that theologians and ethicists can say something useful to the millions of people involved in that dominant economic system; and to summon theology to a rightful and necessary public role. What's more, I agree wholeheartedly with the particulars of its argument. Indeed, the concluding reversal of the *Communist Manifesto*'s rousing climax is worth a host of journal articles. But the tendency to draw a straight line between the Christian Gospel and human action in any economic program, as well as the inordinate claims made for its clericalized model of public theology, deserve criticism. This Calvinist and Catholic enthusiasm invites a dash of Lutheran diffidence. If Lutherans can't or won't supply the zest for social transformation exhibited by our Calvinist and Catholic colleagues, then perhaps we can provide a bit of ballast for the balloons they send up.

THE CALLING OF THE CHURCH IN ECONOMIC LIFE

The economic world in which we live is so vast, dominant, and dynamic that inquiring about the church's role in it is similar to asking each of us individuals what part we have to play in the United States. What role does a single flea play on an elephant? The different scales involved make the topic a bit awesome. But overwhelming size and complexity do not excuse us as individuals from exercising personal responsibility in our own country, no matter how large and bewildering that country might be. Neither is the church exonerated from its calling in economic life simply because economic life is so massive and complex. For the church, as for the individual Christian, the whole of economic life is merely a part of the creation of God, and insofar as we are responsible *to* God, who is the continuing Sustainer and Judge of the world, we are also responsible in some measure *for* the unfolding economic life of the world.

Originally published in *The Two Cities of God*, edited by Carl E. Braaten and Robert W. Jenson (Grand Rapids: Eerdmans, 1997). Amended and reprinted with permission.

In the following pages, I want to sketch what I think to be the nature of the economic world in which we live, the calling of the church in a general sense, and, finally, the specific responsibilities of the church in economic life.

THE ECONOMIC CONTEXT

Although distinctly an amateur in understanding economic matters, I nevertheless accept the obligation to put before you an interpretation of the economic reality in which we live. How we interpret economic reality will in some measure shape our response. Thus the following represents my understanding of the postindustrial economy in which we live and that is spreading across the world.

There are, of course, many things to rejoice about as we look at the emerging economic world. The world is sustaining more people at higher standards of living. There are obviously painful exceptions to this general observation, but they do not obviate the reality of economic progress. The huge productive engines of market economies around the world have lifted the standards of living of many millions of people. Asia provides the most dramatic instances of such progress, but Latin America and Eastern Europe also seem poised for dramatic growth, as does India. Africa continues to provide an especially sad exception to the rule of economic growth.

Along with the growth of middle classes that accompanies economic expansion comes increasing pressure for democracy. The proliferation of democracies constitutes another bright spot aided and abetted by economic success. Even China, which has installed an enormously dynamic capitalism under an authoritarian regime, will experience long-term pressures to liberalize its political life. In Russia another scenario obtains; the Russians must develop their economy quickly enough to stave off the antidemocratic impulses that accompany economic chaos.

Market economies combined with democratic polities have combined to form a remarkable tool for human liberation from abject poverty and oppression. We must be thankful for the many countries in the world that have employed this tool for the benefit of their peoples. All things considered, the last decades of the twentieth century have been a considerable success story for most of the world as far as economic progress is concerned.

These "successes" have been accompanied by serious challenges that render our picture of the world quite a bit more ambiguous. The integration of the world economy has exerted enormous pressures on national and local economies. Instantaneous communication and rapid transportation made possible by technological innovation have made the world a gigantic competitive market. Most business decisions now have to be made with an eye to this emerging world market. Enterprises must be competitive in this larger context or they die. Entire countries who have little to offer to the world economy are in dire straits.[1]

Competition has meant that a good deal of manufacturing has moved from the high-wage countries to the low-wage, or it has meant that simple jobs have been mechanized. Even when firms don't move to low-wage countries, there is a powerful pressure to lower their wages so they can remain competitive. The upshot of this has meant a stagnation since the mid-1970s in the living standards of the American middle and lower middle classes. Some analysts even write somewhat hysterically about the disappearance of the middle class. Although such a judgment is overwrought, it is more accurate to talk of a dividing middle class, the upper end joining the "knowledge classes" who are prospering mightily in the postindustrial world and the lower end being pressed into the working class, which increasingly gravitates toward lower-paid service jobs. The lower class has more difficulty avoiding the "underclass" as good paying jobs demanding little education become more scarce.[2]

Besides this increased competition, and closely related to it, another feature of our modern postindustrial society seems to be a disillusionment with the welfare state. Economic producers, both corporate and individual, have become heavily burdened with taxation to support the welfare state. In a competitive world economy with stagnant middle-class living standards, a likely target to reduce costs is the redistributive apparatus of the welfare state. Efforts to diminish the welfare state are strong in the United States, as well as elsewhere in developed countries. In this situation the fate of the poor is increasingly precarious.

A closely related feature of our world after the collapse of communism is the waning of the socialist ideal. Only Cuba and North Korea hold out for the Marxist-Leninist version of socialism. Even democratic socialism, a favorite of religious intellectuals, is speechless before the emerging new world. Little creative initiatives come from this quarter. Even the venerable Labor and Socialist parties of Europe are competing with conservatives to demonstrate who can tend capitalism the best and preserve the necessary safety net of a trimmed down welfare state. For the near future, it seems, utopian and even moderate socialist schemes have lost their currency.

The pace of technological change has affected social life dramatically. Marx was right in this regard; change in the means of production results in change in the relations of production (society). Our health system is currently undergoing major changes precipitated by technological change, as well as by resistance to inflating prices, which are in part caused by technological change. Great fears abound in the world of education that similar changes are in store for it. This commotion makes jobs less secure and tends to break holistic practices into smaller, specialized parts. Constant job redefinition is a result. In short, it becomes more difficult to see one's work as a life-long calling. Work itself becomes ephemeral and its meaning diffuse. On the other hand, increasing competition amid technological innovation make entry into the economy easier for those who are adept at creating new enterprises. The technologically adept have a chance to prosper in this open economy.

We could not responsibly catalog the ambiguous effects of modern economic life without mentioning ecological effects. More people at increasing standards of living has meant more demands on the environment. Many thoughtful people, such as

Christopher Lasch, believe we have nearly reached our limits.[3] But others argue that more sophisticated technology will allow more of us to live at a high standard without destructive demands on the environment. At any rate, ecological concerns accompany economic development.

Economy—the efficient production of goods and services exchangeable in the marketplace—affects culture as well as society. Capitalism is revolutionary, as Marx pointed out. The massive effects of dynamic capitalism on the meanings and values of the life of the people is only now beginning to be recognized by ordinary people. We are beginning to get populist resistance to the cultural changes wrought by capitalism.[4]

It is now widely recognized that capitalism produces some values that contradict its need for disciplined work.[5] Goods and services are pushed toward the unwary at every turn through the most ingenuous advertising one can imagine. The hedonistic value of short-term pleasure is powerfully promulgated. As people are captured by the consumer ethos, their capacity for and interest in hard work wanes. We begin to wonder what has happened to the work ethic; we live in fear that the more disciplined Japanese and Chinese will outperform us in every strenuous task.[6]

Further, we are beginning to recognize that the biggest business of all, popular entertainment, is effectively undermining the traditional moral values that hold together the basic communities of marriage and family life. Driven by the need to sell their products, the entertainment industry constantly appeals to the new, the titillating, the bizarre, the perverse, the forbidden, the immodest, and the shocking. The jaded consumer needs increased stimulation to notice, watch, or listen. In this process the borders of the permissible are steadily pushed back, first in the realm of imagination, then later in the realms of attitude and behavior. Certainly it is true that an imagination stimulated by the inducements of modern popular culture does not automatically issue into actions of a similar sort. But it seems naive to think that there are no connections between imagination and action, particularly among the less sophisticated. I think of the depredations of pop culture as little doses of poison that may not pervert and destroy taken singly over the short run, but taken as a whole over the long run they can destroy the souls of our young, as well as the young in other countries who are increasingly the "beneficiaries" of our most important export.

Because any decent and orderly social life depends on restraints on impulse and desire, the breakdown of these restraints in both imagination and behavior become threatening to our common life. Expressive and utilitarian individualism, to use the helpful phrases of Robert Bellah, subvert the capacity to keep the commitments that are essential for the elementary republics of our common life.[7]

A final effect I want to mention with regard to the ambiguous effects of our dynamic economy is the tendency for economic rationality to be applied to sectors of life where its approach is inappropriate, if not downright destructive. Because an economic way of thinking is so successful in shaping economic life, there is a great temptation to think that it will be helpful and benign in other areas of human life. Indeed, the Noble prize-winning economist Gary Becker has argued that this economic way of thinking is the most illuminating way of understanding marriage and family life.[8] Further, we find economic rationality increasingly applied to medicine, education, sports, etc., in ways that erode the practices that are the essence of those respective activities.

Although the foregoing is certainly not an exhaustive picture, this sketch of the economic world in which we live provides a context for us to discuss the calling of the church in economic life.

THE CALLING OF THE CHURCH

The primary calling of the church has little directly to do with economic life. At best, its responsibility in and for economic life is one of its many moral concerns and, truth be known, not preeminent among them. The church has a different, unique calling that is of greater ultimate importance.

That calling is to proclaim the Word of God as Law and Gospel and to enact that Gospel in the proper administration of the Sacraments. God has directly called the church to be that earthen vessel through which He reaches out in Word and Sacrament to retrieve all His lost and erring creatures. No other institution on earth has that calling, and none will carry it out if the church fails in its essential mission. It is a sacred calling. It deals with ultimate things: the earthly and eternal destinies of all created but fallen human beings.

The church invokes the Holy Spirit to make its proclamation fruitful in gathering a community of believers around Word and Sacrament. The church is not a disembodied megaphone; it is the Spirit-gathered body of Christ. It is a people. As a people it carries a vision, exhibits a discipline, and nurtures virtues through the practices of its living tradition.

As a trinitarian and catholic church, however, it views the world as the arena of God's continuing, sustaining activity. It cannot turn away from or neglect the world. God's will applies to the whole of reality, not just the church or private life. Likewise, the vision of the church is comprehensive; it has a distinctly public character to it.

Thus the church's calling extends to economic life, just as it does to political, social, and intellectual life. This extension of mission follows from the central core of the church's mission and in no way supplants or precedes it. It is an implication of the mission of the Gospel in history. The church's economic involvement proceeds from the flaming center of the core, just as flames spread outward from the point of hottest combustion.

The integrity of the church's essential mission, as well as the radicality and universality of the Gospel, are protected and maintained when the church is guided by a set of themes that provide a framework for its involvement in economic life. These themes are:

- There is a qualitative distinction between the saving action of God and all human effort.

- The church is primarily called to announce that saving action of God.

- God rules in two distinct ways—through the Law and the Gospel.

- Christians are a paradoxical mixture of God-given sacredness and self-attained fallenness.

- Human history cannot be completed or fulfilled by human effort.

These theological themes provide the necessary clarity, boundaries, and realism for the church's involvement in economic life.[9]

THE CALLING OF THE CHURCH IN ECONOMIC LIFE

If we are clear about the above considerations, then, the next question before us becomes: *How* does the church exercise its calling in economic life? *How* does it perform its responsibilities to and for this facet of God's creation? Those are practical questions, and in the following paragraphs I hope to provide practical answers. To do this I will employ a typology I have used in other places, but here I will apply it to economic life in particular.[10]

The typology breaks into two major parts: indirect and direction connections between the church and economic life. "Indirect" means that the church as an institution does not become involved in economic life; it does not become an economic actor as an institution. Rather, it relies on indirect modes of influence and action through its laity or through independent associations organized by its laity and/or clergy. Neither individual nor associational efforts are under the control or direction of the church itself. In contrast, "direct" means that the church as an institution becomes a public actor. The formal institution itself directly engages the economic sphere. The church's statements and actions vis-à-vis economic life are controlled and directed by its formal authorities.

The following discussion will not include an account of how economic life affects the church and its members, which would be a major inquiry in itself. Interactions of church and economic life are definitely a two-way street. But here the focus is on how the church affects economic life.

INDIRECT CONNECTIONS

Before we enter into our study of the indirect connections between the church and economic life, we need to understand several other terms. By "unintentional" I mean that the church has no definite, conscious intent to affect economic life. It has no blueprints for proper economic behavior in the world; in fact, it may not direct its attention to "the world" at all. Rather, it communicates its core religious and moral vision to its members and allows them to draw the implications of that vision for their own lives in the world. Connections are not intentionally drawn between that core and the economic life of society; it leaves that task to its members to carry out on their own.

"Influence" means that the church relies on persuasion, in this case persuasion of its own members. By compelling example, by convincing narratives, by alluring rituals and practices, by preaching and teaching, and by cogent argument the church persuades its communicants to consent to the core religious and moral vision it bears. "Influence" emphasizes noncoercive means of enlisting people into the church's ethos. "Power," on the other hand, refers to more coercive means to get persons or institutions to behave in certain ways. It includes a variety of strategies ranging from subtle threats to outright force to get persons to do what one wants them to do whether or not they want to do it.

Shaping heart and mind: indirect and unintentional influence. The first indirect approach, "shaping heart and mind," concerns the inward formation of heart, mind, and soul according to the core religious and moral vision of the church. It points to the church's efforts to form the inward parts of its communicants—their dispositions, outlook, and habits of heart.

When proceeding effectively along these lines, the church as a divinely formed community around the scriptural narratives shapes people at a profound level. Their outlook and character is patterned according to the core vision of the tradition. When the church is really the church, its preaching, teaching, worship, and discipline form and transform persons so their innermost being is powerfully fashioned.

Affecting people by catechetically and sacramentally affirming their identity in Christ is arguably the most fundamental and potentially the most effective way the church affects economic life. Laypeople in their various callings in the world express the core vision that has formed them. Through them the religious tradition spontaneously and often pervasively affects its private and public environment.

Many historical studies have traced this kind of indirect and unintentional influence. One of the most celebrated is Max Weber's *The Protestant Ethic and the Spirit of Capitalism*.[11] In this work Weber argues that Reformed piety of a certain sort, which he calls "inner-worldly asceticism," was crucial to the development of Western capitalism. Those Calvinists were not intentionally shaping a new economic order, nor were their religious institutions coercing that order, but they formed persons in such a way that Protestantism became the harbinger of a new economic order.

How does piety affect the economic attitudes and behaviors of contemporary Christians? Although there is much material on how religion ought to affect economic life, we have much less information on the empirical relation between religious values and economic behavior. Robert Wuthnow has addressed precisely this topic in a recent book entitled *God and Mammon in America*. This massive study has increased dramatically our empirical knowledge of the subject. In his summary of the book, Wuthnow says: "My argument is that religious commitment still exerts a significant influence on economic behavior in the United States, but that its influence is often mixed, leading more to ambivalence than to informed ethical decisions or to distinct patterns of life."[12] It seems that Wuthnow was hoping to find real Calvinists among his sample but came upon mostly Lutherans!

Wuthnow goes on to show that Christians *are* vitally affected by their religious commitments in a broad array of personal issues—career choices, job satisfaction, commitment to work, willingness or unwillingness to cut corners, honesty at work, views of money, financial worries, views of materialism and advertising, attitudes toward economic justice and the poor, and charitable giving. The more intensely religious are more likely to show distinct effects than the less religious.

Nevertheless, Wuthnow argues that though faith nudges our attitudes this way or that, it does so "in ways that are seldom as powerful as religious leaders would like and that do little to challenge the status quo."[13] Wuthnow calls for a more powerful and distinctive formation that would lead to more distinct and disciplined patterns of Christian behavior in those areas.

Thus we come to the major challenges to the indirect and unintentional mode of influence. First, we simply are not forming our people strongly enough into a distinctly Christian vision of life. When weakly formed persons move into secular spheres of life that are dominated by another way of understanding and acting, they adapt too easily to that way of understanding and acting. In fact, the church itself does some powerful adapting and often loses its own soul to secular temptations. And we must emphasize that the economic world has a powerful ethos of its own that is often difficult for the Christian vision to penetrate. It is little wonder that economic attitudes and behavior are only "nudged" by Christian commitment.

Added to this difficulty—experienced in every sector of secular life—is the tendency of many laity to view their religious commitments as separate from their worldly economic activities. Sunday and Monday are two different worlds for them.

Nevertheless, the indirect and unintentional type of churchly influence is still an obvious one for the church, as Wuthnow and Lasch have pointed out. Many persons in both church and society would like to stop with this way of relating religion to economic life. This approach seems to fit the traditional doctrine of the church's mission.[14] If the church really does form hearts and minds, people will act differently in other areas of life, including economic life. Further, this approach does not encourage the church to claim competence and spend more energy on issues peripheral to its central mission. It tends to unify Christian communities around their central convictions, not divide them over issues about which Christians of intelligence and goodwill often disagree. Many laypersons, perhaps a majority, believe that if the church really does its job of character formation well, that is all it need do. The church would do its job, then set the laity free to do theirs.[15]

For the reasons listed above, however, as well as for its reluctance to allow the church directly to address the Word directly as Law to the economic world, this indirect and unintentional approach is to my mind insufficient. Without denigrating its importance, we must supplement it with other approaches.

Awakening the conscience: indirect and intentional influence. The key difference between the first and this second type of indirect approach has to do with the element of intentionality. In this second type the church does not rely completely on the spontaneous connection between the Christian laity's hearts and minds and the complex and often overpowering economic world. The church certainly does not deny this unintentional connection, but it aims to augment it with more intentional strategies. It strives to bring its religious and moral vision to bear consciously and intentionally on the economic challenges facing it and its laity.

If the unintentional approach could be called the "ethics of character," this second indirect but intentional approach might be called "the ethics of conscience." It intentionally awakens the conscience of the laity by bringing them into a lively dialog between the social teachings of the church and the economic challenges they face in the world.

The vision applied. The word *apply* is a bit wooden for my purposes here because it implies a one-way street. In any genuine encounter between a religious tradition and the economic challenges around it, there is real interaction. The tradition's core vision has been extended by the church into social teachings about economic life. But each step from the core to a social teaching is open to discussion and debate. Some extensions—such as the church's evaluation of capitalism—are much more open to debate than others, for example, the church's teaching concerning the obligation of Christians to be honest in their economic dealings. But all applications of the moral heritage of the church need to be specific if they are to be helpful to the laity in connecting religion and economic life.

We could start these applications with the more personal dimensions of economic life. Instead of constantly focusing on policy matters, about which the laity can generally do little, the church can begin dealing with applications in the personal life of the laity. The issues that Wuthnow has studied are particularly apt: work and its meaning, ethics in the workplace, orientations toward money, materialism, the poor and economic justice, and charitable behavior.[16] One could add other topics to his list: how to choose real goods in the marketplace of entertainment; how to live in an ecologically responsible manner; how to manage one's wealth in life and at death; and how to help empower in a personal way those who struggle economically.

Certainly the Christian heritage has rich teachings to address all these topics. Christian notions of calling, of gratitude, of modesty and humility, of compassion and justice, of covenantal existence, of respect for the natural world, and, above all, of justification by grace and not by economic works are pregnant with meaning for life in the modern economic world.

Fortunately, we now have much material before us to help the laity apply their heritage to their economic life. William Diehl's many works are particularly noteworthy. His practical efforts to make specific applications are both challenging and helpful.[17] Other recent efforts come to mind. David Krueger has written a useful book that contains much stimulus for lively discussion of these matters.[18] John Schneider's *Godly Materialism: Rethinking Money and Possessions* is a Reformed approach to responsible Christian management of one's resources.[19] One could add many other titles to the list.

The question, however, is whether the church is intentionally making use of these materials to strengthen the Sunday-Monday connection in the lives of the laity. I suspect that it is not. Perhaps if the national and regional judicatories would spend as much time and energy on helping congregations do this sort of intentional connection as they do on statements, we would have more evidence of conscience formation at the parish level. But parishes do not need to wait on the higher levels of church organization to carry out the kind of dialog I am suggesting.

Parishes can begin to stimulate such a discussion by simply providing contexts for laity to talk about their callings in the economic sphere. When this is done, it is pleasantly surprising to find how many laity in fact do connect their Christian commitments with their work in the world. As they articulate those connections publicly, they encourage other Christians to make similar connections.

Other occasions in parish life might focus on more specific issues: stewardship of one's income, ethical challenges at work, tendencies to justify oneself by one's work, the possibilities and problems of retirement, and the economic insecurities felt by so many. The possibilities are endless. Suffice it to say that without this disciplined reflection on Christian values and economic life, the powerful forces of secular thinking in the economic sphere will dominate and marginalize those values. The next generation will not have nearly the impact on economic life that Wuthnow sees in this current generation.

Opportunities for similar approaches are obvious at higher levels of the church's life. We need American versions of the Evangelical Academies of Europe, where laity are brought together with theological ethicists to ponder the challenges facing them. Some gatherings can be devoted to particular occupations, others to common issues across the occupations, and others to points of conflict between occupational groups. The church need not necessarily "take a stand" at any of these points. Rather, it can act as a "mediating institution," mediating in a grace-full context the competing and conflicting claims of various groups in our society.

These efforts could frequently be aimed at the church's elite laity, who are rarely given the opportunity by the church to be challenged by sophisticated theology and ethics in an authentically dialogical manner. There are many high-level Christian owners and managers who simply are not given the benefit of theological/ethical challenge commensurate with their level of sophistication and power in the secular world.

These strategies can also be employed to discuss public policy issues that have direct relevance to economic life. The church, I believe, has spent too much time on encouraging discussion of public policy items about which most people have little say. More attention and effort should be given to the direct vocational challenges that lay Christians experience in the world.

The spawning power of the vision. Before we leave this inquiry into the indirect ways the church carries out its calling in economic life, I want to mention briefly another important indirect effect. This has to do with the propensity of Americans whose conscience has been awakened to join or create independent voluntary organizations to deal with economic concerns. Many Christians join secular organizations devoted to dealing with economic issues or problems. Other Christians begin organizations of their own. One thinks, for example, of Habitat for Humanity, which was organized by Christians and which has been joined by many others who give money and time to its efforts to build low-cost housing. Bread for the World is another such voluntary organization, one that is more directed to affecting public policy on economic issues. Scores of other organizations could be listed.[20]

There is real wisdom in this indirect spawning of voluntary associations. Such associations can deal with controversial issues without implicating the church. Further, because they are not under the direct control of the church, they have a freedom and flexibility often lacking in church organizations. They also have funding that the church frequently does not have or cannot get.

I have spent so much time on these indirect approaches because I believe they have been neglected by the church. We have neglected the task of forming and persuading our own laity to be serious Christian actors in the economic realm. This is partly because this task has been squeezed out by other priorities in the life of the church, partly because church leaders have not known how to do it adequately, but also in good measure because of an undue emphasis on church involvement in public policy concerns. The churches, especially the mainstream Protestant churches, have increased their institutional involvement in public policy "advocacy" in inverse proportion to their capacity to and interest in persuading their own laity to witness to their Christian convictions in economic life. It seems that the churches become more interested in coercing the society through policy as they fail in persuading their own laity to take their message seriously.

Direct Connections

Nevertheless, despite what ought to be the church's preference for indirect connections to economic life, there are good theological reasons for direct approaches. The church's calling is not a call only to individuals in their private roles, it is also a call to the whole society in a public manner. The church believes that the whole of reality is subservient to God's authority and will; therefore, as the body of Christ the church has an obligation to articulate the Word of God as Law to the structures of society. That task is certainly part of its public witness.

In this direct mode the church as an institution becomes a public actor in economic life. The church attempts to affect economic life through its formal institutional statements and actions. Both statements and actions are direct and intentional. But the first kind of direct connection, "articulating social conscience," relies exclusively on persuasion, while the second, "the church exercising power," tends toward more coercive strategies.

Articulating social conscience: direct and intentional influence. Typical examples of this approach are papal encyclicals, Roman Catholic bishops' pastoral letters, and the myriad of social statements made by the mainstream Protestant churches. Lately these efforts have been joined by the newly awakened evangelical and fundamentalist churches. These statements are not only meant to be tools for teaching the laity of the various traditions but also are aimed at public centers of power. They are intended to give moral direction to the decisions made in the public sphere.

Pope John Paul II was an extremely effective practitioner of this approach. He addressed economic life with vigor and incisiveness. His *Laborem Exercens: On Human Work* (1981) and his *Centesimus Annus* (1991) both mounted major arguments about the proper nature and direction of economic life. To a lesser degree, the American Catholic Bishops' *Economic Justice for All: Pastoral Letter on Catholic Social Teaching and the U.S. Economy* (1986) was an effective tool to stimulate general public discussion. The Lutheran Church in America's social statement *Economic Justice* (1980) was a solid piece of work that, like most other Protestant documents, received little public notice.

Catholic articulations of social conscience gather wide response; every director of every editorial page of every daily newspaper seems constrained to comment on Catholic contributions. But scant attention is paid to Protestant efforts. Why? One obvious difference that cannot be remedied quickly is the size of the churches; the Catholic church dwarfs most Protestant communions. Further, the pope as leader of such a large institution has enormous visibility and carries a moral weight that cannot be duplicated by Protestant leaders. But there is more to it than that. If we look carefully at the qualities of the Catholic statements, perhaps we can identify certain guidelines useful for all to follow.

First, it seems evident that the Catholic statements on economic life draw from their own unique tradition of social teaching. There is a long history of such statements, and the pope and bishops draw their guiding principles from their own tradition, not from fashionable ideologies of the day. Particularly important in this regard are Catholic notions of the common good and subsidiarity. Such principles give the Catholic statements an integrity and credibility that are too often lacking in Protestant statements, which frequently seem to reflect the secular ideological biases of the church officials who draw them up.

Second, statements issued by the Catholics are relatively few and well-prepared. They do not try to address everything. They devote time, effort, and expense to the process. The Catholic bishops' letter on the American economy, for example, went through three different drafts over at least three years, and the drafts changed perceptibly as feedback from critics was taken seriously. Lay expertise is invited to complement the theological acumen of Catholic theologians and ethicists.

Third, the Catholic pastoral letters distinguish between the central, core religious and moral vision of the church and the important extrapolations from that core. They recognize that as they move from core to social teachings to social policy there is a gradual diminution of churchly authority. Moving through each concentric circle from the core entails moral argument that is open to disagreement among Christians of goodwill and intelligence. For example, core Christian convictions lead to the conclusion that all persons should receive just recompense for their labors, but Christians of goodwill and intelligence disagree over whether the market or the state should determine what is just and who should set that level of recompense. The Catholic letters invite discussion about public policy; Protestant statements too often draw a nonnegotiable line between the core and the periphery. Unfortunately, evangelical and fundamentalist churches have recently taken up some of the vices of their mainstream colleagues.

There are, of course, times when statements of sheer protest can become a powerful and necessary witness of the church. When social practice—for example, the raw economic exploitation of children—becomes obviously discordant with the core religious and moral vision of the church, then the church can speak with an unequivocally proscriptive voice. Indeed, it is often much more persuasive to call attention to or protest unjust conditions than to try to prescribe public policy options to alleviate them. The church is a better social conscience than an economic director.

There is another variation on this direct, persuasive address to the society that is perhaps more influential than mere words. That variation entails an embodiment of social conscience in institutional form. In a famous essay on "The Responsibility of the Church for Society," H. Richard Niebuhr argued that the most persuasive way the church could exercise its social responsibility was by incarnating its vision in its own institutional life. He called this activity "social pioneering."[21]

The church has incarnated its own sense of compassion in its many social ministry organizations, which often deal with those who are unable to survive in economic life. The church also models its sense of economic justice when it arranges its own internal life and the life of its institutions in accordance with its own values. In some places it provides the means for the poor to enter economic life through training and job placement. It sets up cooperatives in poor lands. It trains farmers and entrepreneurs in other lands. It engages in "responsible investing." These are all examples of "social pioneering." They are done out of the desire to make the church's actions consistent with basic Christian values, but they also have the added effect of awakening the conscience of the secular authorities and giving them models for effective economic practice.

These forms of direct and intentional influence are more controversial than the indirect forms because they put the church's spiritual and moral weight behind certain policies and practices. Therefore, direct influence—with the exception of the "social pioneering" variation—should be done carefully and sparingly. The church simply does not have the authority and expertise to advise the world on complex policy issues. The church should not be left powerless when a really crucial issue comes up because it has depleted its moral capital on a plethora of issues best left to other agencies. It should save its "prophetic power" for the right occasions.

Exercising power: direct and intentional action. The first Sunday I attended a Lutheran church in a changing neighborhood on Chicago's South Side in the early 1960s, the young social activist pastor announced from the chancel that right after church he and other members of the church would be picketing a local dairy company because it had not hired enough blacks. He would wear his clerical collar and carry a sign identifying the local parish. Further, he proposed that all members of the church boycott the dairy's products until it relented. That was direct action at the local level. It entailed the church as an institution becoming an economic actor. It engaged in action, namely, in the coercive activity of picketing and economic boycott. And it did not go over well among the congregants. Many fumed and left. Others withheld their pledges and argued with the pastor. Most felt that there was something wrong with the church engaging in such a conflict methodology.

The era of the 1960s was a time of church involvement in community organizations of all sorts, and, by and large, the result of such involvement was not a happy one. Similar results are accruing around our 1990s versions of direct action. Those versions, though of a softer variety than the community organization movement, are expressed in the church's "advocacy" efforts. These attempts are generally directed toward the realm of public policy, that is, they take a political form, though the policies they aim at affecting often have economic effects. Other attempts, however, aim directly at the economic decision-making of business enterprises.

These latter usually take the form of "ethical investing." Church funds—stocks, savings, pensions—are used as bargaining chips to urge secular economic agencies to conform to the values the church ostensibly holds. Strong arguments can be marshaled in support of such direct action. The church, so the argument goes, is more likely to support causes of justice for the vulnerable than are powerful, self-interested economic organizations. To limit the church's role to individual Christian witness is to refuse to support worthy causes when we have the chance. The use of the church's economic power is an important tool for serving the neighbor in the modern world. If the church does not use its power intentionally, the secular world will use the church's economic wherewithal for its own purposes. Not to decide is to decide, as the 1960s slogan had it.

However, there are also compelling arguments on the other side, which become much more insistent when the church's action is made painfully public. (Usually the "socially responsible" use of the church's funds is done quietly and unobtrusively.) The current fracas about the use of pension funds in the ELCA is a case in point.

In cases such as this the problems with direct action become visible. Advocacy gets the church involved with power, contrary to its nature and mission. The church often does "lobby" for its self-interest and, therefore, engages in hypocrisy when it claims to be advocating for others. Advocacy is usually partisan; it reflects the political and economic disposition of the bureaucratic elite rather than the membership of the church. In doing so it coercively uses the money of the church against the wishes of its members. It extends far beyond what the church has actually said in its social statements, and it has little warrant for much of what it does. It divides the church unnecessarily and usurps the economic vocation of individual Christians.

Do the noble intentions and presumably good effects of advocacy overturn the presumption against direct action? Only partially, it seems. The furor surrounding advocacy is a signal of its borderline legitimacy. The church needs to think clearly and carefully about its involvement in direct action, which *is* fraught with theological, ecclesiological, and practical difficulties. It should engage in direct action rarely. If the church wants to enter the arena of economic decision-making in the secular world, it should remember that calling attention to problems rather than "calling the shots" is more appropriate to its mission of persuasion. Further, when the church invests its money, it should focus on extremes but leave the great middle ground alone. It should invest money wisely in obviously constructive economic activities and divest or avoid investing in the obviously unwholesome. These limiting principles would inhibit the more activist and coercive uses of the church's funds. It is wiser for the church to leave the more vigorous and controversial agitation to voluntary associations independent of the church.

In some places around the world, however, there are not as many other actors on the scene to witness for justice in the economic world. The church may be the only major independent institution with moral and economic weight. The Catholic church's support of Solidarity in Poland is an example of such a contingency. Its support of community organizations among the poor in Latin America may be another. At any rate, there are specific historical occasions when direct action is warranted.

The presumption against direct action is still an important one. Evidence for overturning it should be strong. As one commentator has put it: "Not to put too fine a point on the matter, religion's capital is frequently maximized when it is not a capital religion."[22]

CONCLUSION

I have argued that the church does indeed have a calling in economic life. I have contended that more disciplined attention should be given to indirect forms of that calling. I have certainly left room for direct approaches, though without the enthusiasm shown by so many of our mainstream brothers and sisters who have now been joined by their evangelical and fundamentalist compatriots. (I must admit that I do harbor enthusiasm for the pope's direct address to the world, though I suspect that may be in part because I agree with him on so many items. My Catholic intellectual friends are not so enthused.)

With regard to worldly activities, the church's main calling is to nurture many callings—the callings of the specialized auxiliary organizations to which it is related and the callings of its millions of individual laypersons. These are the primary links the church has with the world, and the church should do much more to strengthen those links than it currently does.

The church's ministry through its laity and its institutions has the capacity to reach the deepest levels of human society—the hearts and minds of its people. Economics and politics are much less able to affect the most profound guidance systems of the people. If religion is indeed the substance of culture, the church is at the front lines of the battle for society's soul. Its public role as an institutional actor has far less potential than does its indirect role as shepherd of souls. What political party or business wouldn't give its right arm to have more than one hundred million people in its lair on a given morning of the week?

Moreover, the indirect mode is most fit for modern economic life, which itself is complex and specialized enough to make it impossible for the church as an institution to speak to or affect it adequately. But laypersons who are deployed into all areas of our dynamic and variegated economy will be most able to make creative connections between religion and economic life. Further, modern society, with its penchant for autonomy, will be more inclined to listen to articulate Christian laypersons than to the church. Laypersons will be able to speak and act with the authority of their own economic callings and will be able to translate the Christian vision into economic language and behavior in those callings. All this depends, of course, on the strength of lay formation in the churches. It is to that task that we must give our utmost attention. Much will follow from that.

So we should seek first the kingdom of God, trusting that much more will be given to us. This priority will lead us to take the economic world seriously, but not too seriously. By pointing to a kingdom of another quality in a dimension of another sort, the church relativizes the pretensions of the world and its powerful economies. It ministers best to the world when it is not of the world.

Notes

1.   See, for example, Michael Porter, *The Competitive Advantage of Nations* (New York: Free Press, 1990).

2. An excellent comprehensive view of the emerging world economy can be found in Robert Reich, *The Work of Nations: Preparing Ourselves for 21st Century Capitalism* (New York: Knopf, 1991).

3. Christopher Lasch, *The True and Only Heaven: Progress and Its Critics* (New York: Norton, 1991), 22ff.

4. A fascinating book tracing populist criticism of capitalist "progress" is Lasch, *True and Only Heaven*. Interestingly, Lasch, who became more religiously committed before his death in 1993, found the most resistance to the incessant, restless search for a higher standard of living in the classical Republican ideal of political life and in the Protestant notion of "calling."

5. Daniel Bell's celebrated work, *The Cultural Contradictions of Capitalism* (New York: Basic Books, 1976), argued this point persuasively.

6. For an unsettling view of this challenge, see Lester Thurow, *Head to Head: The Coming Economic Battle among Japan, Europe and America* (New York: Morrow, 1992).

7. Robert Bellah et al., *Habits of the Heart: Individualism and Commitment in American Life* (Berkeley: University of California Press, 1985).

8. Gary Becker, *The Economic Approach to Human Behavior* (Chicago: University of Chicago Press, 1976).

9. I have elaborated these themes in detail in my book *The Paradoxical Vision: A Public Theology for the Twenty-first Century* (Minneapolis: Fortress, 1995). They furnish the underlying structure for my argument in this essay.

10. See, for example, Benne, *Paradoxical Vision*, 181ff., and Benne "Religion and Politics: Four Possible Connections," in *Discourse and the Two Cultures: Science, Religion and the Humanities*, ed. Kenneth Thompson (Latham, Md.: University Press of America, 1988).

11. Max Weber, *The Protestant Ethic and the Spirit of Capitalism* (New York: Scribners, 1958).

12. Robert Wuthnow, *God and Mammon in America* (New York: Free Press, 1994), 5.

13. Wuthnow, *God and Mammon in America*, 5.

14. Among the family of Lutheran churches, The Lutheran Church—Missouri Synod represents this indirect and unintentional mode well. It generally confines its efforts to implanting its core vision into its laity, then allowing them to take it from there.

15. One of the important serendipitous factors of this unintentional mode is the formation of Christian intellectuals who go on to connect their faith and learning in the field of economics. Lutherans have produced a number of distinguished economists who do in fact think seriously about the relevance of their theological convictions to their economic work. Paul Heyne, for example, has not only written a standard text in the field of economics but has also authored at least one book and many articles on the interface between Christian theology and economics. David Beckmann, current president of Bread for the World, is another theologian/economist. Lutherans also have produced a number of intellectuals in theology who have grappled with economic issues. These examples show the power of formation in the churches. There is no way a church could intend that these persons arise within its ranks to become Christian agents in economic life. But it formed them and they arose.

16. Wuthnow, *God and Mammon in America*, xvii.

17. Diehl has written a number of books in this vein: *Christianity and Everyday Life* (Philadelphia: Fortress, 1978), *Thank God It's Monday* (Philadelphia: Fortress, 1982), *In Search of Faithfulness* (Philadelphia: Fortress, 1987), and *The Monday Connection* (San Francisco: HarperSanFrancisco, 1991) are excellent examples. Each provokes the laity to think seriously about what it means to live as a Christian in one's life as a worker, consumer, and citizen.

18. David Krueger, *Keeping Faith at Work* (Nashville: Abingdon, 1994).

19. John Schneider, *Godly Materialism: Rethinking Money and Possessions* (Downer's Grove: InterVarsity, 1994).

20. A recent book has chronicled a number of organizations and their organizers spawned by the church's vision of economic justice. *Loving Neighbors Far and Near: U.S. Lutherans Repond to a Hungry World* (Minneapolis: Augsburg, 1994) tells the encouraging stories of church organizations such as Lutheran World Relief, as well as those of voluntary associations such as Bread for the World. Persons formed deeply in the ethos of the church are inevitably the instigators and leaders of such organizations.

21. H. Richard Niebuhr, "The Responsibility of the Church for Society," in *The Gospel, the Church and the World*, ed. K. S. Latourette (New York: Harper & Brothers, 1946).

22. N. J. Demerath, "Religious Capital and Capital Religions: Cross-cultural and Non-legal Factors in the Separation of Church and State," *Daedalus* (Summer 1991): 21.

AM I RIGHTEOUS OR WHAT?

I DRIVE A HONDA CIVIC THAT GETS 40 MPG

After filling up on a recent trip from Ohio, I had my wife calculate the gasoline consumption of our spiffy new Honda Civic. "You're going to like this," she said. "It comes out to 45 miles per gallon." Although aided by a strong tailwind, I was still enthused. But not as enthused as I was when I found out that driving such a car was exactly what Jesus would do. Wow, I was not only frugal and fascinated by the efficiency of small engines, I was righteous. My righteousness was inflated further by the facts that we own only one car and I ride a bicycle to work. My goodness knows no bounds.

This is in stark contrast to the sinful ways of my children, who trundle their families around in SUVs or vans, who own more than one car, and who definitely do not ride bicycles to work. Unperceptive as usual, I thought their transportation choices had to do with a desire for room and safety for their fam-

Originally published in *The Journal of Lutheran Ethics*, vol. 3, no. 2 (February 2003). Available online at www.elca.org/jle. Amended and reprinted with permission.

ilies. But in actuality, those practical choices concealed wickedness. They were disobedient to what Jesus would drive.

The Evangelical Environmental Network is waging a campaign organized around the question "What would Jesus drive?" It is trying to get Christians to buy fuel-efficient cars and to put pressure on manufacturers to make more of them and fewer SUVs. Their pledge contains this statement: "Obeying Jesus in our transportation choices is one of the great Christian obligations and opportunities for the twenty-first century." It goes on to suggest practical steps that leave little doubt that I am doing what Jesus wants and my children definitely are not.

Why is this campaign so silly? Not in the goal it is commending—diminishing air pollution. Almost everyone can affirm that. And many of the people who have signed the pledge—some of whom I know and admire—are fine Christians. But it is silly, if not outrageous, to enlist Jesus in both that goal and the particular means to achieve that goal. The silliness is borne out by the many tongue-in-cheek quips that have been offered to contest the campaign's confident claim that Jesus would drive a Civic. For example, it is clear from the biblical record that Jesus preferred donkeys for ground transportation and boats for other occasions. He also was not averse to air travel on His own power (the ascension). Further, it seems that Jesus would drive a Honda, but a model several steps up from my Civic, for He said, "For I did not speak of my own *accord*" (John 12:49). These jokes indicate that we don't have much of an idea about what Jesus would commend when it comes to transportation. He never really had to face that question.

But there are more serious theological and ethical issues here. The Evangelical Environmental Network is too easily co-opting Jesus for one of its admirable social projects. In this facile co-optation evangelicals are now following their liberal compatriots in the faith, those who have claimed Jesus' authority for almost every social or political cause imaginable. Liberal Protestants have claimed that Jesus would support an ever-expanding welfare state, a higher minimum wage, abortion rights, recycling, the nuclear freeze of the 1980s, and a nonviolent approach to Saddam Hussein. In fact, when I first heard of this campaign, I was sure it was the effort of the National Council of Churches or the Methodist Board of Church and Society. As Richard Neuhaus once quipped: Liberal Protestants refuse to utter any religious statement that is not socially redemptive.

Jesus taught a radical religious and moral vision. He taught an unwavering love for God and a sacrificial love for the neighbor. He sharpened and deepened the commandments so they became what Reinhold Niebuhr called "the impossible possible." They are impossible for us to fulfill and, therefore, condemn us before God, yet Jesus fulfilled them. (Before this radical ethic, claiming righteousness for driving a Honda Civic not only seems far too easy but even blasphemous.)

It is a dubious practice to reduce and domesticate Jesus' teaching to one's favorite social cause. Jesus' teaching *is* related to complex social and political matters, but only indirectly. It has to pass through a number of phases of deliberation before one comes to a judgment, then that judgment is often ambiguous. For example, Jesus taught an ethic of nonviolence, but most Christian traditions have interpreted that ethic as applying to personal relations, not to international relations. (Jesus did not seem critical of the soldiers who appeared before Him.) Rather, the church has developed through the centuries a theory of justified use of violence. That theory is applied to modern international relations, as it is now with regard to war with Iraq. Christians come down on different sides of that particular issue, but all sides wisely refrain from saying that Jesus commands their course of action.

Such it is with questions of consumption—such as what kind of vehicle to purchase. So many competing values and trade-offs enter into a decision that it is ridiculous to claim that we know the mind of Jesus on this matter. My children weigh the convenience and safety of owning a van against the fuel-efficiency of my Civic and come down for a larger vehicle. The claim that Jesus would frown on this is quite a stretch.

Another problem with the "What would Jesus drive?" campaign as well as with the earlier "What would Jesus do?" approach is that they wrongly assume that Jesus had the same vocation as we do. Jesus' vocation was to be the Savior of the world, who "died for us while we were yet sinners." Because of that unique calling, he did not marry and have a family, did not work for pay, and did not exercise a political role. However, the great Reformation traditions teach that each Christian has worldly callings that entail distinct worldly responsibilities. One of those callings for many Christians is marriage and family life. They have to make practical decisions about where to live, what schools their children attend, what to buy, and what to drive. Jesus gives no simple directives about those matters.

Rather than claim to know the mind of Jesus on these matters, it would be far better for the Evangelical Ecological Network to call Christians to express the virtues of humility, modesty, and compassion in their practical decisions. That might lead to abstemious patterns of consumption, but it may not. The overall pattern of generosity with one's time and money is far more important in the Christian life than the choice of a vehicle.

Part 5

CHRISTIAN HIGHER EDUCATION

THE DARKNESS
BEFORE THE DAWN?

Although it has become something of a parlor sport to criticize James Burtchaell's massive work *The Dying of the Light:
The Disengagement of Colleges and Universities from Their Christian Churches*, the major thrust of that work is most assuredly
right. The vast majority of mainstream Protestant and Catholic
schools have suffered the darkening trends Burtchaell has so
clearly traced. One doesn't have to spend much time at those
schools to experience the dramatic marginalization of their
sponsoring heritage from all facets of their lives—intellectual,
social, institutional.

That work and the numerous other accounts of the secularization of church-related colleges and universities has generated a wave of stock-taking among a large number of schools
that were not secularized in the last fifty years. Catholic colleges
and universities have had the additional impetus of Pope John
Paul II's call in his "Ex Corde" letter to become more seriously
Catholic. There is much reflection among Protestant and
Catholic colleges. That reflection has been further aided by networks such as the Lilly Fellows Program in Humanities and the
Arts and the Rhodes Consultation on the Future of the Church-

Related College. Moreover, a number of denominations—the Lutherans and the Baptists come to mind—are also supporting a renewed commitment to the religious identity and mission of their colleges and universities.

However, one doesn't have to be a professional historian to perceive that these conversations ebb and flow. One need only look at the 1966 Danforth Study to see that all this talk has gone on before. Each denomination has its own history of alarms about the secularization of its colleges and universities. Yet with all these warnings and their resulting resolutions, the secularization process continued. Such a trajectory makes Burtchaell's elegiac fatalism plausible indeed; the darkening trends seem to have a certain inevitability about them.

It is quite possible, though, that the conversation about strengthening ties between the schools and their churches might be more fruitful this time around. Why would one hazard such a dubious proposition? First, the cultural situation has changed dramatically since the earlier conversations. That change has provided more fertile ground for the renewal of religious identity and mission among church-related colleges and universities.

Second, we are now aware of a number of impressive colleges and universities who "kept the faith." With clearer knowledge of the "whys" and "hows" behind the maintenance such schools demonstrate of a robust connection to their heritage, other schools can duplicate those strategies. The robustly connected schools—which are also schools of high quality—can provide models for those who want to maintain and even strengthen an already close relation to their heritages. (I tell the story of six of those colleges and universities in *Quality with Soul: How Six Premier Colleges and Universities Keep Faith with Their Religious Traditions.* The institutions I take up are Calvin, Wheaton, and St. Olaf Colleges and Baylor, Notre Dame, and Valparaiso Universities.)

Third, there is evidence that a significant number of partially secularized schools are trying to reconnect with their heritage. An impressive number of such schools have joined the Lilly Network of Church-Related Colleges and Universities and the

Rhodes Consultation on the Future of the Church-Related College, both of which are well-funded efforts to help schools strengthen their connection with their sponsoring tradition. These schools are responding both to the new cultural situation and to the examples provided by those schools who have maintained quality and soul. Although such schools are unlikely ever to achieve the full measure of a Christian college or university, they are taking steps that can lead them toward a more meaningful relation to their sponsoring heritage. The secularization process may be halted and reversed among these schools.

I.

There are at least two dramatic changes in our cultural situation that encourage the reconnection of colleges and universities with their parent religious traditions. The two changes involve a loss of direction in both our national and academic cultures that opens the way for the return to the religious traditions that first spawned those institutions of higher learning. The first change involves the general loss of coherence in our American culture. The complex of meanings and values that once provided the guidance system for our society has been dethroned from its normative status. The culture shaped by mainline Protestantism—what Martin Marty has called the *the* culture or what Daniel Bell has named the Protestant Ethic—once served as the glue for the general society. Schools could assume that boards, administrations, faculties, and students were shaped by a shared American cultural consensus about the aims and norms of higher education. The schools themselves did not intentionally have to shape an ethos among those groups. Rather, the American ethos shaped and guided them. They were held together by the inertia of that American consensus.

From the 1960s onward, that consensus has evaporated. Although the old culture is not dead, it survives as only one option among many cultures. This shattering of consensus was first wrought by the upheaval of the 1960s, when the old myth of American innocence (and the culture it uncritically bore) was turned into the myth of American guilt. The protest movements initiated in the 1960s—feminism, multiculturalism, ecologism, gay liberation—grew into full-fledged cultures of their own. In their "long march through the institutions" these cultures claimed their own epistemologies, their own perspectives on the world. Colleges and universities became the battleground between the old culture and the new. Any sort of integrating American vision was lost, even among the majority of church-related schools. They lost their props. The schools reflected the larger society's confusion.

If the American culture's consensus was broken by the 1960s and their further unfolding, the academic culture's confidence was shaken by unsettling challenges to the so-called "Enlightenment project." The Enlightenment, with its haughty claims for autonomous reason, seemed at first to transcend our society's confusion and to give colleges and universities a firm epistemological foundation. Its claims had already marginalized the role of religion in the public and private schools yet seemed to offer a reliable substitute. Alas, that was not to continue. Various sorts of postmodernisms, fueled in part by the movements of the 1960s but also by larger epistemological shifts, have called into question the Enlightenment's proud assertions. Christians should not have been too surprised by this; the Enlightenment was always more parasitic upon the Judeo-Christian tradition than it admitted.

The upshot of these two developments—the decentering of American culture and the challenge to Enlightenment hegemony—is that universities and colleges have to search for other integrating visions if they are to have any coherence at all. This is a new situation for American higher education. Church-related schools ought to ask: "Lord, to whom shall we go?" And they ought to answer: "To You, Lord. You have the words of eternal life."

The various Christian traditions that founded and nurtured church-related colleges and universities often have exactly what those educational enterprises need: a coherent and comprehensive moral and intellectual vision that can shape their identities and missions. Indeed, those who have never lost their connection to their nourishing traditions rejoice in their good sense. Those who have a less robust relation to their traditions are beginning to realize what they have lost, and many are making efforts to retrieve a stronger connection. They have realized that our new cultural situation closes some doors but opens others with which they are familiar. They need to step through those half-forgotten doors, and many are doing just that. In their cases, necessity may be the mother not of invention but of remembrance.

II.

If a significant number of schools are attempting to reconnect with their sponsoring traditions, they will be aided by the example of those who have never disconnected. Those robustly connected schools never succumbed to the temptation to replace the Christian paradigm with the American or Enlightenment paradigms. They have kept the faith through thick and thin and offer models of thriving ventures in Christian higher education. "Keeping the faith" means they insisted that the Christian tradition—as intellectual vision and as ethos—remain the organizing principle of their school's identity and mission. The tradition continued to be publicly relevant to all facets of the school's life, from its curriculum to its student residential life.

It was not that the leaders—boards, administrations, and faculty—of the schools that succumbed to secularization were always bereft of a solid Christian faith. There were few real scoffers among those who presided over the displacement of the Christian vision by others. The vast majority were Protestant liberals who wanted their version of the faith to remain relevant to modern life and thought. In their search for relevance, however, they gradually replaced the Christian account with the American and Enlightenment accounts. If they did not lose their personal faith, they did lose confidence in the public relevance—the intellectual and moral potency—of the Christian account of life and reality.

But not all colleges and universities were so accommodating to the *Zeitgeist*. Calvin College, for example, never succumbed to the replacement of the Christian account with the American or Enlightenment. Indeed, it had enough confidence in the Reformed version of the Christian account to continue to use it as the organizing vision of its life and mission. It also had enough philosophical sophistication to be suspicious of exclusive Enlightenment claims. It did not do obeisance to them. On the contrary, the college did "worldview analysis" of the presuppositions involved in many secular approaches to knowledge. Finding that such approaches were built on faith claims less persuasive than the Christian, it critiqued those claims and integrated their chastened offerings into the Christian vision it cherished. This it called "the integration of faith and learning." It continues this project with vigor and sophistication to this day and serves as a beacon of "Christian scholarship" to many other Protestant colleges and universities.

Even as Calvin College took seriously the intellectual dimension of the Reformed tradition, it also attended to the spiritual and moral dimensions of that stream of the larger Christian tradition. As a Reformed institution, the college believed in the transformation of its students and its social surroundings, as well as the knowledge it offered them. There is, according to Calvin, a definable Christian "way of life" that can be communicated to its students through many sorts of practices. These efforts at transformation permeate the institutional life of the college. No area of life is "unclaimed for Christ," to put it in the words of the college's theological progenitor, Abraham Kuyper.

Such a strong mixture of vision, ethos, and educational excellence has produced an impressive array of Christian intellectuals. It has also formed laypersons who have gone on to exercise their vocations in many other areas of life. The college has been able to combine both quality and soul. But there are a goodly number of excellent colleges and universities who have kept the faith. Some are evangelical schools that have been strongly Christian in ethos but lately have been inspired by Calvin's intellectual approach, for example, Wheaton and Baylor. Some are Catholic colleges and universities that operate from quite a different theological model of Christian higher education, for example, Notre Dame, Holy Cross, Scranton. Others are Lutheran and work with yet another model of faith-learning engagement, for example, St. Olaf, Valparaiso, Luther, Concordia of Moorhead. Yet others are shaped by other religious traditions.

Besides educational excellence, all seem to share the characteristics that Paul Griffiths (*Religious Reading*) attributes to genuinely serious religious persons and institutions. Griffiths argues that those who are religiously serious hold the Christian account of life and reality to be comprehensive, unsurpassable, and central.

By *comprehensive*, Griffiths means that the Christian account encompasses all of reality—private and public, personal and historical, intellectual and moral. The Christian account has universal scope. This certainly does not mean that the Christian account provides all the knowledge within that universal horizon. There is much essential knowledge ascertainable through science, reason, and experience. But the comprehensive claim of the faith means that we attempt to organize, critique, and fit such knowledge into the Christian world of meaning. Thus a college that operates with a comprehensive Christian account does not let other claims to knowledge operate with complete autonomy. Rather, it insists that the Christian account engage other accounts and vice versa. The various theological models belonging to the several religious traditions project different views of what such engagement entails, as well as how it should be resolved. The comprehensive criterion also demands that serious theology be taught at the school and that it be an ever-present partner in faith/learning engagement. Without serious systematic theology, faith cannot make credible comprehensive claims. Comprehensiveness also means that the Christian account involves "ethos," or lifestyle, claims, as well as intellectual claims. One does not leave the life-shaping potential of, say, the student life office up to purely secular approaches. The whole school comes under the umbrella of a comprehensive Christian account.

Unsurpassable simply means that the Christian account will not be given up for another account. The leadership of the college or university firmly believe that the Christian account is the true account of human meaning and flourishing. It is the rock upon which are built the identity and mission of the college. Sadly, in the larger story of secularization, it was precisely this criterion that was bargained away in the efforts of many a school to live up to the standards of excellence set by the great research universities. Those standards were almost always set by the Enlightenment paradigm, which then gradually brought about the displacement of the Christian account in favor of its own. On the opposite side of the ledger, however, many colleges of a pietist bent held to the unsurpassability of the Christian account but were not able to meet the comprehensiveness criterion. Those colleges then located their Christian identity primarily in the extracurricular ethos of the college rather than in the heart of the educational enterprise itself.

Centrality means that an account addresses the central issues of human existence—one's relation to oneself, to others, to the natural world, to God. Centrality, of course, is one of the main strengths of a serious religious account. It responds to the deepest and most crucial questions of human life. A Christian college grapples with centrality in both its academic and its extracurricular life. These issues are of both the mind and heart. Although a secular college often avoids these central issues, they are so irrepressible that they inevitably emerge in some fashion. But the best the secular college can do is respond to them with a cacophony of answers. This throws the weight of decision on the mind and heart of the immature student. Serious Christian colleges "privilege" Christian answers to the constellation of central questions, though wise ones allow freedom to dissent from those answers. But there are no qualms about making those central answers normative.

III.

Thus the full-fledged Christian college or university makes the Christian account comprehensive, unsurpassable, and central for its life and mission. The schools I studied for my book start from such a conviction, then move with various degrees of success to realize that conviction. The most successful have had the courage and confidence to hire an overwhelming majority of faculty and administrators who believe that the Christian account is comprehensive, unsurpassable, and central.

But most church-related colleges no longer hold the Christian account in such a normative position. Yet there is a minority of strong Christian believers on their boards, administrations, faculties, and in their constituencies. Is there any hope for such colleges and universities? Not only is there hope, but a number of them are on their way to reconnecting with their heritage in more meaningful ways. The lists of colleges and universities in the Lilly and Rhodes networks are dotted with schools that have lost a robust relation to their heritage but want to reclaim something more meaningful than they currently have. They do so for reasons I have alluded to above. Christian perspectives seem more viable with the erosion of confidence in the Enlightenment and American accounts. Moreover, a number of seriously Christian schools have shown both quality and soul; one does not have to choose between faith and intellectual excellence.

For such colleges and universities, a strategy I call "intentional pluralism" is most appropriate. If the Christian account is no longer the organizing principle of the college or university, it can at least be guaranteed a voice among the other voices that contribute to the educational enterprise of the college. If other voices—feminist, multiculturalist, humanist, Marxist, Africanist—can be represented in the school, why shouldn't the Christian, which has the additional claim of continuity with the originating vision of the school? In our postmodern age such an approach seems persuasive indeed, not only for church-related schools but also for public colleges and universities.

The strong Christian believers remaining at the school—the remnant, if you will—can activate such a strategy by directing "religious" money to places in the school where the Christian account can be magnified. Individual givers from the sponsoring tradition can be sought out to establish endowments for the chaplain, for professors who do research in and teach the sponsoring tradition, and/or for centers or institutes that take seriously the Christian account as it has been refracted through the parent heritage.

When such a strategy gains momentum, it becomes possible for such an intentional pluralism to become the policy of the school in all its facets. Then the Christian voice can be heard not only in the curriculum but also in deliberations about student life. Although it is unlikely that such colleges and universities will ever "re-privilege" the Christian account, their commitment to intentional pluralism represents a more defensible relation to their sponsoring Christian heritage than they currently have. In the long run perhaps such a strategy can lead to enrichments we cannot now foresee. At any rate, the light is not dying in all church-related colleges and universities. In a significant number the light is shining brightly. In many others it may be glimmering before a dawn.

INTEGRITY AND FRAGMENTATION

CAN THE LUTHERAN CENTER HOLD?

There is much discussion today about whether a "Lutheran center," or identity, can hold in many Lutheran colleges. In my view, the Lutheran center cannot hold in many, if not most, of our colleges because it was never there in an articulated form in the first place. How can they hold now what they never held in the first place? A few Lutheran colleges have been able to articulate and hold a distinct religious center that has shaped and organized their lives as institutions. Although that center may be under constant discussion, it still provides the identity and mission of the college as a whole. Whether it can remain the organizing paradigm for the college of the future is an open question. But the fact that it is under intense public discussion is a good sign.

Mere discussion is not enough though. Discussion can lead to chaos or paralysis. (The whole faculty of Calvin Seminary was once dismissed by its board because they had argued themselves to an impasse. The good Calvinist pastors on the board held the quaint thought that the seminary should have a clear position on important matters of faith.) Ongoing discussion can also lead to notions of a center that in fact will marginalize or subvert any persisting Lutheran identity. That nuance, too, will have to be unpacked.

It is important to define at least provisionally and formally what is meant by "center." I would argue that the center for Lutheran liberal arts colleges ought to be religiously defined. That is, a religious vision of Christian higher education should be at their center. This religious vision, which like the Christian faith is comprehensive, would have within it an interpretation of the role and nature of human learning. (This provision, of course, eliminates a lot of our colleges that would currently find it quite embarrassing to admit that their mission was religiously defined.)

The religious vision comes from a living religious tradition. Alasdair MacIntyre has famously argued that a living tradition is "an historically extended, socially embodied argument about the goods which constitute that tradition."[1] Traditions extend through many generations. Lutheranism is such a tradition—or better, such a constellation of traditions—and it has sponsored many colleges and universities.

In giving a rationale for its involvement in higher education, Lutheranism has never exhibited unanimity. Something in these Lutheran bodies impelled them to establish colleges. The problem for many Lutheran colleges is that they were not conceptually clear about what they were doing. The impulse was there, but the sharp rationale—particularly a theological rationale—was not. These colleges were "Christ of culture" colleges.

H. Richard Niebuhr, in his renowned book *Christ and Culture*, identified five classic ways that Christian traditions have related Christ (the Christian vision) to culture. One of those, the "Christ of culture" tradition, identifies Christianity with the best of high culture. For example, during the Enlightenment many of the elite identified Christ as a sublime teacher of morality. He was a hero of culture along the lines of Socrates. The way I am using the Christ-of-culture category is a bit different. I mean that for many Lutheran groups that established colleges, the Christian vision was deeply and unconsciously entwined with their particular ethnoreligious culture. They were fairly homogenous groups that wanted their young to be educated within the ethnoreligious culture they prized. They wanted their laity-to-be to be immersed in the "atmosphere" of their culture. Moreover, they wanted that culture to encourage candidates for the ordained ministry who would then attend seminaries of that tradition.

Midland Lutheran of my college days was such a college. We were children of the German and Scandinavian Lutheran immigrations to the Midwest. Most of us had parents who hadn't gone to college, but we were encouraged by them and our local parishes to go to "our" school. We were taught by faculty generally of that same ethnoreligious culture. Ninety-some percent of us were from those backgrounds. How could such education not be Lutheran? Almost everyone at the college was Lutheran. Similar statements could be made about Gettysburg and Muhlenberg a generation or so earlier. Many Lutheran colleges exhibited these characteristics.

But was there anything more specifically Lutheran about that Midland of yore? Not a whole lot. Religion was a pretty inward, nonintellectual matter. We had pietist behavioral standards that prohibited premarital sex and alcohol. We had Bible courses offered at a low level of sophistication. We had required chapel of a distinctly nonliturgical sort. We had faculty who had committed their lives to the college and who now and then would connect their Christian perspective with their teaching. By and large the faculty and administration encouraged us as young Christians.

But there was no articulated center that sharply delineated the mission of the college. The theological acuity to do that was simply absent or was felt not to be needed. Lutheran theology and ethics were not taught. Lutheran history was nowhere to be found. The Lutheran idea of the calling was not explicitly taught to young people who had had it bred into them in their parishes. There was no concerted intellectual effort to interrelate the Christian vision with other fields of learning. We were simply Lutheran by ethos. We were immersed in a Christ-of-culture educational enterprise.

When the colleges expanded their student bodies and faculties in the late 1950s and 1960s, students and faculty members were recruited who no longer were part of that ethos. Indeed, the ethos itself was melting into the general American culture. Because the colleges had no articulated center, the colleges lost whatever integrity and unity they had. Soon faculty members appeared who were not only apathetic about the tradition that originally sponsored them but actually hostile toward it. Raising any question about a religious center disturbed and offended them. The culture that was friendly to Christ became one that either ignored or rejected Him—and the college went with that culture.

Now the loss of such a religious, Christ-of-culture orientation did not mean death for the colleges. Some of them found new ways to define themselves. Some, like Gettysburg, went for high quality and highly selective pre-professional education. They have an integrity and unity, but it is not religiously defined. At most, religion is a grace note, a flavor in the mix, a social ornament but certainly not the organizing center. It remains to be seen whether such an identity is satisfying enough to either college or church to maintain it.

Other Lutheran colleges, which James Burtchaell calls the "confessional colleges," did have a more articulated center.[2] That is, the religious vision that sprang from their religious tradition was more specific, often theologically stated. They didn't mind being viewed as "sectarian," an appellation from which the Christ-of-culture colleges fled. This theological distillation of the religious vision served as the paradigm around which was organized the whole life of the college—its academic, social, organizational, and extracurricular facets.

Two Lutheran colleges that I studied in the formation of my book *Quality with Soul—How Six Premier Colleges and Universities Keep Faith with Their Religious Traditions* (2001) are representative of these "confessional colleges." St. Olaf College in Northfield, Minnesota, a college of the Evangelical Lutheran Church in America, and Valparaiso University in Valparaiso, Indiana, historically linked to The Lutheran Church—Missouri Synod, are both highly articulated colleges who have kept a robust connection with their sponsoring Lutheran religious traditions. They have organized their identities and missions around the Christian vision and ethos.

St. Olaf, stemming from a strong Norwegian Lutheran religious tradition, has had a long history of tending its Lutheran identity. In its early days, St. Olaf was so pervasively Norwegian Lutheran that it scarcely had to attend to its identity, but it did, mainly through the charismatic leadership of its clergy presidents. They were able to draw to St. Olaf some giants in the world of literature and music—for example, the author O. E. Rolvaag and the choral conductor F. Melius Christianson. From the beginning the Lutheran idea of the calling of all Christians was a central organizing motif; it pervaded the consciousness of faculty, students, and staff.

As the Norwegian ethnic identity waned after World War II, St. Olaf began serious theological reflections about its identity and mission. These affirmed St. Olaf's commitment to an engagement between secular learning and Lutheran theology. They also ensured a strong commitment to teaching required courses in Christian theology and ethics and to encouraging exchanges between the Christian vision and secular fields of learning.

This reflection and commitment continue at St. Olaf. It is a self-consciously Lutheran Christian college. This articulation of the Lutheran identity of the college is bolstered by the ethos maintained at the institution. More than 50 percent of the students are Lutheran, and the college would like to keep that percentage high. There is a highly developed daily chapel program presided over by a distinguished chaplain and his staff. There are many active Christian groups on campus. Further, the famed St. Olaf choral and instrumental music programs draw participation by almost half the student body. These programs are not only aesthetically oriented but also religiously serious. Students are invited into a deeper exploration of their Christian commitments through them.

Much of a similar nature could be said about Valparaiso University. Its theater, choral, instrumental, and visual arts program are flourishing, led by capable young Christians. These programs become vehicles for the Christian formation of the students. Although Valparaiso doesn't have the percentage of Lutheran students that St. Olaf does, it appeals to large numbers of Roman Catholics. Together these two religious groups constitute roughly 60 percent of the student body. They worship together in daily chapel services in the stunning Chapel of the Resurrection, the largest and most architecturally interesting building on campus. The chapel was built to symbolize the Christian center of all learning. Emblazoned on its front is Valparaiso's motto: "In Thy Light We See Light."

Valparaiso is informally related but not legally tied to the theologically conservative Lutheran Church—Missouri Synod. Lutheran theology has provided the defining vision for Valparaiso from its inception as a Lutheran school in the 1920s. That vision was given charismatic articulation by Valparaiso's longtime, larger-than-life president, O. P. Kretzmann. In his long tenure at the university he gathered a large group of impressive Lutheran intellectuals who taught and wrote at the university. He also founded literary journals, an honors college, and a liturgical institute, among other things. Throughout his tenure and beyond, the university has enjoyed a conspicuous flowering of Christian humanism, Lutheran style.

The university continues this heritage, though its relation to The Lutheran Church—Missouri Synod is ambiguous. It continues to be led by Lutheran leaders in its board, administration, faculty, and alumni. The Christian vision and ethos continue to be the organizing paradigm for its life and mission. It has strengthened this commitment by garnering a number of externally funded centers, institutes, and programs that contribute directly to its religious identity and mission. It also fosters an ongoing public discussion about its Lutheran Christian character, which witnesses to the fact that its church-relatedness is the crucial element in its self-understanding.

These two schools continue to exemplify a centered Lutheran version of Christian humanism. They have been led by people who have had a clear rationale for what they were doing. This rationale has sprung from their religious tradition and has been theologically articulated. It has been supported by a board that has explicitly supported and prized that tradition. Above all, the schools have had the courage to select faculty who have supported such a notion of Lutheran humanism.

These two, and a number of other such Lutheran colleges, still exist, but they have an uphill battle to maintain themselves. Some institutions had a clear rationale but are losing it. A number of reasons for that are obvious. Some colleges fight for survival and are willing to adapt to market conditions, even if it means giving up their religious center. Others are seduced to give up their religious center by a glorious worldly success that goes far beyond mere survival. Some have increasing numbers of administrators and faculty who simply do not see the point in trying to operate from a religious center. They do not believe that the Christian vision is any longer an adequate vision for organizing the life of a college. For many of those administrators and faculty, religion is a private, interior matter that should not be publicly relevant to the educational enterprise. Some colleges can no longer agree on the center and fall into a kind of chaotic pluralism. Then they cannot summon either the clarity or the courage to hire faculty that support Lutheran humanism in higher education.

A number of our colleges fall between these two depictions. They are a bit more intentional than the Christ-of-culture types but less defined than the Lutheran humanist types. I do not wish to set up exclusive categories. But it does us no good to continue with self-congratulation concerning our fidelity to a Lutheran center when so many of us have little or no semblance of one.

II.

All this brings us to the question: What is an adequate Lutheran "center"? Let me say that a Lutheran center is first a Christian center. Lutherans share with other major Christian traditions a common Christian narrative—the Bible and the long history of the church. From those narratives emerged early on what we could call the apostolic or trinitarian faith, defined in the classic ecumenical creeds. In the long history of the church much theological reflection took place; a Christian intellectual tradition was shaped. This intellectual tradition conveyed a Christian view of the origin and destiny of the world, of nature and history, of human nature and its predicament, of human salvation and of a Christian way of life. This larger Christian tradition also bore Christian practices such as worship, marriage, hospitality, charity, etc.

The Lutheran Reformation and its ensuing history arose from and expressed a Lutheran construal of this general Christian tradition. Many of the facets of that construal are ensconced in the Lutheran Confessions. Some of the more particular elements of that Lutheran construal will be discussed a bit later as I further delineate the Lutheran center for Christian higher education. This Lutheran Christian vision of reality, particularly in its intellectual form, constitutes the center. But how will it work out in the life of a college? How will it provide the organizing paradigm for the identity and mission of a college? How will it make a difference? What difference will it make?

Mark Schwehn, in a recent address at the University of Chicago[3] provides a wonderful starting point. In his address he attempts to define the characteristics of a Christian university, one that, as I put it, employs the Christian vision as the organizing paradigm for its life and mission. Schwehn talks generically about "Christian" institutions, but I will transpose his language for specifically Lutheran colleges. Also, I will abbreviate the rich elaboration of each of his characteristics.

First, Schwehn lists what he calls "constitutional requirements." A Lutheran college must have a board of trustees composed of a substantial majority of Lutheran persons, clergy and lay, whose primary task is to ensure the continuity of its Lutheran Christian character. This will mean appointing a majority of

Lutheran leaders who are committed to the idea of a Lutheran Christian college.

These leaders will in turn see to it that all the following things are present within the life of the institution. First, a department of theology that offers courses required of all students in both biblical studies and the Christian intellectual tradition; second, an active chapel ministry that offers worship services in the tradition of the faith community that supports the school (Lutheran) but also makes provision for worship by those of other faiths; third, a critical mass of faculty members who, in addition to being excellent teacher-scholars, carry in and among themselves the DNA of the school, care for the perpetuation of its mission as a Christian community of inquiry, and understand their own callings as importantly bound up with the well-being of the immediate community; and fourth, a curriculum that includes a large number of courses, required of all students, that are compellingly construed as parts of a larger whole and that taken together constitute a liberal education.[4]

Second, Schwehn develops three qualities that ought to be present in a Lutheran Christian college that flow directly from its theological commitments. The first is unity. By that he means the conviction that because God is One and Creator, all reality and all truth finally cohere in Him. Thus the Christian college quests for the unity that follows from this theological principle. The second quality is universality, that all humans are beloved of the God who has created and redeemed them. All humans must be treated with dignity and respect. The third is integrity, which involves the belief "that there is an integral connection among the intellectual, moral, and spiritual dimensions of human life, and that these therefore ought where possible to be addressed concurrently within a single institution rather than parceled out into separate and often conflicting realms."[5] Although these qualities may be grounded in other views of life, they are thoroughly grounded for a Christian college in trinitarian theological principles.

Schwehn's fourth principle deserves more attention because it gets at, at least for this essay, the particularly Lutheran qualities of a Christian college. Schwehn argues that a "Christian university privileges and seeks to transmit, through its theology department, its official rhetoric, the corporate worship it sponsors, and in myriad other ways, a particular tradition of thought, feeling, and practice."[6]

Although one could spend a good deal of time on a Lutheran college's "feeling"—its aesthetic tone—and "practices"—its worship, its arts, its sense of corporate and institutional calling—I would rather focus on its tradition of thought, its approach to higher learning. This is shaped by the particular way that Lutherans relate Christ and culture, Gospel and Law, the right-hand kingdom and that of the left. And because the Lutheran approach is complex and dialectical, it is highly vulnerable to distortion.

The first thing to say is that Lutheran colleges respect the independence, creativity, and contributions of the many "worldly" ways of knowing. The disciplines are prized in their full splendor. Luther roared: "How dare you not know what you can know!" He also argued that Christians have to be competent in their secular callings; a Christian cobbler makes good shoes, not poor shoes with little crosses on them. Lutheran teacher-scholars teach and write well; their piety will not excuse incompetence.

However, the disciplines are not given idolatrous autonomy because they, too, are under the dominion of finitude and sin, and they often claim too much for themselves. Rather, the disciplines are to be engaged from the point of view of the Gospel, and here "Gospel" is meant to refer to the whole trinitarian perspective on the world, not just the doctrine of the forgiveness of sins. That is, a Lutheran college aims at an ongoing dialogue between the Christian intellectual tradition—Lutheranly construed—and the secular disciplines. This is what is meant by a lively tension and interaction between Christ and culture, the Gospel and the Law, and the two ways that God reigns in the world.

A genuinely Lutheran college will aim at such an engagement, rejoicing in the areas of overlap and agreement that may occur, continuing a mutual critique where there are divergences and disagreements, anticipating that in the eschaton these differing views will come together in God's own truth, but in the meantime being willing to live with many unresolved questions. Thus in some areas of inquiry, a Lutheran college will recognize paradox, ambiguity, and irresolvability. But this recognition takes place at the end of a creative process of engagement, not at the beginning, where some of the proponents of "paradox" would like to put it. Those proponents simply avoid real engagement by declaring "paradox" at the beginning, essentially allowing everyone to go their own way and do their own thing.

Let me enter a caveat here. This sort of engagement does not go on all the time and by everyone in every classroom. A good deal of educational time in a Lutheran college is given over to transmitting the "normal knowledge" of the field or the freight of the liberal arts core. But in probing the depths of every discipline, in addressing perennial and contemporary issues, in shaping a curriculum, in the kind of teaching and scholarship it prizes, and, above all, in the kind of faculty it hires, a Lutheran college nurtures this ongoing engagement between the Christian intellectual tradition and other ways of knowing.

Contrary to the Reformed approach, a Lutheran college does not give an automatic privilege to the Christian worldview, which in the end can "trump" the other ways of knowing. Contrary to the Catholic approach, which sees all knowledge rising to a synthesis organized by Catholic wisdom, the Lutheran approach lives with more messiness. But it respects those models of Christian humanism and finds itself closer to them than to the modern secular tendency to marginalize and sequester into irrelevancy the Christian view of life and reality.

This genuine Lutheran approach also guards against its own Lutheran distortions, the prime one being the separation of Christ and culture, Gospel and Law, and of the two ways that God reigns. This separation occurs in this way. The Gospel is narrowly defined as the doctrine of justification. This Gospel is preached in the chapel and taught by the theology department. But it is not the full-blown, comprehensive vision of life explicit in the trinitarian faith. It does not have the intellectual content of the full Christian vision. In this flawed view, the Law (culture or the left hand of God) embraces everything else. All disciplines are under the Law, and reason is the instrument for understanding them. Indeed, Luther's understanding of reason is often appealed to. His understanding sounds like an affirmation of autonomous reason set free from Christian assumptions. If that is the case, then a Lutheran college simply allows all inquiries shaped by reason to proceed freely. The results of these inquiries are respected and left pretty much unchallenged. The best available faculty can be hired for this exercise of autonomous reason without regard to religious convictions or interest in the theological dialogue I outlined above. A Lutheran college, in this view, is simply one that encourages the exercise of autonomous reason. Or, in postmodern terms, it respects the various perspectives that people bring to learning from their social locations.

There are enormous problems with this approach. For one thing, it assumes that Luther meant the same thing by reason that we do. On the contrary, the reason that Luther respected was thoroughly ensconced in a Christian worldview. It was a reason that could affirm the Good, the True, and the Beautiful in a way that was consistent with Christian presuppositions. But such a view of reason is long gone. Reason has been removed from the religious traditions within which it worked. Now reason operates from different assumptions, usually characterized by a pervasive philosophical naturalism (the modern) or by an arbitrary epistemological tribalism (the postmodern).

Allowing such an exercise of reason to go unchallenged in a Lutheran school is irresponsible. It leads to bifurcations of the minds of students and faculty alike. For example, Christian faculty who worship God on Sunday teach a view of the world that shuts out God and human freedom on Monday. Students live their faith and intellectual lives in two separate compartments. To combat this unhappy situation, the disciplines must be engaged by the Gospel, namely, the Christian vision with its comprehensive claims to truth. However, the Christian vision is not immune to challenge itself. The disciplines engage the Christian vision. In any genuine conversation there is the chance that both conversation partners' views may be changed. What's more, Christian claims are often of high generality, the claims of a discipline more detailed and concrete. One often needs the other. Engagement is not always conflictual; it is often complementary.

The distorted Lutheran approach I have depicted above splits Christ (the Christian vision) and culture (the academic enterprise), the Gospel (in its full elaboration) from the Law (the exercise of reason). This separation of the Christian intellectual tradition from secular learning is as dangerous to Lutheran colleges as the separation of the Gospel and politics was to the Germany of Nazi times. Certainly the stakes are quite different, but such a separation will lead to a realm of secular education unchallenged by the Christian vision, just as it led in Germany to a political movement unchecked by that same Christian vision.

Such an approach, which often is used as a rationalization to disguise the prior lapse into secularization, can well appeal to paradox, ambiguity, and uncertainty because it will have nothing but a cacophony of voices, each claiming their little corner of the college. Such a condition, which is not too far from the one prevailing at many of our colleges, led one of our graduate students who attended a summer conference a few years back to say: "From what I gathered there, a Lutheran college is a wonderful place because everyone can think and do whatever they wish. It's a free-for-all."

In summary, a Lutheran college fosters a genuine engagement of Christ and culture. It encourages a creative dialectic between Gospel and Law by giving the Gospel in its fullest intellectual standing. Such a college stands at the lively junction between the two ways that God reigns. All this flows from the Lutheran Christian center that guides the college. Such a college is willing to make the hard institutional decisions that ensure that such a vision lives on. It will hire an administration and faculty that not only tolerate such a vision but also support and participate in it. Indeed, they will feel called to it. Such a college will recruit students who are open to such an enterprise. And if it executes such an enterprise well, it will have something special to offer the church and world. It will become more than just a pretty good generic liberal arts college.

III.

Those colleges that approximate such a view of Lutheran higher education—Lutheran humanism, if you will—will have a good idea of what to aim at. The practical aspects of that task will be difficult and challenging, but the principles are pretty clear. In actual fact, a few of our colleges have a fighting chance to move closer to the ideal. I wish them well and Godspeed.

But what of the many colleges who long ago lost a Lutheran center, a religious vision that shapes the life of the college? What of the many colleges that find my ideal Lutheran vision simply impossible. One might answer that we can't put Humpty Dumpty together again. We can't unscramble the eggs in our omelet. We simply have little chance of regaining such a robust center. Some might be saying that we shouldn't do that even if we could. But an intentional, robust pluralism can be a goal, a pluralism in which the college guarantees that the perspectives of Lutheran Christianity are represented in all the departments and divisions of the college. The Lutheran vision may no longer be the paradigm that organizes the college's life, if it ever was, but it can be intentionally represented among the many voices of other perspectives. The college at which I work, Roanoke College, has adopted such a model, though it is far from complete. From a point in the early 1980s, when the institution almost lost any meaningful church connection, Roanoke College now encourages the strong representation of the Christian perspective among the other voices that constitute the college's life. It appears there is strong momentum to increase our movement toward a more intentional pluralism.

Why is it not possible that Christian public intellectuals— those who in their teaching and scholarship embody the dialogical model I elaborated above—be intentionally sprinkled among the departments? Could we not ensure that the Christian perspective on our life together be represented in student affairs along with the more secular ones? Could college leaders not articulate a Christian rationale for our involvement in service, as well as the more generic reasons?

It seems only honest to press for such an intentional pluralism—affirmative action for Christians generally and Lutherans specifically—in a college that still claims a relationship to the Lutheran tradition. If a provision for such a pluralism can be made, our appeal to Lutheran donors and Lutheran students would have more plausibility. The kind of hypocrisy that takes donations for projects that lead to further secularization of the college can be avoided.

Certainly boards of trustees, presidents, deans, department heads, and faculty could be persuaded to see the cogency of such a proposal. If being related to a religious tradition means anything significant, it must mean that that tradition can speak within its "own" institution. If we can't muster at least that commitment, why in heaven's name should we continue the relationship?

NOTES

1. Alasdair MacIntyre, *After Virtue* (South Bend, Ind.: Notre Dame University Press, 1981), 207.

2. James Burtchaell, *The Dying of the Light* (Grand Rapids: Eerdmans, 1998), 499.

3. Mark Schwehn, "A Christian University: Defining the Difference," *First Things* 93 (May 1999): 25–31.

4. Schwehn, "Christian University," 26–27.

5. Schwehn, "Christian University," 28.

6. Schwehn, "Christian University," 29.

Reconnecting

A COLLEGE
RECOVERS ITS CHRISTIAN HERITAGE

For much of this century, the waning influence of religion in American colleges and universities was viewed as a natural concomitant of modernization, and it was generally seen as a necessary or even a good thing. In recent years, Christian scholars such as George Marsden and James Burtchaell have offered a new interpretation of that history, arguing that the marginalization of religion in higher education has been lamentable and assigning the blame to institutional leaders, not to the inexorable forces of modernization.

Of course, not all Christian colleges have been secularized. Notre Dame, Baylor, Valparaiso, St. Olaf, Wheaton and Calvin are among the schools that have maintained a robust relation to their sponsoring religious heritages.

More typical, however, are the church-related colleges and universities that have experienced significant secularization and that have maintained only a thin connection with their religious heritage. Some of these schools maintain this connection simply as a social ornament—a gentle hypocrisy. Others have made new efforts to reengage their heritage. Roanoke College in Virginia is one such school.

Roanoke is a liberal arts college affiliated with the Evangelical Lutheran Church in America. Is is the second oldest Lutheran college in the U. S. Its clergyman founder, David Bittle, was from the beginning committed to a broad, nonconfessional approach to higher education. He regarded Lutheran ethnic or religious isolation as something to be avoided. Many sorts of Christians and non-Christians were invited into the enterprise, though it was clear that Lutherans were responsible for directing it.

Through most of its years the college was recognizably Christian—its intellectual, moral and social life guided by Christian principles. Immersed deeply in enlightened evangelicalism, it was never troubled by serious conflicts over evolution or biblical interpretation. Its Christian humanism was borne by the informal consensus of southern Lutheran gentlemen, led by rather impressive and learned clergy presidents. Its Christian character was reinforced by the religious culture of southwestern Virginia, whence many of its students came. Relations with supporting Lutheran bodies were unsteady, however, since the synods were unable or unwilling to provide the financial support the college needed.

However, in the late 1950s and '60s, the college was led by lay presidents who did not tend to the earlier Christian consensus, partly because that consensus was more tacit than well-articulated. During the expansion of the school in the 1960s and the cultural upheavals of that era, administrators, professors, and board members were recruited without regard to their religious convictions.

A familiar story unfolded. The statement of purpose no longer claimed that the college was Christian or that intellectual and moral development there took place in a "Christian atmosphere." Rather, it vaguely stated that the college "honors its Christian heritage and founding by Lutherans." The two required religion courses were made electives. Chapel attendance was no longer required. Christian moral standards were no longer publicly claimed as guides for conduct; the honor system was abandoned. In the '70s Roanoke was listed in *Playboy*'s catalogue of top party schools.

New faculty were influenced heavily by the Enlightenment bias that religion has no reliable intellectual content. The increasingly large secularist wing of the faculty mounted at least one attempt to disengage the college from the church. Religious practice was marginalized and religious organizations declined. The chaplain focused on crisis intervention among the many students caught up in alcohol and drug abuse. Any sense of common life nearly vanished, and the faculty adopted a kind of social libertarianism—it kept the common educational core as minimal as possible. And the church became increasingly suspicious of the college.

By the early '80s, the religious factor seemed to be ignored in all facets of the college's life. The number of Lutherans in the administration and on the faculty was so low that the few who were left appealed to the president for some Lutheran affirmative action. Religion was no longer considered publicly relevant. As a powerful member of the board put it in the midst of a debate about whether the president should be required to be Lutheran: "It is a matter of indifference to the board what the president does on his weekends."

As the college stood poised on the brink of total disengagement from the church, the president, a midwestern Lutheran used to more robust connections, and the dean, a Presbyterian, quietly but deliberately began to take steps to reverse the process. They raised Lutheran money for an endowed chair in religion and for a center for church and society. I was recruited for that chair, then the only endowed professorship at the college, and to be director of the center. I was asked to find ways to strengthen the Christian character of the college. Several new board members of strong Lutheran conviction were appointed. A young and vigorous new bishop of the Virginia Synod came onto the executive committee of the board. The college provided space for the Virginia Synod headquarters, and the bishop and his staff became a familiar presence on campus. A director of church relations was hired who opened the college to many church functions—youth events, synod assemblies, continuing education events and synod council meetings. So successful has she been in recruiting Lutheran donors for the specifically religious activities of the college that the chaplaincy and its staff recently became completely endowed.

Through a combination of providence and design, a significant number of Christian faculty who are willing to be public about their convictions and to integrate their faith with their teaching have been gathered. A second endowed professorship— this time in English—was filled by a Christian intellectual committed to church-related education.

Near the beginning of this process, a majority of the faculty would not have supported the college's reengagement with its Christian heritage. If the issue had been brought to a public vote, the Christian partisans would certainly have been trounced.

Crucially important to winning support for these reforms has been a grass-roots group on "faith and learning" which meets regularly to reflect on the college's religious character and to support efforts to strengthen it. The president and most of his cabinet participate regularly. Now with nearly 40 members, the "faith and learning" organization has given the administration stimulation and support. It has broadened faculty support by making a persuasive case for the viability of the Christian intellectual tradition.

The college has joined both the Lilly Network of Church-related Colleges and Universities and the Rhodes Consultation, and participates vigorously in the Evangelical Lutheran Church in America's summer conferences on the calling of the Lutheran college and in its Lutheran Academy for younger scholars.

Roanoke's current president came from a midwestern Lutheran college with a robust connection to its Lutheran heritage. He is a theologically reflective Lutheran layman who has through the years strengthened his support for our Christian heritage. His public rhetoric has become more boldly Christian. His cabinet of six includes four Lutherans. He has been committed to raising endowments for the particularly religious elements of the college's identity and mission. Working with development personnel and faculty, he is raising endowments for chairs in Lutheran studies, evangelical studies, and Christian ethics, as well as for the Center for Religion and Society (the name was changed so as to include the Jewish studies program for which the college received a major ongoing grant).

A high-quality religion department is essential to a church-related college. In the present buyer's market in religion and philosophy, we have been able to recruit some of the best graduates from top graduate schools. Their exemplary record in both teaching and scholarship is one of the school's most potent signals that we are serious about religion. Most of them speak not only about but for the Christian tradition. The number of religion majors has increased from one in 1983 to forty in 2000. We are again supplying a steady stream of students (four to six per year) to a wide range of seminaries.

Guided by a Lutheran chaplain who is bold in his proclamation of the Word, religious life on campus has grown. The meetings of many study groups, InterVarsity, Lutheran Student Movement, Baptist Student Union and a Catholic Campus Ministry fill the college calendar. Weekly morning chapel has returned as an option, while several other worship services are held in the evenings. The last decade has also brought the development of one of the marks of Lutheran college education—a vigorous choral music program. The college has also adopted a required cocurricular program that emphasizes service to the community. The service opportunities are organized by the chaplain's office.

Despite determined efforts to recruit Lutheran students, the Lutheran composition of the student body remains low—about 8 or 9 percent—mainly because our region is sparsely populated with Lutherans (but Lutheran students seem to make an impact beyond their numbers). Evangelical students drawn from the region provide the strongest religious presence in the student body. Our effort to endow a professorship in evangelical studies is intended both to nourish and recruit more of these students, as well as to study a major American religious movement.

Because of the presence of the Center for Religion and Society, major public lectures and conferences include the religious perspective among others. The center provides our weekly convocation with a number of Christian speakers each term. It encourages interdisciplinary conversations and courses; and last year a symposium on religion and psychology was held by the two departments. The center is now embarking on a series of hour-long programs on religion and society issues for our local public television outlet. After a 20-year absence from the curriculum, the college has again instituted a required religion and philosophy course called "Values and the Responsible Life."

The introduction of the course in the early '90s prompted the first public showdown between those supporting reengagement and those resisting it. The faculty narrowly voted to allow a "values course" to be developed by the religion and philosophy department. When faculty realized that this course would include the Judeo-Christian tradition as a source of religious and moral values along with other perspectives, many grew suspicious. The course was monitored more closely than any other in the core curriculum. When evaluation of the core curriculum took place in the mid-'90s, a number of faculty protested anonymously that the course was "Sunday school proselytizing" with weak intellectual content.

In response, the college held a summer workshop to prepare faculty outside the religion and pilosophy department to teach the class. The word spread that indeed there was intellectual challenge in the course and that the department wasn't coercing the students to faith, if indeed that were possible. Since that workshop there has been little further carping, and the college touts the importance of the course far and wide.

The momentum toward reconnection led last year to important revisions in the college's statement of purpose. One of those revisions brought about a second showdown. The new statement not only puts a greater emphasis on spiritual growth and participation in religious and service activities, but spells out what it means to "honor our Christian heritage." The new version states that the college "honors its Christian heritage and its partnership with the Lutheran church by nurturing a dialogue between faith and reason."

Anticipating a lively debate on the new wording, the "faith and learning" group arranged for articulate spokespersons from the group to defend the amendment against possible objections. Curiously, the skeptics did not argue against it. The ensuing vote resulted in a tie, which the faculty moderator, a devout Catholic, broke by voting for the proposal. When a later attempt was made to reconsider the change, the faculty defeated it by a comfortable margin.

The "faith and learning" group is now organizing a series of programs about what a dialogue between faith and reason entails. The group's most recent venture featured a lecture by a distinguished historian of Christian thought on the Christian intellectual tradition. The group's hope is that more faculty will accept the notion that Christian higher education means an intellectual encounter between the Christian account of life and reality and other perspectives implicit in other fields of learning.

Roanoke College is still a long way from being a robust Christian college. Perhaps a third of the faculty—including many Christians—remains indifferent to the changes that have been made. A smaller group is disturbed by and suspicious of recent developments. Half the department heads still believe that religious considerations ought to be irrelevant in faculty recruitment and hire accordingly. Too many of our students do not participate in religious life. Chapel attendance is low. The college is still bashful about articulating explicitly Christian standards of moral conduct. As on most campuses, parties continue to be one of the main attractions of student life, and only a fraction of the students are awake on Sunday mornings. Piety is not exactly the campus rage.

Even so, the past 15 years have seen a significant reengagement of the college with its Lutheran and Christian heritage. If Roanoke's story can be duplicated—as I believe it can—colleges that have come close to losing their connection can reverse that process and make important headway in the opposite direction. A determined but patient group of leaders who believe that the Christian account of the world is publicly relevant to all facets of the college's life and mission can move such a college toward a new relation to its religious heritage. And that new relation may be more intentional, meaningful and fruitful than its earlier one.

CHRISTIAN COLLEGES
AND CIVIL SOCIETY

I remember first coming across the concept of "intermediate groups" or "mediating institutions" or "voluntary associations" in graduate school at the University of Chicago. We were given an assignment to read William Kornhauser's *The Politics of Mass Society* (1959). In that book the author laments the erosion of intermediate groups and the ensuing emergence of "mass society," a condition in which isolated individuals unconnected to intermediate groups are vulnerable to domination and manipulation by an ever-expanding state. I was so fascinated by Kornhauser's ideas that I wrote my dissertation on responsibility in mass society.

Of course the idea of intermediate groups was not at all new. De Touqueville, that inexhaustible source of insight into American society, pointed out the importance of voluntary associations in the life of early America. He believed they were key to self-governance and hence to a stable and flourishing democracy. Berger and Neuhaus, in their influential *To Empower People* (1977), made a strong argument for using "mediating institu-

Originally published in *The Cresset* (Summer 1996).
Amended and reprinted with permission.

tions" to perform many social functions rather than expanding the state.

Now the concept is really flourishing. Communitarians commend "social unions" as a continuing source of social solidarity. Those who study formerly communist societies are especially interested in what they call "civil society," those free, private, and independent organizations that connect people with one another and play important roles in societies with states that are limited not only constitutionally but also in terms of capabilities. In such countries the reemergence of a flourishing civil society is crucial for the preservation of democracy. Reconstituting them is no simple matter, however, because totalitarian regimes destroy both civil society and the habits of the people that can sustain it.

I.

Obviously, churches are crucial in this schema. They are "intermediate associations" par excellence. In American society they are numerous and varied. Only recently have churches been given their due as bulwarks of civil society, partly, I suspect, because of the secularist bent of most social scientists. They simply do not like to admit that religious convictions—and the institutions they sustain—play an important role in modern societies.

But important role they do play, and the "they" includes the many church-related institutions besides the churches themselves. When one thinks of the kinds and numbers of institutions founded and sustained by the churches, one is duly impressed with their role in civil society. Nursery schools, kindergartens, elementary schools, colleges and universities, orphanages, social service agencies, homes for the elderly, hospitals, cause-oriented voluntary associations, service and recreational organizations—the list goes on and on.

Theorists of intermediate organizations point to the many functions they play. They provide services that the state need not supply; thereby they obviate an ever-growing Leviathan. They are schools of virtue; they shape the character traits that sustain good citizenship. They communicate values and shore up identity. They provide structures of belonging so people do not feel isolated and alienated. They represent groups of people to higher levels of power and authority. They protect people from arbitrary intrusions by the state. They increase social solidarity. Their multiple claims on persons give those persons a variety of sources of information and loyalty; such persons are not inclined to paranoid politics.

II.

Certainly one of the most important of these intermediate organizations are church-related colleges and universities. They perform many of the above-listed functions as well as their primary function—education. For Lutherans these colleges and universities have been highly prized vehicles for transmitting their heritage to succeeding generations. In doing so they also play an important role in sustaining civil society.

Private, church-related colleges and universities, however, are an endangered species. All of us experience the admissions "crunch" each spring where we try to maintain our numbers. The consultants tell us that there are simply too many colleges basically like us. They encourage us to develop marketable "margins of difference." They suggest that a lot of us won't be around in the twenty-first century. Although there is no doubt there is some self-serving alarmism in these consultants' message, there is enough truth in it to give serious pause.

Os Guinness, in *The American Hour* (1993), argues that civil society has been caught in a pincer movement from above and below. From above we have the continuing expansion of the state. It takes over more and more functions once performed by voluntary associations, families, and individuals. (Think, for example, of the diminishing percentage of students attending private schools though their absolute numbers are at least holding their own.) What the state does not take over directly it regulates. Because of its vast resources, it becomes indispensable to the survival of private institutions, and when it pays the piper, it calls the tune. (Most faculty members in private institutions take the required nondiscrimination rules to mean that one cannot intentionally hire members of the sponsoring religious tradition to carry on that tradition.)

Also from "above" come the huge economic organizations that demand an education that will prepare people for business. If our graduates are to get employment, they need to go easy on the liberal arts and "get practical." Indeed, as the culture is shaped increasingly by commercial values, the liberal arts seem to take on decreased importance. An additional worry is that private for-profit schools offering practical education at a low price will further erode the place of private liberal arts colleges.

Finally, as George Marsden has pointed out, the graduate schools from which our faculty come have worked mightily to eliminate religious tradition—in both its intellectual and moral dimensions—as a relevant factor in education. Education is supposed to be neutral and objective, based on rational criteria of truth. Religious tradition, so the graduate schools often claim, will soon become irrational and intolerant if it plays any meaningful role in the educational process. Therefore, to talk about it at all, one must understand it in other more respectable secular categories.

So, Guinness suggests, state, economy, and university constitute one arm of the pincer that is putting the squeeze on private colleges from above. From below, he says, we have a galloping individualism fueled by a commercial culture that idolizes choice and an atmosphere of individual rights and freedoms that refuses to grant authority to any corporate tradition. Utilitarian and/or expressive individualists are not inclined to connect with colleges with demanding liberal arts and religious traditions.

III.

Where does this leave the sector of civil society in which many of us have our callings? Squeezed indeed. Interestingly enough, however, this is exactly the time when such colleges and universities are so sorely needed. Faced with the growing centrifugal forces of multiculturalism and postmodernism, public institutions, I believe, will have increasing difficulty coming up with coherent visions of education, especially those kinds of education that effectively form citizens, let alone those kinds of education that transmit a religious and/or cultural heritage. The public behemoths of education will simply be dispensaries of useful knowledge to meet the demands of the individuals who come to them. They will be unable to fulfill some of the key functions of civil society precisely when our society badly needs them.

What will be doubly tragic, though, is that just when society will need colleges with real character, the colleges themselves will have in many cases squandered whatever distinctiveness they had. That is, precisely when we will need colleges anchored in living religious and liberal arts traditions, we will find that the colleges have been deracinated by the pincer movement described above and by their callow capitulation to it. They will have lost the characteristics that make them valuable contributors to civil society; they will have adapted to the bland mold of others who have capitulated.

As I have indicated, there are many external forces that push toward the deracination of these colleges; it is no simple task to survive amid them without losing one's soul. But I am convinced that most colleges have been deeply complicitous in their own undoing. Their leadership and faculties have either failed to discern what has been going on or, if they have, have failed to muster the courage to provide a constructive alternative to the deracinating process. Perhaps a combination of ignorance and cowardice made up the formula for that complicity.

What has been going on? In brief, this is the way I see it. The external forces mentioned above have slowly marginalized the religious traditions that once were crucial in the social, moral, and intellectual life of church-related colleges. The sponsoring religious heritages have gradually lost their public relevance for the main functions of the respective colleges. Except for a few exceptions among the colleges, the religious heritage has been pushed out of the center. In some colleges it remains one tiny note among the booming peals that issue from secular sources. In others it is tolerated only as an ornament that graces the ritual events of the college's life. In yet others it is represented only by the first few chapters in the college's bicentennial history.

It would be difficult to plead total ignorance of this process, but it is plausible to plead that these secularizing processes have been operating piecemeal over a long period of time. Past leaders may be partially excused from seeing the reality of the emerging situation. But it takes willful blindness not to discern their massive presence now. Even in the face of unmistakable evidence, however, some leaders still rationalize the situation. They claim that the colleges still stand for the unfettered search for truth. Isn't that a Christian value, they ask? Meanwhile, however, those very schools eliminate the Christian intellectual tradition as a significant source of truth. It is a bystander at best. Why then, one might ask, do we bother to keep up appearances?

IV.

A few Catholic and mainstream Protestant colleges and universities have had the courage to maintain the public relevance of their religious heritage in their hiring policies, curricula, intellectual life, moral life, and overall ethos. I dare say, though, that the vast majority have not. They have amalgamated into the generic private, church-related liberal arts college, which is under threat of extinction.

The evangelicals, fundamentalists, and conservative Catholics have fared better. They have had the courage to insist that their religious heritage have public relevance in their colleges and universities. Sometimes the fruit of their efforts has been impressive: Wheaton and Calvin, for example, are among the best liberal arts colleges in the country. Fundamentalist institutions such as Liberty University are probably better than most liberal Protestants think, but even so they do not provide models for any of our Lutheran colleges. Their ways of relating Christ and culture are simply not an option for us. But it is difficult not to admire their courage and resolve in making the Christian vision relevant to higher education.

Lutherans, it seems to me, have a wonderful tradition of Christian humanism. Our particular way of relating the Christian vision to secular human learning might be termed "dialectical." Following from our paradoxical theological tradition, we tend to see the conversation between Christ and culture as full of creative but unresolved tension. Such a dialectical Christian humanism should be attractive in a modern world in which past certainties—such as the Enlightenment confidence in reason and science—are being eroded. It is time for the Christian vision to take its rightful place in the conversation about what human flourishing is all about. Such conversation in our colleges will guarantee that we will make strong contributions to civil society.

But do we have the zeal and courage to make such a Christian humanism live in our colleges and universities? For some the game is over; they have no meaningful relation to their historic Christian heritage. Others have a chance. A few stand in positions of strength. But even those few must tend their gardens with care. We should tend them not only or even primarily because we want to play our constructive role in civil society but also because we believe that such a Christian humanism has intrinsic truth and merit. We want to carry on not only because it is useful to society but above all because it is true.

Part 6

SEXUAL ETHICS

REINVENTING SEXUAL ETHICS

In its August 2001 Churchwide Assembly, the Evangelical Lutheran Church in America (ELCA) took three steps—two of them potentially momentous—with regard to its moral assessment of homosexuality and homosexual relations. The assembly decided (899–115) to do a "churchwide study on homosexuality, including matters related to the blessing of same-gender relationships and ordination of gay and lesbian people in committed relationships."[1] The action also called for a final report and action plan for implementation to be presented to the 2005 Churchwide Assembly.

In a related but separate action, the Assembly voted 624–381 to ask the Church Council, the Conference of Bishops, and the Division of Ministry to "create a specific plan and timeline leading toward a decision concerning the rostering of homosexual persons in committed relationships."[2] That plan is to be placed before the Churchwide Assembly in 2005. A third action that asked for the initiation of a process to lead to a social statement on human sexuality passed 581–386.[3]

Originally published in *First Things*, 121 (March 2002).
Amended and reprinted with permission.

The momentous part of the first two actions is that they may result in a straightforward decision to ordain gays and lesbians in committed relationships and to bless same-sex unions. Although it is widely believed that the church bureaucracy solidly supports both innovations, that bureaucracy certainly didn't want to be rushed into a real decision in 2005. After all, the ELCA already has plenty of internal organized resistance on its hands from those incensed about the concessions concerning the office of bishop that the ELCA made to establish fellowship with the Episcopal Church.

The ELCA bureaucracy would have preferred to muddle along without any precipitating action for a decade or so until the "crabby old guys" died off. After all, it holds all the cards—a self-perpetuating headquarters ethos that, combined with a quota system for church officers, guarantees "enlightened" thinking, control of the official communication instruments of the church, and the capacity to set agendas and frame questions. The ELCA leaders could afford to wait out the opposition on this issue, anticipating that the practice of "irregular ordinations" and blessing of same-sex unions would outrun and finally overturn traditional teaching. These revisionist practices are already doing just that in some synods of the ELCA. When challenged by conservatives, the violators formally have their wrists slapped, while informally they are embraced. The juggernaut is moving.

This assessment may sound a bit cynical, but I have personal experience with the workings of the ELCA on this particular issue. After the storm of protest that greeted the first ELCA attempt at a statement on sexuality during the 1990s, I was asked to serve on a select committee to discuss how the ELCA might engage in "moral deliberation" on issues of sexuality, especially homosexuality. (I was lecturing at The Lutheran Church—Missouri Synod's Concordia Seminary in St. Louis when the first ELCA study came out. A local newspaper greeted the study with the banner headline: "Lutherans Endorse Masturbation!" It was more than a bit embarrassing to be ELCA on that day.)

When I attended the task force's first meeting of about a dozen persons, I quickly found that I was the only one willing to articulate the classical Christian teaching on sexual ethics. Eight or nine of the group were vocal proponents of the homosexual agenda. The other participants—one a bishop—remained silent. After a good deal of fruitless bickering, the group decided that all of us should depart for home grounds to develop models for discussion of the issue. We would gather again in several months to see what sort of models we had developed and how they fared.

I held a "Disputation on Homosexuality" at Roanoke College at which I invited Gilbert Meilaender to argue the classic case and Paul Jersild, then of Lutheran Theological Southern Seminary, to present the revisionist view. We printed up and taped the proceedings. (Interestingly, Meilaender got Jersild to admit that one couldn't support the revisionist agenda on biblical or confessional grounds; one would have to rely on social science and contemporary experience.)

When we gathered again to report on our experiments in "moral deliberation," I was appalled. The other "models" were either unchallenged expositions of the revisionist position or, more commonly, tapes of gays and lesbians "telling their stories" to one another and to other Lutheran pastors and laypeople. Not one decent representation of the classic Lutheran teaching on sexuality was evident. Theological and biblical reflection was nowhere to be found. Indeed, as is often the case in ELCA deliberations, theology was viewed suspiciously as "hegemonic" in nature and, therefore, to be treated as but one interest among others. The consensus of the group seemed to be: The issue is settled. Let's enlighten the masses who sit in darkness. However, the bureaucrats—leery following the protests over the poposed earlier statement—put something of a brake on that sentiment.

The Meilaender and Jersild essays and tapes got wide exposure in the following ELCA study materials because they were the only theologically articulate pieces the"moral deliberation" models had turned up. Sad to say, though, the study materials that came out of our task force deliberations turned out to be heavily biased toward the revisionist agenda.

There are good reasons to suspect that the study process leading up to 2005 will resemble what I have just described. After all, that first venture took place under a presiding bishop, George Anderson, who believed in the Lutheran moral tradition on these matters but whose influence on the latitudinarian draft statement was not much in evidence. The new bishop Mark Hanson, from the notably liberal St. Paul Area Synod of the ELCA, has already shown tacit support both for ordaining gays and lesbians in committed relationships and for blessing same-sex unions. The governing Church Council maintains a thoroughly "progressive" posture, as witnessed by its elimination of a reference to the normative status of marriage in a Church and Society statement on sexual exploitation. Furthermore, most of the same ELCA executives hold sway now as then, and they will make sure that a "reliable" person will attempt to direct the four-year process in their preferred direction.

The ELCA in general acts as if it has no normative tradition on Christian sexual ethics. Since its creation in 1988, it has been confused about whether the statements on sexual ethics of its predecessor bodies have any real authority. Detached from its history, it tends to view the various perspectives on sexual ethics as equally valid. We just have to find out where the majority of the 2005 Churchwide Assembly comes down, and, voila!—we have a new teaching on sexual ethics. Furthermore, it is argued that these revisionist changes are not so important because they are peripheral to the Christian Gospel. "Don't we have something more important to argue about?" liberals dismissively argue.

These blithe attitudes are oblivious to the gravity of treating the classic tradition as optional and of viewing the issue itself as one of relative insignificance in Christian life and teaching. These items are peripheral only to Lutherans who want the acceptance of the Gospel without the commands of Law. To many within the church, the sober warning of Wolfhart Pannenberg sums up their own posture:

> If a church were to let itself be pushed to the point where it ceased to treat homosexual activity as a departure from the biblical norm, and recognized homosexual unions as a personal partnership of love equivalent to marriage, such a church would stand no longer on biblical ground but against the unequivocal witness of Scripture. A church that took this step would cease to be one, holy, catholic, and apostolic.[4]

An acceptance of the revisionist agenda by the ELCA in 2005 would be the last straw for many in a church that has gradually joined the Protestant mainsteam and accommodated itself to liberal secular culture. The commitment to "inclusivity" is the only new impulse in the ELCA. Unlike its surface meaning, "inclusivity" has not meant the vigorous evangelization of many sorts of people at home and abroad. Rather, it has meant an interest-group liberalism that has led to quotas, identity politics, and factionalism, just as it has in secular society itself. The ELCA has more or less followed the culture on issues of abortion, divorce, and the acceptance of premarital sex and cohabitation. Factionalism, or more precisely an aggressive feminism, has prevented it from clearly affirming traditional teachings on any of those issues. "True love waits," the simple slogan of the evangelicals concerning premarital sex, would be far too uncomplicated for the ELCA.

What, then, will happen in 2005, and what will the "losers" do thereafter? As I have already indicated, I believe the ELCA will capitulate to the revisionists, who have momentum and bureaucratic power on their side. Moreover, the militant gay and lesbian lobby has shown itself to be willing to push an agenda that may lead to the loss of one to two million members of the church. Chances are good that both items—the ordination of homosexuals in committed relationships and the blessing of same-sex unions—will pass.

It is possible that an organized resistance could emerge that would awaken the ordinary laity to what is going on and prevent the revisionists from gaining the two-thirds majority vote they will need in 2005. There is already one organized resistance movement in the ELCA—the WordAlone Network—but that group seems fixated on its rejection of hierarchical authority in the church. It might well fracture if it were to focus on anything else. Perhaps another group will step forward, but that would take leadership that as yet is nowhere in sight.

If the revisionist agenda triumphs in 2005, what will the "losers" do? A small number of clergy will, as one of my Greek Orthodox friends invited me to do, "swim the Bosphorus." A larger number—yet still fairly small—will go to Rome. A significant number of laity are likely to migrate to evangelical or conservative churches, including the more conservative Lutheran Church—Missouri Synod. Perhaps the estimate of one to two million persons is too high, at least in the short run. As in most church fractures, those electing to leave are always fewer than predicted. People focus on their local parish and try to ignore what is going on at higher levels of the church.

If the revisionists win in 2005, however, ordinary laity will have a hard time ignoring what will be going on above them. If the ELCA's record on "inclusivity" is a reliable sign of what will happen on homosexual issues, no one will be able to hide. The ELCA has driven "inclusivity" into the ground. Every featured picture in *The Lutheran*, every worship team at every Assembly, every text, every committee, every Sunday school lesson now has to reflect the "official" inclusivity of the ELCA.

I can visualize the future. Three weeks after the 2005 Churchwide Assembly votes in the revisionist agenda, *The Lutheran* will have a cover picture of the blessing of a gay union before a Lutheran church altar. Sunday school materials will depict two mommies or two daddies who are in idyllic committed relationships. Quotas will include required places for gays and lesbians. Seminaries will have a growing homosexual population, as will Lutheran pulpits.

When these changes become widely visible, defections will begin to take place on a massive scale. Much of the laity will simply not tolerate their children being taught what the ELCA will try to teach them. Because many congregations can take their property with them as they withdraw, many will do so.

However, instead of leaving the ELCA (who wants yet another denomination?), a significant group of pastors and congregations will withdraw their benevolence to and cooperation with the ELCA and its synods. They will treat those "higher" expressions of the church as "mere associations in the left-hand kingdom, not the church," as one Lutheran theologian put it. In other words, the ELCA as a unified church will come to an end. Traditional Lutheran clergy and laity will seek out congregations that adhere to classical teaching and will refuse to support the ELCA or synods supportive of the ELCA. Revisionist clergy and laity will gather in the congregations that support the ELCA and in synods that move with the ELCA. The ELCA will resemble the Episcopal Church that it has courted so ardently. In due time it may even merge fully with the Episcopal Church—and dwindle further with it into the peripheral irrelevance that liberal Protestantism has made of itself.

NOTES

1. *Assembly Action*, CA 01.06.28.
2. *Assembly Action*, CA 01.06.36.
3. *Assembly Action*, CA 01.06.45.
4. From *The Church Times of London*, 1996.

GOD'S HOLY ORDINANCE

I. OUR SITUATION

What is assumed is not understood," said a wise but anonymous person. That wise saying is certainly applicable to the ethic of sex and marriage. For so long a particular Judeo-Christian version of that ethic was embedded in our culture, and few paused to understand and defend it. Even the churches did little to understand it; they, too, floated on the momentum of the culture.

I can remember no one—neither parent nor church nor school—instructing me about the immorality of premarital sex, about the indissolubility of the marriage bond, about sexual fidelity in marriage, about the joyful obligation to have children, and the heterosexual nature of the bond. But I knew what was right, as did my compatriots growing up in the 1950s. Everything in the culture reinforced the ideal, including the popular entertainment of the day. (Ingrid Bergman had to flee Hollywood when it became known that she had a child out of wedlock.) I astound my students when I tell them that in my growing up years I knew no one whose parents were divorced.

Portions of this essay originally published in *Lutheran Forum*.
Amended and reprinted with permission.

I am not so naïve to think that the ideal was followed scrupulously by everyone. There certainly were those who went astray. My wife and I were attendants in at least one "hurried" wedding. But the ideal was strong enough that it was not difficult to find a prospective mate who held to those ideals, which we did when we found each other.

The culture has come a long way since then—mostly downward with regards to a wholesome ethic of sex and marriage. One of the most helpful analyses of this culture was offered some time ago, and recently updated, by Robert Bellah. In his *Habits of the Heart*, Bellah argued that the two great normative visions of life that made up the United States of America—what he calls republican and biblical virtue—have been subverted by two new forms of radical individualism: the utilitarian and the expressive. The older visions of life bore and were transmitted by practices—including marriage—that enfolded intrinsic goods into their performance. These visions with their attendant practices were carried by communities shaped by formative narratives. The newer individualisms have no narratives that gather them into communities of vision and are corrosive of strong connections among persons and communities.

Utilitarian individualism—aiming at personal success through disciplined self-interest—tends to view marriage as a limited contract between two wary, self-interested parties. (The prenuptial agreement is vividly illustrative of this utilitarian view.) Expressive individualism—devoted to the free expression of internal states—views marriage as desirable only as long as individuals can express and satisfy their needs within a tentative agreement to be together. When the bells no longer ring, it is time to move on.

Because both forms of individualism view institutions with suspicion because they involve persisting commitments outside the self, they are also wary of marriage. Thus we get an exponential growth in cohabitation, in which public commitment is not required. Cohabitation is the fitting fruit of both kinds of individualism.

We have also witnessed an exponential growth in sex outside of marriage. Everybody's doing it, says the popular media in every possible way. A Martian visiting Earth from afar might guess that sex only happens outside marriage. In our popular culture, sex has been detached from commitment; it also has been detached from procreation. And, increasingly, it is being detached from bodily form. Sex has been plunged into what Daniel Bell, following Freud's usage, called "polymorphous perversity."

We are now aware of the terrible toll that this transformation in sexual behavior has wrought in broken marriages and families, troubled children, venereal diseases, and chaotic personal behavior. No doubt some good has come from this transformation, but on the whole the effects seem to me to be perverse.

Meanwhile, the church has not taken seriously this powerful cultural shift. The last two generations have been powerfully influenced by the unfolding individualism I spoke of above. They are likely to hold unstable mixtures of Christian and cultural notions of sex and marriage. The church continues to meander along while a dramatic battle is going on for the soul of its young. This complacence is evident in the lack of Christian education programs—including both religious and moral elements.

At any rate, we now have a world in which the Christian ethic of sex and marriage is neither assumed nor understood. It is time to rebuild our understanding of the Christian marriage and sexual ethic because we can no longer assume one. The following is meant to offer a Christian theological and moral vision of marriage and, by implication, a Christian view of proper sexual norms of behavior. It will discuss homosexual behavior in that larger context.

II. Marriage as a Place of Responsibility

To this day in Germany, couples go to the magistrate for a civil marriage and to the church for a Christian marriage. This duality indicates that Lutherans believe the institution of marriage has a civic status independent of the church's blessing of the same.

Lutherans inalterably argue that God has not left the world bereft of His creating, governing, and judging presence after the fall. God has preserved certain forms—called "orders of creation"—to order and sustain the human community. In the Old Testament this "first institution," in Luther's words, was founded before the fall: "Therefore a man leaves his father and his mother and cleaves to his wife, and they become one flesh. And the man and his wife were both naked, and were not ashamed" (Genesis 2:24–25 RSV).

This "place of responsibility" is something that is found throughout the whole world, whether Christian or not. As an estate of God, it is oriented toward preserving and sustaining the creation. It is a barrier to sin, it provides for permanent loving unions, it is the place for bearing and nurturing children, and it is a platform for service to the world. Many religions and cultures endorse these basic ends of marriage, though they may define marriage in different ways. Even in our dissembling culture, those ends are still held in high esteem yet ensconced in law and custom. In all societies marriage is a crucial institution. That is why there is widespread alarm in almost all the countries of Europe and North America, where marriage is less practiced and less stable than earlier.

The orders of creation and the obligations that go with them—Lutheranism's version of natural law—have been thought to be accessible to human reason and experience. But they—like Catholic versions of natural law—are best viewed in the light of the revelation of God in the Old Testament, where God reveals His will for our life together. He wills a covenantal existence for us in the varied places where we live out our responsible lives, marriage being the primal covenant that God offers man and woman in their mutual needs and possibilities. That covenantal existence is ordered by the Law of God, which sometimes operates incognito in the consciences and experiences of people and at other times explicitly through the commandments of God. The Law of God contends in human existence with human propensities toward sin so every concrete historical manifestation of covenantal existence is marred by sin. Even so, all cultures at their best reflect the pull of God's Law by shaping bonds between men and women that are faithful, fruitful, and permanent.

It seems that marriage in the Old Testament gradually moves from polygamy toward monogamy, so by the time of the New Testament, the latter provides the normative model. That certainly seems to be the moral norm taught by Jesus and Paul. Although there were a variety of models of marriage in Old Testament Judaism, as well as in other world religions, there is overwhelming unanimity that the structure of marriage is heterosexual, again as in all other world religions.

The unanimity on heterosexual marriage is matched by the unanimity of opposition to homosexual relations in general. There is an overwhelming consensus that there is a divinely created structure to sexual life. Women and men are meant to complement each other in sex and marriage. They "fit" together physically, emotionally, and spiritually. They have the possibility of procreation. Some of this "fit" is of course culturally constructed, but that construction is built on solid biological, even ontological, grounds. God created them male and female, and they are meant to be together in the bonds of marriage. This is near universal in human historical and cultural experience. And it is crystal clear in the Hebrew and Christian Scriptures; one does not need proof texts to demonstrate the heterosexual nature of marriage and sexual relations in the Bible. Indeed, that fact is even conceded by the proponents of homosexual unions, only they call the phenomenon "heterosexism."

If what I said in the first section is true, our ideals about and practice of marriage are in disarray not only in society but also in the church. The general agreements suggested in the second section have diminished in normative power. We have weak assumptions and even weaker understandings. The corrosive individualism that disturbs society also affects the people of the church. So it behooves us to come to a better understanding of and training for marriage in the Christian community.

MARRIAGE AS A CHRISTIAN CALLING

Building on the theological notion that God wills the ordinance of marriage throughout the world, we will now move on to a particularly Christian understanding of marriage. We are now moving from marriage as an ordinance or estate to marriage as a *holy* ordinance or a *holy* estate. Or we are moving from marriage as a place of responsibility to marriage as a Christian calling.

The church brings three great Christian virtues to bear on the ordinance of marriage to make it a *holy* ordinance—faith, love, and hope. Likewise, well-formed Christians bring those virtues with them as they transform a place of responsibility into a calling.

First, *faith* is faith in the justifying grace of God in Christ that affirms and forgives those who believe in the Gospel promises of God. That grace is radical and universal, offered to all who cast themselves upon the mercy of God in Christ, whether they are married or unmarried, young or old, rich or poor. This is the "vertical" dimension of faith. But for the Christian who receives the Gospel through the power of the Spirit, that same Spirit makes faith practically effective in the world. This is the "horizontal" dimension of faith, if you will.

FAITH

The first effect of faith is to discern the deeper level of meaning and reality that inheres in the institution of marriage. Marriage is discerned as an estate founded and willed by God. His will undergirds the deep purposes of marriage—faithful union, procreation, and service to the world. Marriage is not simply an emergent of cultural evolution, a purely human construction, or the product of necessary repression for the sake of an orderly civilization. Rather, "The Lord God in his goodness created us male and female, and by the gift of marriage founded human community" (*Lutheran Book of Worship*, 203). Jesus quotes Genesis 2:24 as to the divine origin of marriage when He debates the nature of marriage vows with the Pharisees (Mark 10:7–8). Luther affirms that the "lawful joining together of a man and a woman is a divine ordinance and institution" (LW 1:134). Dietrich Bonhoeffer certainly delineates the divine, objective character of Christian marriage when he writes to a young couple about to be married that though love is a "private possession," marriage is a unique and sacred office in life, one with rights and promises. Bonhoeffer emphasizes that love does not keep the marriage strong; rather, the marriage keeps the love strong (*Letters and Papers from Prison*).

The sacred canopy that is marriage hallows our life together, shielding us from the confusion and disorder of the world. It provides the protected space under which marital love can grow. When we live in accordance with God's establishment, we move with God's will. When we ignore it or violate it, we rebel against something more than human convention. Lord help the church that rebels against God's establishment by violating or distorting it.

The second practical work of faith is to enable persons entering marriage to see their roles as a calling from God. They come to see themselves playing a role in the covenantal existence that God has provided for them. They enter Christian marriage in a disciplined fashion, responding to God's call to be formed into the Christian vision of marriage.

This Christian vision can be discussed briefly under two rubrics—the context and time frame of the marriage vow. First, let us look at the context. Far from being limited to a private vow between two persons, as our individualistic culture seems to maintain, Christian promise-keeping has many contexts, all of which are publicly important. Like the public and historical nature of God's vow to Israel and Jesus' vow to the church, Christian marriage vows are historical and public.

There is of course the interpersonal nature of the vow: "I take you to be my wife/husband from this day forward . . ." But that is preceded by an intrapersonal vow: I promise myself that I take the other in faithfulness. I agree to bind myself to that vow. From there the context broadens. Promises are made before family and friends, who witness its solemnity and vow to support the couple in their life together. Further, the vow is made in the context of the church—the pastor symbolizing that context. Vows are made to conform to this universal community's particular understanding of marriage. That understanding has been blessed by Jesus "who gladdened the wedding at Cana in Galilee" (*Lutheran Book of Worship*, 202). The vows are also made in the legal context of the state, which has an interest in sound and stable marriage. But finally and most important, the vows are made before God, who has ordained this estate and called the participants to play their roles in the institution He has founded.

These ever-widening contexts bestow a powerful social quality on Christian marriage. It renders pale and insufficient current practices of "living together," which lack the objectivity and seriousness of public vows. Christian promises reverberate far beyond the couple alone. They establish the couple within an ongoing community that finally claims divine sanction for its practice.

The time frame of Christian marriage is as long as the context is wide. The marriage that Christians are called to was created from the beginning by the Lord God, "who created our first parents and established them in marriage" (*Lutheran Book of Worship*, 203). That foundation extends continuously throughout history through many generations to the present day.

By vowing to enter this tradition in the present, a Christian couple makes a sharp break with their earlier life by entering into this new covenant. Their vows indicate a powerful rite of passage. After this moment loyalties are rearranged, financial responsibilities change, a new home is founded, and the "two become one." This moment of transition opens the way for sexual relations; properly so, for it marks the moment of public commitment and validation. It is fitting that the access to the most intimate and life-promising of exchanges be given at that time. Just as priests do not baptize or marry, judges do not render decisions, and presidents do not issue presidential orders until vows are made and validated, so new privileges—as well as responsibilities—come with the vows.

Christian marriage has a future dimension as well. There are solemn intentions toward a permanent bond. "I promise to be faithful to you until death parts us." We are to "find delight in each other and grow in holy love until life's end" (*Lutheran Book of Worship*, 203). At the moment of marriage, the partners themselves, as well as their mutualities, are immature. The vows of permanence are assurances that the partners will give each other and their relationship the time to grow and flourish. They recognize with Jesus that what God puts together no one should put asunder.

LOVE

The crown of Christian marriage is its affirmation of agape love, a special kind of reflected love that is characterized by an unconditional, steadfast, other-regarding faithfulness. Love in marriage is to be modeled after God's faithful love for His people and Jesus' love for others. Married love is to remain constant in the "joys and sorrows that all the years may bring" (*Lutheran Book of Worship*, 203). Fidelity includes commitment to the other's good, even amid the changes that each shall undergo. It includes the willingness to forgive and begin anew. It means affirmation and acceptance of the partner as partner, no matter what the judgments of the world are with regard to life in the world. It obviously means fidelity in sexual matters so the deepest intimacies are never violated by moving them outside the bond. It means the willingness to become dependent on the other—physically, emotionally, and spiritually. It means enduring partnership in bearing and nurturing children and in broader service to the world.

Married life under the bond of agape love is not all heavy and serious. It is within the comfort and security of faithful love that many kinds of spontaneities can flourish. It provides space for fun, for secure delight in all the pleasures of marital life.

This transcendent love builds upon earthly loves—erotic, pragmatic, romantic, and friendship—that the Creator has built into creation to draw woman and man together. A number of these mutual loves have to be strongly present in the relationship of married lovers. But such loves, important as they are, are unstable because of human sin and finitude. Partners change over time, they intentionally and unintentionally violate each other and their relationship, and they have rough edges that never are completely ironed out and thereby become sources of discontent.

Agape provides the capacities for steadfastness and reconciliation that can overcome the turbulence caused by the disruption of mutualities that are bound to occur. Agape disposes each partner to repent, initiate forgiveness, and work at building up the bond that simply cannot be free of problems. Agape also lures both partners from focusing on themselves to caring for others, first to bearing and nurturing children, if that is their aim, and to the service of others in their callings in work, church, society, and world.

HOPE

One salutary dimension of Christian hope is that our salvation is finally not dependent on our performance in marriage. Our acceptance by God is dependent on His free grace in Christ, not our work. This is a source of firm hope for several reasons. First, we are freed from placing ultimate trust in a "successful marriage" or even in our spouse. This gives us needed distance from both so we will not have the wrong kind of expectations of any human connection. We need not frantically grasp at perfection and thereby fail to receive the blessings that have already been given. Second, we are assured of the daily forgiveness of God that enables us to pick up our lives and live them anew every day, even amid our flawed marriages. That gives us the needed hope to continue. We can move into the future.

Because we know we are offered anew this grace every morning, we can hope for a time of completion. Our marriage service includes the nuptial blessing that we might "grow in holy love until life's end." Further, this service expresses a hope in the "joy that begins now and is brought to perfection in the life to come" so we "may at length celebrate with Christ the marriage feast which has no end" (*Lutheran Book of Worship*, 202f.).

There may be no giving and taking in marriage in heaven, but certainly those bonds of faithful love that have been shaped on earth as a sign of God's kingdom will not be lost in the fulfillment of that kingdom. As with all approximations of the kingdom, the bonds of marriage will be drawn by the good power of God to Himself in His good time. All the fragile, flawed, and interrupted relations of earth will find their permanence and completion in heaven. In this can we hope.

So we have faith, love, and hope. According to the measure we have been given by the Spirit, marriage becomes transparent to God's presence and will. Shored up and supported by the Christian community, it becomes a calling central to the Christian life.

MAGIC'S MOMENT

SAFE SEX AND BEYOND

Magic Johnson tests positive for the HIV virus. Robin Williams gets sued for allegedly transmitting herpes. Wilt Chamberlain claims 20,000 sexual encounters, some of which must have resulted in discomforting effects.

Beyond these personal tragedies and comedies, however, truly grim realities emerge. Thirty percent of Caucasian babies are born out of wedlock, more than 70 percent of black infants. Many of the children born in these circumstances face lives of poverty and diminished expectations. Abortions continue at roughly 4,500 per day. The divorce rate for new marriages approaches 50 percent. Many of those breakups are precipitated by unfaithfulness. Thousands of gay men die of AIDS contracted from one among multiple partners. The age for first sexual intercourse continues downward, while venereal disease spirals upward. Children have children. The incidence of rape and other sexual abuse of women increases.

And what do we propose as the major solution to these severe social challenges? Condoms. This lowly latex product, once discretely tucked away behind the druggist's counter, is now touted as the great American technological fix for all that ails us.

Universal use of the condom promises that sex will be safe. Magic Johnson, as reported by our local paper, is going to spend his life encouraging safe sex. But what will he be encouraging? More sex or more safe sex or both?

Certainly there is something praiseworthy about encouraging the "sexually active" to be careful. It's the prudent thing to do, like counseling moderation in drinking or smoking. Abuse of such activities can lead to self-inflicted harm, harm to others, and large costs for society. However, in counseling prudence so insistently do we also encourage the very activity we wish to moderate?

That seems to be the effect of the avalanche of commendation of condom use. It assumes that humans are like rabbits; they inevitably scratch when they feel the itch. Given that, we must coax the dumb animals into safe practice. Inundate them with condoms. Put a machine in every restroom in the country. Teach sixth-graders how to use them. Hand them out at church. Include free packages in six-packs of beer. Condoms to the rescue.

But isn't this a terribly wrongheaded and superficial strategy? It neglects and even undercuts higher human sexual morality—which is the true solution to our terrible problems—by appealing constantly to the lowest motive of sexual life: self-protection. It suggests you can and ought to have a lot of cake and eat it too. Condoms will protect you from the baleful effects of your indulgence.

What we sorely need is the renewal of an ethic that connects sex and serious commitment. Let's aim higher. Let's teach our young that sex and long-term commitment go together. We might even aim higher than that: Sex belongs in marriage. Such a revolutionary message—shored up by parents, church, and school—might actually begin to counter the little doses of poison administered in so many ways by our popular culture: music, films, video, magazines, television. Generally speaking, these agents of communication work hard to separate sex and commitment. After watching television for one day, a visitor from Mars would be astonished to find that good sex happens within marriage. Such a setting for sex is rarely portrayed in our mass media.

Such an ethic, even in its most demanding form, is not freakish. The National Opinion Research Center, in its well-known 1989 Smith study, estimated that fully 98.5 percent of married persons had been faithful to each other in the year of the poll. Indeed, 48 percent had been faithful to one partner since they were 18. Seventy-five percent believe that adultery is always wrong. Americans believe in connecting sex and commitment.

So why are we so timid in advocating a sexual ethic that involves few of the fears and dangers worrying our larger society? Why don't we promote an ethic in which love nurtures sex and sex nurtures love within a lifelong covenant of fidelity? That should be our public goal. The young should emulate the fine examples we know firsthand, not the sexual libertines of the world.

In the famous movie *The Graduate*, the young hero asks an adult what he should devote his life to. Expecting something profound, the young man is disappointed to hear his advice: "Plastics, young man, that's where it's at." When the young need direction about a sexual ethic, let's be able to say more than, "Condoms, that's where it's at."

Part 7

CULTURE AND ENTERTAINMENT

THE PLAY'S THE THING

One does not have to be a sociologist of sport to know that sport looms large in American culture. As we have become more affluent, the role of entertainment has expanded to satisfy all the leisure desires of millions of customers. Indeed, our greatest export is entertainment, which should give us some pause. Certainly sport makes up the largest slice of entertainment in America. Signaling that fact, the market rewards professional athletes with salaries that could never have been imagined a generation ago. Sport has taken on idolatrous proportions in America.

I am guilty of participating in this idolatry. I came from a family that loved sports; my father was a semiprofessional baseball player and coach. I grew up playing the mainstream American sports in a small Nebraska town and went on to letter in four different sports at a small Midwestern Lutheran college. But I left those sports behind to concentrate on tennis, which I love too much. Playing all those sports has given me deep appreciation of those who play them well. I played them well enough to know how much better the professionals are than I. So besides playing

Originally published in *The Cresset* (Trinity 2002).
Amended and reprinted with permission.

tennis, I continue my interest by watching many sports in person and on television.

I must say, though, that it is becoming more difficult for me to watch sports on television without becoming angry about the behavior of the players. They just don't seem to want to be players in a single-minded way. They want to take on all sorts of other roles. And, unfortunately, the media, sports writers, and fans often egg them on.

A good player performs certain athletic activities well. He or she has mastered the practices of a sport over time. He or she has matched great talent with hard work. When we watch athletic activities performed with great excellence, we delight in them and the athletes who perform them. Some of them are so good they become "immortal" in our human memories. Moreover, when they perform in a competitive context, another thrill is added to the performance. Not only are the athletes summoned to their highest performance, but we get involved in the competition, hoping for our favorite athlete or team to win.

From ancient times, though, it has been recognized that there is a certain integrity to the role of athlete, just as there is to that of a coach. We expect players to play well and coaches to coach well. But in recent times the integrity of these roles has been violated by athletes taking on roles extraneous to the main role of playing. This violation irritates me, and perhaps many other folks. Let me be more concrete.

Most outrageously, athletes have taken on the role of the onlookers by giving themselves honor. It is not their role to congratulate themselves; others are to do that. They pound their chests, hold up their fists in triumph, do war dances after an ordinary tackle, and prance into the end zone, watch in admiration as their home runs disappear into the stands, and shout that they are the greatest. (Muhammad Ali was one of the pioneers of self-congratulation, for which I've never quite forgiven him. Neither was he gracious to his opponents, especially Joe Frazier.) What is really the role of the fans—the offering of plaudits—has been taken over by the athletes themselves. I'd rather athletes let us do the applauding.

We now have athletes taking on the role of referee. After making a first down, football players beat the referee to the punch by signaling the first down. Further, they take on the role of chums with the referee, patting them on the behind or back. (If I were a referee, I would hiss at the first player that patted me, "Next time you do that it's a technical!") Players and referees are not supposed to be chums.

Athletes take on the role of entertainer beyond the role of entertaining us by playing well. They do dances after a touchdown, wear striking clothing, sing jingles, exhibit wild and wooly tattoos, invent rituals that call attention to themselves. In hockey they fight. I'd rather be entertained by their play.

Athletes and even coaches now commonly take on the role of cheerleader, summoning the crowd to make a lot of noise at crucial times. Besides the dubious sportsmanship of the practice, it seems that their primary roles should demand full concentration on playing or coaching, not cheerleading. Let us—led by real cheerleaders—decide when to cheer.

Many athletes become their own therapists. They maintain that they have to "let it all hang out" to perform well. Screams, grunts, stunts, shouts of triumph, and outbursts of anger are all justified by players as therapeutically necessary venting. Maybe the old days of complete suppression of emotions were too much, but at least the players acted as if they had been in the end zone or had put one in the stands before. Besides, adulthood means the control of raw emotional expression. I for one find it much more dramatic for the baseball player who pitched a great game or hit a winning home run to doff his cap modestly and offer a grin. After all, the play's the thing, not the self-expression.

Added to this accretion of extraneous roles is poor sportsmanship—the brattish and boorish behavior of a MacEnroe or Conners (poor Pete Sampras has always gotten bad press for his good behavior), the trash talking, the taunting, the dirty play, and the putdowns of the opponent. All these things make it less and less appealing to watch big-time college and professional sports. And the oddest thing is that professional football seems to have the worst record. One would think that grown men in a dangerous sport would have more dignity and maturity.

But there is good news. Golf and baseball have not succumbed to the most irritating of these role confusions. Tennis has finally gotten over MacEnroe. College sports are getting their acts together through more stringent rules. Maybe the NBA and NFL will catch on before too long. Maybe players will just play well. I'd like to be a happier camper when I watch them on television.

DOES GOD FAVOR THE YANKEES?

RELIGION IN SPORT

A ny religion worth its salt embraces all of life, not just the recesses of the heart, the sacred hour on Sunday, or the intimacies of family and friendship. A serious Christian, Jew, or Muslim who participates in sport also practices that athletic activity in light of his or her faith. So there is no question that sport—one of the mainstays of life, especially in affluent societies—can be freighted with religious meaning. The more difficult question is: How should religious conviction be expressed in sport?

One option is simply to hide it from view. This approach is taken by many religious people in other areas of life—business, politics, education, and entertainment. Religion for them operates as motivation or perhaps as the hidden ground of ethics that can be shared with other decent people. Many people prefer religion to stay private for some good and many bad reasons. The problem with this "hidden" approach is that all those areas of life can and will be filled with other meanings and values, some of them contrary to what religious people believe. None of these key areas in

Originally published in *The Cresset* (Michaelmas 2002).
Amended and reprinted with permission.

life—including sports—is simply neutral. They convey meanings and values. Why should religious meanings and values be refused their part in defining the meanings and values of sport? Why should sport be completely secular?

As I argued above, it shouldn't. True religion is comprehensive. But religion can also be abused, as it often is in sport. One abuse occurs when the divine is manipulated for the player's own use. Religion is turned into a magical formula in which one tries to wheedle the majestic, omnipotent Creator of all into doing one's bidding. Crossing oneself before a free throw or an at bat or praying for victory fall into that category. Although I am happy to know that a player is Christian, I wonder whether he has a mature understanding of God. Why should God prefer his victory over that of his competitor? More seriously, why should God care who wins in any athletic contest? (One of my moments of religious clarity was refusing to pray for victory in the pregame huddle instituted by the coach of my college football team. Maybe I should have joined in; we usually got beat. But not to worry, I never took our defeats as the judgment of God.)

Another abuse is inserting religious gestures directly into the performance of the sport. The finger poked heavenward, the prayer in the end zone, or crossing oneself after an athletic triumph all seem to violate the integrity of the athlete's primary role. I am disgusted by players acting as the audience by honoring themselves, acting as referees or cheerleaders, or by acting as entertainers who offer us song, dance, and ditty. I would also prefer that players not act as evangelists during the performance of their athletic roles. We could apply Martin Luther's famous saying that good cobblers make good shoes, not poor shoes with little crosses on them. Good players play well without adorning their play with little crosses.

True, it is far better for the player to point heavenward than to point to himself after a particularly good performance. Many young people will receive a positive message from that athlete as he models gratitude rather than arrogance. But it is difficult not to get the impression that the player is fusing his triumph with God's will. If the player were consistent, he would point skyward to mark the judgment of God after he got his shot blocked or was struck out. I haven't seen that done lately.

What room, then, is left for religious expression? First, one can give a public religious interpretation of one's participation in sport. When the sprinter in *Chariots of Fire* tells his pious sister that when he runs he can feel God's pleasure, he is voicing a profound joy that athletes often experience when their performance is at its peak. As an avid tennis player, I sometimes—I wish it would occur more often—have a sacramental (small *s*) sense of union when the mind and body are working in beautiful harmony to propel that ball accurately over the net on a beautiful court in the morning sunshine. One can publicly articulate such a great feeling, though I don't think my opponent would find it fitting for me to kneel in prayer after I made a winning shot.

Many fine athletes have a deep sense of gratitude to God for the talents they have been given, and it is refreshing to hear them mention that to interviewers who want them to talk of their accomplishments. Further, it is heartening to listen to their expressions of gratitude to others who have helped them along the way, including their teammates. Praying before games is a common practice that is certainly fitting if it involves supplication for good play, sportsmanship, and protection from injury. (I must add that it seems curious to pray for safety in a sport that is particularly dangerous, such as football or auto racing. Players intentionally place themselves in a dangerous role and at the same time pray to God to keep them safe. By the end of my football career, I was adding a pregame petition of repentance to God for putting myself in harm's way.)

It is altogether appropriate—indeed, it is moving—for teams from both sides to gather together after a game to offer thanks for the opportunity to play and for safe passage. Such rituals are often occasions for reconciliation after the fierce competition is over. Serious Christians and Jews can also witness to the fact that their faith comes before their sport by refusing to violate their religious practices. Sandy Koufax, the great pitcher, refused to pitch on the Sabbath. Similarly, it is a sign of religious serious-ness when players are able publicly to acknowledge the relative unimportance of athletic contests and their role in them before the more profound triumphs and tragedies of life. Mature persons of faith do not confuse the fate of the Washington Redskins with the salvation of their souls or the fate of the nation.

I certainly do not begrudge athletes the opportunity to use their athletic celebrity to further their religious causes, as many athletes from Bob Richards to Reggie White have done. That is far more noble than selling Viagra™. Finally, religion in sport can and should elevate sportsmanship—fair play, respect for the opponent, and civility toward officials. It is impressive to see play-ers help fallen opponents off the floor or turf now and then, not only their teammates.

VIEWING MOVIES
THROUGH CHRISTIAN EYES

I.

It is disconcerting that we in church and school do so little to help our members, especially our young members, discriminate among and interpret the thousands of films that they see on television, video, and in movie houses. (The *Christian Century* deserves praise on this score, having long included film interpretation in its offerings.) It is no secret that movies are "the literature of choice" for the young, who readily admit that they have seen far more movies than they have read books. Yet we do little to help them choose well among the thousands of offerings and to interpret and critique what they see.

I have tried to remedy this problem in my little corner of the world by developing a film interpretation course over the stretch of thirty years. I drew from two sources in that task. First, I was impressed by the film interpretation done at the end of an inten-

Originally published in *Journal of Lutheran Ethics*. Available online at www.elca.org/jle. Amended and reprinted with permission.

sive weekend retreat called Religious Studies I that was offered by the Ecumenical Institute of Chicago during the 1960s and 1970s. After grappling with key Christians doctrines, they would draw Christian meaning out of a seemingly secular movie, *Requiem for a Heavyweight*. I was also inspired as a graduate student by an important essay written by Preston Roberts of the University of Chicago Divinity School entitled "A Christian Theory of Dramatic Tragedy." In that essay he argued that serious Western literature expresses three visions of life—the Christian, the Greek, and the Skeptical.

I combined these approaches into a method that I call "narrative analysis." It assumes that most serious American movies express a vision of life at their deeper levels. There are at least four different visions encoded in American movies. While movies are characterized by great surface plurality, there are constants at the deeper levels. I identify these primal deep narratives as four—the Christian (implicit and explicit); the Greek, the American (including both Dream and Nightmare), and the Skeptical.

Over the years I could not find books dealing with film that would help me in this approach. So I wrote my own text. Those of you who are intrigued by what I develop below can rush to amazon.com where you can find it under the title *Seeing Is Believing: Visions of Life through Film*. I do not claim that this approach works with all movies; some simply do not have serious intent. They are merely meant to entertain. But more serious film dramas are persuasive and powerful in portraying visions of life. Also, there may well be more primal narratives than I identify. Certainly non-Western cultures would portray different visions of life. But I contend that Western movies do in fact reflect these four formative visions of life, which are embedded in mythic structures that run deeply in our history.

II.

Narrative analysis does not primarily focus on symbols—that is, "Christ-figures"—nor on themes or values. Rather, it focuses on the elements of narrative—plot, character, atmosphere, and tone—as they are combined into a coherent vision. Narrative analysis seeks a comprehensive interpretation. Each of the four primal narratives has a certain "take" on plot, character, atmosphere, and tone. They combine these into a coherent vision that can be identified and interpreted by the educated viewer.

For example, the American Story (we could call it the American Dream) features a character that is talented and ambitious but must leave the confines of comfortable, small-scale existence to achieve success. American characters are not complex but must surmount challenges that strengthen their character. Through force of character and will they prevail and are rewarded with success by a society that is finally open and good. The plot in the American Story begins with the character in a bucolic, wholesome American home, moves through the middle of the story where the character meets great tests, and ends with external success, often defined as land and sons. The "atmosphere" of the movie—the background conditions that set the limits and possibilities of the movie as well as that drive the plot—is a providential context that rewards the virtuous American character. The tone—the attitude or posture of the storyteller toward the American Story he or she has told—is one of approval, if not celebration.

There are many American Dream movies. I take *The Natural* and *Forrest Gump* to be classic contemporary examples. Indeed, I believe the Academy Award winner for best picture—*A Beautiful Mind*—is right in the tradition of great America Dream stories. The 1930s, 1940s, and 1950s were rampant with these sorts of movies. But with the 1960s there was a reversal of vision that I call the American Nightmare. Everything—character, plot, atmosphere, and tone—is reversed. *Easy Rider* and *Death of a Salesman* are pioneers of this type, but there are many examples from the '60s onward to the present day. Oliver Stone has produced a number of them. The *Rocky* movies of the early 1980s were robust, if simplistic, counterattacks on the nightmarish movies of the '60s and '70s.

III.

The Greek movie is rarely produced. People don't like the astringent pleasures of the Greek tragedy. I use *Breaker Morant* in my courses but could use *Das Boot* or *Gallipoli*. The Greek character is internally free and noble but externally bound. He is caught up in forces of life and history that he cannot control. He makes a fatal mistake and is brought to doom, which he accepts with serenity and nobility. There is a recognition scene in the middle where he realizes what he has done and what will happen. Often he has a chance to escape but does not take it. The atmosphere of the Greek movie is inimical to human aspirations. The gods strike down the noble heroes. Life is like that. The tone is one of pity and fear.

The Skeptical Story has come into its own in America since the 1960s, thanks in part to the American Nightmare movies. But skeptical movies were around long before the '60s in European film-making. During college, I enjoyed going to the local art film movie house because it offered some variety from the upbeat American Dream movies. Lutherans have their own skeptical moviemaker in Ingmar Bergman. You can't get any more skeptical than *Winter Light*, whose main antihero is a Lutheran pastor.

The character in the Skeptical Story is inwardly twisted and perverse, but that isn't evident at the beginning. In fact, there are glimmers of normalcy and hope. But the middle of the story reveals the character—under various sorts of pressure—in all his enormous eccentricity or perversity. The end finds the character descending to madness or death or, in a shocking reversal, winning over all, demonstrating that cleverness or might make right. The atmosphere of the skeptical film is absurd, supporting neither religious belief nor morality. The tone the producer or director exhibits is often one of ironic distance or perhaps veiled contempt for the antiheroes he or she has depicted.

There are many examples of the Skeptical Story among current American films. I use *Crimes and Misdemeanors* but will probably use *In the Bedroom* the next time around. I find that many students—especially young men—love to watch skeptical movies, especially violent movies. To satisfy them I sometimes show *Reservoir Dogs* or *The Usual Suspects*. We then have a good discussion about why they are drawn to such movies.

IV.

I have saved the best until last. The Christian reader is no doubt interested in the Christian Story in movies. There are two types—implicit and explicit. The implicit does not have overt religious subject matter in its characters or plot while the explicit does. There are many of both types in the great store of movies we have, though the explicit Christian movie has only recently come to the fore. Moviemakers were and are reluctant to take up explicitly Christian dramas. Robert Duvall had to finance his own venture into Christian filmmaking, *The Apostle*. But since the Christian mythos runs so deeply in Western culture, many more movie dramas are implicitly Christian. These implicit Christian dramas are no doubt more attractive to make in such a secular industry.

As I have argued above, the main freight of a film's meaning is in its narrative structure—its coherent combination of a certain type of character, plot, atmosphere, and tone. Thus a movie can be thoroughly Christian without being overtly so. There are many movies of this sort. I use *The Verdict* and *Ordinary People* in my course, but I could select any number, running from *Midnight Cowboy* to the more recent *American Beauty*.

I'm sure that among the readers who have seen *American Beauty*, there is more than a little reluctance to call that movie implicitly Christian. But I believe it is. The character in a Christian movie begins as internally bound but externally free. The internal bondage is, of course, sin. The Kevin Spacey character in *American Beauty* certainly has his internal bondage. He is dissatisfied with his wife, his job, and his life in general. He is mean and alienated. To find something meaningful he engages in the lustful pursuit of the 16-year-old friend of his daughter. He is responsible for his own mess. In a Christian drama the internal bondage is not blamed on anything external. Externally, he has all the good things of life.

The plot proceeds to more and more intense pressure points for the hero. These are challenges that shake up the character, revealing and cracking his illusions and idolatries. Indeed, the hero in *American Beauty* appears more foolish with every move toward the young girl. Finally, the challenge moment occurs, the moment of turning around, of repentance. He no sooner gets the young girl to the point of seduction, when he backs off, realizing both her innocence and his foolishness. He turns away from his disgusting path, recollects the blessings of his life, and turns toward a new future. The moment of repentance is followed by a moment of grace. However, much like a Flannery O'Connor short story, his brief new life is brought to a quick end by a pistol shot to the head, administered either by his wife or his deranged neighbor.

Crucial to the deeper meaning of the story is a brief scene in the middle when the talented but screwed up son of the deranged neighbor shows a video he has made for the hero's daughter, to whom he is drawn. The video depicts a small sheet of plastic, carried and tossed by a small whirlwind in an alley. It dances up and down with a kind of mystical grace. The young man comments about the video: "There are invisible forces in the world of such beauty and goodness that, when you can grasp them, make you want to cry with joy."

That video is shown again at the movie's end when the hero, after repentance, begins his new life. It is a direct commentary on what has happened to him. The background conditions of life (God) bring the character through difficult changes to a graceful realization of the beauty and goodness of his own life. The tone— the attitude of the creator of the movie—is one of satisfaction in the restoration of the main character, though that earthly restoration is brief.

Christian movies are movies of restoration. They portray in a thousand imaginative ways the movement of the character from inward bondage through repentance under the grinding power of the Law of God, to restoration by grace, and finally to a new life of resolve, intentionality, and hope. In the middle of the story a moment of receptivity immediately follows the rigors of the pressure point, the time of great challenge. That is the moment of grace during which the character is affirmed from beyond the self and freed from the bondage of the past. Then the character moves toward the future with renewed vigor, claiming his or her calling in this life.

One can easily see the trinitarian structure of the story. One is created, sustained, and brought to judgment by God the Father. One is restored by the grace of God in Christ the Son and empowered into the future by God the Holy Spirit.

There are many fine examples of explicit Christian films. These are films with overt religious meanings, themes, and symbols. They also follow the structure and dynamics of the Christian narrative that I have elaborated above. Certainly *Dead Man Walking* is one of the most powerful Christian stories ever made. There are many others, including *Babette's Feast, Tender Mercies, Trip to Bountiful,* and *The Apostle,* to name a few. All of them are stories of restoration by a power beyond the self.

So there you have it. I contend that this narrative analysis helps viewers come to grips with the comprehensive meaning expressed in the many serious movies our people view. The church needs to be active in this process of understanding and critique because there are many contrasting visions of life powerfully presented to our members by contemporary films. They have more influence on our young than we would like to admit. It is important that we steer people to the films that support our faith and help them critically respond to those that don't.

GREEN SHOOTS IN AMERICA

RELIGIONS AND THE RENEWAL OF CULTURE

I.

Os Guinness, in *The American Hour—A Time of Reckoning and the Once and Future Role of Faith*, argues that we are indeed at a time of reckoning. We have prevailed in the world against Communism and Nazism. Our ideas about and practices of democracy and a market economy are now the models for the rest of the world. But deeper than both politics and economics, Guinness argues, is culture, the guidance system for both politics and economics and for the lives of America's millions of citizens.

At this deeper level, Guinness believes, we have a "crisis of cultural authority." By this he means that the commanding truths of our moral existence have been shattered and we are facing a period of debilitating confusion in which America's promise as a beacon to the nations is severely threatened. We are, he thinks,

Originally published in *Public Life and the Renewal of Culture* (Center for Economic and Policy Education). Amended and reprinted with permission.

standing at a fork in the road. One path leads to a renewal of culture and one leads to chaos, violence, and perhaps an authoritarian repression. He looks to religious faith as the crucial variable. The various faiths, but particularly the Christian faith, can and must serve as vital impulses—the green shoots—in the renewal of American culture.

I agree with Guinness. In the following I want to give my own take on our current cultural situation, then move to religious groups and movements that might be candidates for the green shoots of renewal, and finally give my assessment of what is promising and what is not.

Regarding the commanding truths of culture, we've come a long way in my lifetime. My growing up years were spent in an intact normative culture in which there were indeed commanding truths. Daniel Bell thinks the "Protestant ethic" provided the cultural glue for the traditional American society of my youth. Martin Marty called this mainstream Protestant ethos the *the* culture. It provided the normative meanings and norms for the American project.

As a child of the late 1940s and 1950s, I can attest to the reality of such a culture. It was taught in the schools, in the media, and in the institutions of higher education. It was reinforced in church and Sunday school. The few non-Christians in our town were brought up with the same moral ideals that we Christians were. These moral norms were sanctioned by both church and culture. Although there were rebels and sinners, these individuals knew, as did the rest of the town, that they were rebels and sinners.

I knew of no divorced parents in my town in northeastern Nebraska. Illegitimacy was unheard of, though we did know of a number of "shotgun marriages." Sex was connected with marriage: They "went together," as Frank Sinatra assured us in a pop favorite of the day. Cohabiters would have found no place to inhabit in our town. All persons had callings, and, be they ever so humble, their obligation was to do the best they could. Honest work brought blessing; laziness brought hardship. Persons were responsible for their actions; self-reliance was a central principle of life. The deserving poor and the truly unfortunate were the objects of genuine compassion; the undeserving poor had to find their way the best they could. America's role in the world was noble and altruistic; America was a beacon to the nations. Almost everyone belonged to a church. Martin Marty, a fellow townsman of that same burg, calculated that the people in the surrounding county were 105 percent churched.

The *the* culture was real, and I have much affection for it, though I might feel somewhat differently if I were a woman or black. I say "might" because the vast majority of women did not find that culture as oppressive as the feminists were later to aver. Blacks would have a much better case to feel distinctly unnostalgic about that older culture. It was avowedly racist, but not always in a crass or vicious way. For most whites it was a racism of omission rather than commission. And, I've read, blacks themselves enjoyed a more solid and coherent subculture within a generally racist environment.

This Protestant culture (shared to a great extent by Catholics) was substantive. It stipulated what the freedom that Americans enjoyed should be used for. It was not merely procedural, focusing on the "rights" to do what one pleased or entitlements to what one was owed. It said yes to the specific patterns and practices I have mentioned above, and no to attitudes and behaviors that violated them. That old culture was not Christian in any direct sense, but it certainly was to a great extent the product of the churches' mission on this continent.

II.

This old culture has not vanished by any means. It lives strongly in many pockets of American society. But it has definitely lost its normative power for the whole society. The cultural *unum* has been fractured, and we now have only fragments, the key image employed by Alasdair MacIntyre to depict our current condition. We now live "after virtue," to use his famous phrase, though the virtues whose loss he laments are not necessarily those of the older American culture.

Other social philosophers make similar observations. Robert Bellah's work communicates alarm about the loss of what he calls "republican" and "biblical" virtue. Richard Neuhaus decries a naked public square, one denuded of substantive, religiously grounded morality. Robert Putnam fears the consequences of bowling alone. Francis Fukuyama laments the loss of trust that accompanies the decline of reliable moral patterns. Michael Sandel outlines the poverty of the "procedural state" in which "rights" and "choices" gradually liberate us from the moral practices that enable civic responsibility.

One gets the sense that things may get worse. The forces driving this emerging pluralism may turn it into the kind of chaotic pluralism that will threaten the basic order humans need to live in community. I see no abatement of our capitalistic culture's tendency to market hedonism and to entertain us to death while it defines down deviancy and pushes relentlessly at the limits of decency. I anticipate the continued elaboration of "rights" that undermine every local communities' ability to sanction its substantive moral commitments. If the courts on their own don't "discover" more of these kind of "rights" in the Constitution, the ACLU will certainly help them. The adversarial culture, fueled by feminism and multiculturalism and strongly ensconced in our universities, will continue to deconstruct the older culture as a socially constructed instrument of oppression.

This is not to say that there are not genuinely liberating impulses in this postmodern world. There was and is much in the old culture about which to be skeptical. Besides, too many of us enjoy the freedoms we have to do as we please. As Roger Scruton has observed, we're not ready for virtue, much as Chicago was not ready for reform. Things will have to get a lot worse before we divert our freedoms toward communal purposes. Virtue, like socialism, leaves too few free evenings.

But I must admit to being uneasy in this world of fragments. I often feel that the common world we inhabit is in terminal decline and the best thing to do is to retire (literally and figuratively) to some isolated home in the Blue Ridge. But that seems premature, if not paranoid. Besides, there is much I like about the modern world. So I cast about for different strategies that might make sense for serious Christians at the dawning of a new millennium. That brings me to religion and the possibilities of renewal.

III.

We might begin with several "optimistic" interpretations and responses. One of them might be termed the "progressive" orientation, to use the language of sociologist James Hunter. These are the folks in charge of the mainstream Protestant churches. Progressives would simply disagree with the alarmist tone of the interpretation of the modern world given above. They believe the old culture needed thorough purging and revision. It was racist, sexist, classist, heterosexist, and imperialist with regard to the rest of the human and the natural world. The emancipatory impulses that shattered the *unum* were necessary and overdue. Good riddance! Green shoots are definitely visible in this culture, and the progressive church should take its cue from the culture.

For the progressives, it is only natural that we should go through some rough phases as we pass through a transition from the old to the new. In the progressive view the new promises to be much more just and harmonious than the old, though we don't know exactly what that new order will look like. We must undergo with hope the confusion that necessarily arises as the tradition is revised powerfully by the liberating experience of the present. So go with the flow; participate in the "progressive" movements of our time and hope for a new and brighter *unum*.

Less optimistic but yet hopeful are the communitarians, who seem to be popping up as rapidly as mushrooms these days. They participate in the lamentations I have elaborated above, but they believe that the good society—with a common culture—can be rebuilt by attending seriously to civil society. The intermediate organizations between state and family need to be strengthened, and they seem to think American culture has the capacity to rejuvenate the civic virtues. The communitarians are much more skeptical of the centrifugal forces of "progress" than are the progressives; therefore they are much more inclined to honor the traditions of the older culture. They are coming more and more to recognize the important role that religious institutions have played in the past, and they look expectantly to the churches to play their part in rebuilding civil society. Indeed, many important communitarians—such as Elshtain and Bellah—are Christians.

These first two interpretations and strategies are held by elite sectors of American society. A third "optimistic" orientation is much more populist in character, located among Christians in the lower middle and working classes. Just as apocalyptic in its interpretation as anything outlined above, the populists believe they can storm the walls of American institutions and reinstall the "Christian" culture that has been dismantled by the progressives. A group such as the Christian Coalition, which draws on popular sentiments among religious and cultural conservatives of all religious traditions, is an example of such populism. The religious right argues that because political levers were used to tear down the old culture, the same levers can be used to reinstate it. The silent, moral majority can exercise its muscle and "take our country back."

Such hope accrues to groups that are growing in numbers and confidence. And the world of religious conservatives—evangelical and fundamentalist—is a large one indeed, mostly invisible to the mainstream Christian and secular worlds. American elites hold that "other" world in such contempt that they do not even bother to learn about the huge counterculture that has been constructed, a culture with its own music, books, radio, TV, and organizational life. And different from the religious conservatives of a generation ago, this counterculture is not a reclusive and retiring one. It is a transformative movement bent on reviving many of the older cultural norms.

There are far more pessimistic interpretations of our present situations than those already examined. Among the Christian elite, there is a party that could be called neo-Augustinian. It believes the barbarians have pretty much taken over our world. Heavy hitters such as Alasdair MacIntyre, Stanley Hauerwas, and John Milbank tend in this direction. While remaining "worldly" in an external sense (they hold prestigious university positions), these intellectuals commend a disciplined construction of a churchly Christian culture. Thoroughgoing historicists, they believe that civilization is formed by particular religious "cultural-linguistic systems." Christendom, imperfect though it was, was such a civilization but it has been thoroughly subverted first by the Enlightenment and then by modern secularism, especially liberalism. There is not enough left of Christian substance in the common culture to rescue, and, moreover, Christians should not be in the business of imposing their will by political means. Better to be about constructing real Christian communities that will begin to build a churchly culture and civilization from the ground up. In this scenario the church would provide the "world" that we inhabit. It would not aim at transforming or managing culture. It would simply abandon its attachments to a dying pagan culture and build its own on Christian grounds. "Lord, to whom else shall we go? You have the words of eternal life"—and, one might add, cultural well-being.

This, of course, is a long-range strategy of renewal. The green shoots would be nourished by a far more disciplined church than we currently have. This church, like the early church, would simply wait until the current culture collapsed into the kind of violence and chaos that engulfed the dying Roman Empire. The City of God would simply replace the City of Man.

An unusual variant of this perspective is offered by James Skillen in his provocative book *Recharging the American Experiment*. Skillen does not recommend that we give up serious citizenship in America but that we limit it to a loose set of procedural rules that would order our public lives. That would be the extent of the *unum*. In his vision of "principled pluralism," however, the real cultural content of our lives would be provided by full-blooded traditions supported indirectly by the public sphere.

Skillen draws on the Dutch Calvinist theologies that have led to what some sociologists have called the "columnization" of Dutch life. That is, the public treasury helps support the schools, neighborhood associations, social agencies, newspapers, etc., that each tradition employs to maintain and communicate its vision.

Skillen believes that such an arrangement is the most persuasive and honest for Christians and others who want both to be Americans and to possess a coherent culture. Any effort to have a common culture, a substantive *unum*, will necessarily be an imposition and will be met with distrust and resistance, much as we are experiencing today. So why not admit that there can be no common culture and instead concentrate on developing a rich pluralism that lives and lets live? Christians could then focus on building a strong subculture. They could really create a seriously Christian culture that would be attractive to those in the larger society that wanted a challenging way of life. Skillen seems to think that Christianity would fare well in competition with other ways of life.

There are, of course, more populist versions of the pessimistic interpretation. On the violence-prone fringe, we have those militia movements that fervently believe a centralized state is forcibly pressing an alien culture on them. Other unarmed survivalists have similar interpretations. And there are many grassroots fundamentalist Christian efforts to create a separate Christian culture for themselves and their children. These groups do not enter the political sphere because they believe things are too far gone and that it is better to withdraw to their own enclaves. They become energized only when something directly threatens them, for example, when their homeschooling arrangements are threatened by legislation.

Where, then, does this leave me? I find the "progressive" attitude far too optimistic about our current chaos. Deconstructing traditions simply does not lead to stronger and more coherent ones. The progressives are reaping the whirlwind of their attack on the *the* culture. I think the communitarians beg the question by assuming the health of the churches. They do not grasp the depth of our cultural and ecclesial decline.

I have some affinity for the populist Christians who are entering the political fray. I am particularly drawn to their commitment to a robust and orthodox Christianity and to their zeal in transmitting and spreading it. But I shy away from their direct interventions into politics and their near identification of partisan political agendas with Christianity. However, I find myself giving money to their organizations because they seem to be the only groups courageous enough to resist the depredations of our current culture. Raw as it is, Don Wildmon's American Family Association is a force to be reckoned with, whereas I cannot imagine Lutherans protesting the trash on network TV. That would make us appear too, well, unsophisticated.

I am attracted to the neo-Augustinians because I think the churches have to get much more serious than they have been about forming their own participants, but I am reluctant to give up serious engagement with the public world, which they, and Skillen, seem to commend.

That leads me to endorse something similar to the proposal that Os Guinness makes in *The American Hour*. Unlike the progressives, Guinness does not downplay the "crisis of cultural authority" that he and I think is at the heart of our current unease. He believes with the neo-Augustinians that Christians first have to deal seriously with the crisis of religious authority in their own religious communities. But he also suggests robust engagement with the civil and political spheres at the same time. He calls for a "chartered pluralism" wherein each faith community enters into "principled persuasion" with other perspectives to find an overlapping consensus on cultural norms. In this scenario, there is neither a naked public square nor a mere procedural republic nor an imposed common culture. Rather, there is an ongoing process of public deliberation to find the common ground for a common culture. Guinness hopes, as do I, that such an ongoing process would lead to neither chaos nor conformity but to some semblance of a renewed and common culture.

This brackets the question of whether the historic mainstream faith communities—Protestant and Catholic alike—can experience the green shoots of renewal in their own communions. Can they become green shoots? I do not expect the mainstream Protestant denominations to experience such a renewal because they are in the hands of the progressives. But I do see a realignment going on whose particular contours are not yet clear. Orthodox Protestants are searching out those in other communions with whom they share a common vision. Such a realignment will be closely connected with that segment of the Catholic tradition that also longs for a more robust and clear definition of the Christian life. Catholicism is one big tent, and it is unpredictable from whence will come its green shoots.

So it is not at all clear in my mind the external shape of a Christian renewing movement will be. But my hunch is that it will embrace evangelicals, Catholics, and classic Protestants who are all passionate about the core of the apostolic faith. They will provide the religious substance—the green shoots—of a renewed culture.

DOWN WITH DIVERSITY

When a word or phrase achieves the status of an unexamined mantra or buzzword in American society, it is time to focus some critical scrutiny on it. The nation celebrates and promotes its diversity. All colleges and universities, it seems, are in headlong pursuit of "diversity." All one has to do is chant the word and many sorts of policy proposals spring to action. What school doesn't have an office of multiculturalism or a policy of diversity for its students and faculty? Those of us in the Evangelical Lutheran Church in America have already been conditioned to this national mantra of diversity by the church's commitment since its founding in 1988 to "inclusivity."

That commitment is the only discernible new thrust in the new church. It has meant the goal of achieving 10 percent minority membership in a church that—after fourteen years of effort—includes at best 2 percent. (It is interesting that only some ethnic or racial groups are included in the tally. Blacks and Hispanics are included but Slovaks are not, though many use a language other than English.) However, instead of robust evangelizing among those minority groups, inclusivity has been more and more

Originally published in *The Cresset* (Easter 2002).
Amended and reprinted with permission.

reduced to an obsession with symbolic representation. Members of prescribed groups are enlisted, if not hounded, to act as representatives of their "group" in sundry offices and positions, with the full expectation that they will think like their group is supposed to think. The church's polity is permeated with an interest-group liberalism that blocks bold missional decisions.

Now why would anyone protest this move toward diversity in a society that is more and more pluralistic? Shouldn't our institutions "look like America"? After all, when it came time for me to go to graduate school, I went to Chicago at least partly to experience the incredible array of ethnic groups in that great city. I had grown up in a section of Nebraska where everyone pretty much looked alike. We were all of northern European heritage who had been assimilated into Midwestern American culture. Later I found out that the founding figures of the University of Chicago sociology department were from backgrounds similar to mine. They, too, were fascinated by the city's diversity and were drawn to study it. Weren't they and I seeking "diversity"?

Of course we were, but that pursuit seems so innocent compared to the purposes that now define many of the efforts at diversity. Some of those purposes are simply confused and thoughtless, while some of them are more sinister. Let's start with the first category—confused and thoughtless.

First, it seems obvious that any institution, but particularly colleges, universities, and above all, churches, desire diversity in some areas but shared meanings, if not complete unity, in others. Racial, ethnic, religious, and gender diversity—the currently prescribed categories—is a worthy goal. But why not add categories such as political orientation and social class? The latter categories seem to be off-limits in the pursuit of diversity, though the hegemony of upper middle class political liberalism is often a stifling blanket over lively discussion in many educational and religious institutions. It would be wholesome if faculties and church bureaucracies would overcome their monotonous liberalism by inviting articulate political conservatives into their midst. Blue-collar cultural conservatives would add immensely to many faculties and student bodies. But social class, particularly if it is white, and political persuasion are not "in" as diversity categories. Perhaps they should be, if we truly want diversity.

Although we might pursue diversity in these areas, however, it would be more reasonable in other areas to pursue unity. For example, why wouldn't a church-related liberal arts college aim at unity in faculty commitment to a liberal arts education in which religious perspectives have a serious voice in the scholarly conversation? Do we in liberal arts colleges really want faculty committed to a research university model in which engagement with students is considered at best a burden? Do we want faculty committed to utilitarian vocational education for the sake of diversity? Do we want militant secularists on our faculties who believe religious perspectives are illegitimate expressions in the academic world? Do we want faculty who believe that service to our fellow human beings is a sentimental diversion? Do we want faculty diversity on these fundamental issues? I think not. Likewise, I think we want to recruit students who wish to pursue a liberal arts education in which religious convictions are honored and in which service is prized. Although we obviously get diversity of opinion on these issues from students, we certainly do not seek it.

The ELCA, in its headlong pursuit of diversity, has also been confused about where it really wants diversity and where it wants shared convictions. Diversity has been applied to theological matters, as well as racial and ethnic matters. Indeed, suspicion toward the inherited Lutheran tradition on the part of some multiculturalists and feminists has meant a profusion of perspectival theologies that simply bewilder those folks in the church who believe we ought to be operating from a common Lutheran theology. The low point of this emphasis on theological diversity occurred when an ex-Catholic pastor demanded on the floor of a churchwide assembly that his Caribbean Catholic perspective be given equal weight to the Lutheran in the discussion of an important theological issue. After all, he argued, weren't we interested in diversity? Were we to take such sentiments seriously, we soon would not have a church worthy of the name.

Another bad effect of diversity mongering is its tendency to neglect priorities. It is not unusual for less-then-competent people to be appointed to positions simply for diversity's sake. Quality then suffers and the appointees suffer under the suspicion of being a "diversity" hire. Our Lutheran college is rapidly running out of Lutheran representation on its faculty, but few are concerned about that, though great enthusiasm has been generated for increased diversity. On another front, colleges neglect the crucial need for a lively intellectual conversation across disciplinary boundaries. Addressing this need would mean the recruitment of that rare breed—intellectuals—no matter what color or race or ethnic background they may be.

The above confusions are the result of careless thinking about the whole concept of diversity. But some diversity schemes are certainly not careless or unthinking. They are fueled by ideological commitments that intentionally subvert the shared meanings necessary for a coherent identity and mission. Colleges, universities, churches, and even our nation are struggling with the effects of these destructive ideologies.

Let's begin with the nation. The ethnic groups that fascinated me in the Chicago of the early 1960s did not doubt that they were assimilating into American culture. They knew that in due time their grandchildren would observe their ethnic inheritance as more or less a hobby. In the meantime, however, they celebrated and expressed their roots. Above all, they admired the American constitutional order and were fiercely committed to it. They shared deeply in the American experiment.

Not so now, however, with certain multicultural ideologies that aim at keeping the diversity of cultures permanently that way. They encourage their people to shun American society and live in enclaves hostile to the larger culture. Moreover, they are deeply skeptical of the American political order and abide by it only for temporary advantage. They are intentionally unassimilated and prone to paranoid resistance. A small number of persons from such anticommunities have participated in terrorist acts. Although most new immigrants are casting their lot with America, a disturbing minority are guided by an ideological multiculturalism that will spell trouble ahead.

September 11 was a wake-up call to the nation to examine more critically the claims of multiculturalists that all cultures—and the political ideas they carry—are equal. Some sorts of "difference" we don't want in this culture. Some sorts of political ideas and actions have to be judged by the normative criteria of the American political tradition. By this I do not mean that we should outlaw or suppress nonviolent dissident groups. Rather, we should assess their claims more critically and dismiss them as wrong when warranted. True tolerance has its limits.

The emphasis on diversity in colleges, universities, and churches has had ambiguous results. That emphasis has actively invited minorities to participate in many institutions where they were not present in significant numbers in an earlier time. That is all to the good. But some of that emphasis is fueled by a harmful multiculturalism that undercuts the normative traditions that give those institutions a coherent identity and mission. The strands of multiculturalism shaped by a pervasive hermeneutic of suspicion attack any normative framework as "hegemonic." They wish to "deconstruct" it to head off its oppressive tendencies. Even schools of robust Christian identity are not immune to this deconstruction. Indeed, Christian normative frameworks are under suspicion in many colleges and universities, even if the Christians have no chance to dominate. Just the fact that their outlook makes comprehensive truth claims is enough to send some proponents of diversity into the nervous vapors. Those proponents want Christian perspectives to be less equal than others, if not completely absent.

The hyper-individualism of faculty and students makes it difficult enough for institutions of higher learning to pass on traditions, whether they are intellectual, moral, or religious. Add to that the "epistemological tribalism" generated by militant multiculturalists and those institutions fall into even more chaos. Then the educational public square is evacuated of substantive notions of purpose and ends. Schools are held together by a minimal set of procedural agreements that keep things going, even if they know not where.

Such is the state of most public colleges and universities. Besides these procedural agreements, they are held together for the most part by the circuses of big-time athletics and the bread of government research grants. Sadly enough, however, the same corrosive trends are at work in church-related schools. Those who have retained a coherent identity and mission should be wary of both the thoughtless and intentionally subversive approaches to diversity I have written about above. Those who haven't retained that coherence will fall into even more chaotic pluralism as they carelessly pursue diversity.

Unsurprisingly, the churches' efforts at diversity also include these centrifugal tendencies. In their commitment to diversity, the mainstream Protestant churches have cultivated an "epistemological tribalism" that has further weakened an already anemic effort to pass on central religious and moral meanings and practices. Catholics and evangelical Protestants are faring better because they think more carefully about where they cultivate diversity and where they affirm shared meanings.

Where does this leave us then? Am I a grouchy defender of vanilla homogeneity? I don't think so. I admire the Roman Catholic Church because it is *catholic*; it embraces all sorts and conditions of humankind throughout all earthly time and space. I, too, would like to see our nation and our institutions welcome all sorts and conditions of people. But I am not overly embarrassed if some of those institutions are predominantly white (as is the ELCA), or black (as is the NBA), or Jewish (as is Hollywood), or Catholic (as is Notre Dame), or men (as are airline pilots), or women (as are teachers)—if they do not engage in discrimination. However, I oppose the efforts at diversity that thoughtlessly forget about the need for fundamental agreement on basic values, that put diversity ahead of the central needs of the organization, and that intentionally undermine the normative traditions of our nation and our institutions.

THE BURDEN
OF CULTURAL CORRECTNESS

The term "political correctness" has entered our language, much to the consternation of those who actually spawned the term through their practice of coercive liberalism. Dictionaries now list and define the phrase as: "marked by or adhering to a typically progressive orthodoxy on issues involving especially race, gender, sexual affinity, or ecology" (*Random House Webster's College Dictionary*). Political correctness has led to enforced orthodoxies that suppress contrary opinion and shut down a good deal of public debate on some of the most important issues facing our country. It has led to laws that ensconce progressive opinion into the legal apparatus of the state.

However, the most powerful currents of political correctness do not operate in the political sphere, where politicians have to represent the opinions of their constituents, whose opinions are often not politically correct. Rather, political correctness operates most powerfully in the cultural sphere, in those institutions most responsible for the communication of meaning and values.

Originally published in *The Cresset* (Lent 2003).
Amended and reprinted with permission.

It would be better, then, to call this progressive orthodoxy "cultural correctness," which I believe more accurately describes the phenomenon.

The institutions in which cultural correctness operates most coercively are the national newspapers, especially the *New York Times* and the *Washington Post*, followed by large regional papers such as the *Los Angeles Times* and the *Chicago Tribune*; the major publishing houses; the headquarters, presses, and seminaries of the mainline Protestant churches; the elite universities and colleges and their presses; National Public Radio and to a somewhat lesser extent the Public Broadcasting System; and the three commercial television networks—NBC, CBS, and ABC.

Leaders of the youthful revolutions of the 1960s promised a "long march through the institutions" after they found out that "the revolution" would not succeed politically. To a great measure their prediction has come true. The "commanding heights of the culture" are now controlled by the "progressive" elements of a generation that has had a major quarrel with traditional American politics and culture. Because traditional American culture has had and continues to have a major impact on what happens politically, the progressives took the path of least resistance—the cultural route.

I first encountered the coercive power of this march through the institutions when I became a conservative in a liberal Protestant seminary in the late 1970s. In addition to being a public conservative, I made the additional mistake of thinking I could be a conservative and teach in the field of Christian ethics in such a context. I was on "the wrong side of history" on most of the issues that stirred the students of the day: divestment from South Africa, "inclusive language," support for revolutionary movements in South and Central America, the moral equivalence of Soviet socialism and American democratic capitalism, and the celebration of newfound sexual freedoms that emerged from the revolution of the 1960s. I found out that contrary opinions on these matters were most unwelcome. Dissenters from cultural correctness quickly learned to be quiet, which then obviated any real debate in the community on these matters.

Because the seminary was something of an avant-garde institution, it has taken progressives a little longer to consolidate their power in those other institutions that occupy the "commanding heights of the culture." But cultural correctness is now a force to be reckoned with in almost all the sectors I listed above. Indeed, it operates with such force that it suppresses debate and deliberation in the very institutions that should prize such practices. That is the burden of cultural correctness.

I experienced a particularly dramatic example of such suppression at an annual conference of the Society of Christian Ethics. An opening plenary luncheon was to feature an "open hearing" on just-war criteria and their application to American foreign policy with regard to Iraq. Naïvely expecting an objective initial presentation by a distinguished university professor, I attended the meeting. Instead of inviting arguments from both sides of the question after an introduction to the just-war tradition, the professor proceeded to indicate that scarcely any of the requirements for a just war were met by current government intentions. A series of cartoons ridiculing George W. Bush and his policies projected on an overhead accompanied the presentation. These brought much laughter, but the fun was just beginning. A line of "discussants" took turns lambasting American policy, several even comparing America to Nazi Germany. Two brave souls made some oblique comments that suggested the discussion was not representative and that American policy might be more clever than it appeared, but both had to couch their remarks in derogatory comments about the Bush administration.

I felt moved to rise in protest of this charade but decided not to. Later I found out that almost all the conservatives in the society (a pretty small group) found other things to do during the lunch hour. They anticipated a pep rally instead of a fair debate, and they were right. This exercise in cultural correctness intimidated dissenters within an organization that pats itself on the back for its capacity for moral deliberation. Cultural correctness, however, simply couldn't be suspended on such an important matter.

There are many examples of this sort of intimidation. In each case the approved opinion is protected by the use of epithets that fend off anyone courageous or unaware enough to challenge it. For instance, it is increasingly difficult to argue for the traditional teaching on homosexual practice in the institutions mentioned above without being called a "homophobe." Such a psychological reduction of honest dissenters is now whipped out even in the churches, which should be careful about jettisoning traditional teaching on this matter. In the current debate within the Evangelical Lutheran Church in America, it is increasingly difficult to find persons who are willing publicly to defend the traditional teaching that proscribes homosexual practice. Who wants to be called a "homophobe"? Not only have the seminaries weeded out most of the persons who might have such Neanderthal opinions, but those who do manage still to hold them are intimidated into silence.

Militant feminism has contributed its share of approved opinions to our fund of cultural correctness. For example, it would take a lot of courage to argue against our liberal abortion laws in any of the aforementioned institutions. At our college, which is several notches below the elite heights, faculty women created such a furor over a privately funded "pro-life" leaflet included in the college newspaper that the editors of the paper had to apologize and pledge never to run anything so offensive again. Likewise, one would either be foolhardy or brave to criticize publicly the way Title IX has been interpreted in college athletics or to suggest—particularly if you are a male—that there are real differences between men and women.

Feminism has joined with the guardians of approved opinion on racial matters to propose and enforce certain language rules. Few persons in the commanding heights of the culture will use masculine pronouns with regard to God. They would be called "sexists." In many seminary catalogues there are pages of rules for proper "nonsexist" language and Augsburg/Fortress sends to its authors a compendium of "inclusive language" rules that forbid the use of the word *manhole*! If one violates those rules, the language police will strike and snip all the offending words. It takes an established writer to resist these depredations; neophyte writers wouldn't have a chance.

Such sensitivity over language has led to some odd results. John Rocker, the former Atlanta pitcher who used some stupid and offensive language regarding gays, New Yorkers, and blacks experienced the full wrath of the cultural elite. He was hounded out of baseball for a time. Yet Ray Lewis, the star linebacker for the Baltimore Ravens, was actually involved in murders but was not punished as severely by the cultural elite as Rocker. Indeed, he is now something of a hero in the sports media, while Rocker is the object of universal contempt.

Saying certain words violates such powerful taboos that the offender can lose his career and reputation overnight. Who says we have passed beyond the primitive stage when violations of taboos brought instant death, generally through inward turmoil? Instant "death" can occur to current violators, but now through the external outrage of the enforcers of cultural correctness.

Multiculturalists have joined the protectors of gender and racial correctness in prohibiting any speech that might offend any member of any approved oppressed group. This means that no serious debate can go on about real differences in these matters. At best conversation must be managed by "diversity trainers," who duly enforce cultural correctness. A ridiculous extreme of this sort of "sensitivity" happened to an acquaintance of mine whose daughter went to an elite Eastern liberal arts college. This poor girl introduced "Hawaiian pizza" in the college pizza parlor that she managed, only to be faced by an organized group who demanded her resignation because of her "insensitivity" to Hawaiians.

Perhaps cultural correctness is most vigorously wielded on religious conservatives, especially those who are called "funda-mentalist." (The enforcers do not distinguish between evangelicals and fundamentalists.) Public action by members of these religious groups—categorized as the "Religious Right"—is perhaps most closely guarded against because these groups represent the cultural conservatism that is abhorred in all of the instances I wrote of above. At any rate, these groups are unprotected by cultural correctness.

John Leo writes on USNEWS.COM that Rutgers banned a Christian group from its campus and stripped it of its funding because it selected its leaders on the basis of religious belief, a practice proscribed by the university rules of cultural correctness. Leo writes that the real purpose is not to prohibit groups from electing leaders based on common commitments, otherwise the Democratic Club would have to allow a Republican to run for its presidency. Rather, the ban was directed at groups that opposed homosexuality as a means to cause them to disband.

This is not an isolated instance. It is a parlor sport among members of the cultural elite to equate American Christian "fundamentalists" (remember again that no distinction is made between fundamentalists and evangelicals or religious conservatives) with violent Muslim fundamentalists. Therefore the opinions of the "Religious Right" can be dismissed from public debate on all issues at the cultural heights.

However, they cannot be dismissed in the political sphere. Thank God for politics! Because cultural correctness has less sway in politics than in the realms of culture and increasingly in business, honest debate can actually exist. Representatives and Senators who are beholden to nonculturally correct constituencies can and do represent them. Conservatives who did not agree with all of Jesse Helms's political opinions nevertheless admired him because he cared not one whit for the negative—even hateful— opinions of the enforcers of cultural correctness. Many other more moderate political conservatives also violate the canons of cultural correctness and thereby keep genuine political debate alive in the political sphere.

What of the cultural sphere? Is it a closed matter? No, though cultural correctness is intimidating, it is not completely oppressive. Brave souls can and do speak out in the bastions of cultural correctness. I was free to speak and should have spoken my mind at the Society of Christian Ethics; it would have been good for me and the society. Conservatives should refuse to be intimidated. Further, the pervasiveness of cultural correctness at the cultural heights has spawned many alternative organizations and agencies to speak for cultural and political conservatism. Some of them have invaded the cultural heights—newspapers such as *The Washington Times* and *The Wall Street Journal*; journals such as *The Weekly Standard*, *Commentary*, and *First Things*; presses such as Eerdmans and Regnery; conservative think-tanks such as The American Enterprise Institute, The Hoover Institution, and The Ethics and Public Policy Center; and networks such as the Fox Network, though I resist using the word "heights" with anything Fox does. Talk radio operates below the radar screen of the culturally correct and gathers audiences that are far more educated and sophisticated than the debunkers realize.

However, it would be far better if the cultural heights were more open to dissent. They would then live up to their promise of being genuinely liberal.

MUSIC MATTERS

When a friend and I go to the local swim and tennis club on Saturday morning for a serious game of tennis, the rock music comes on loudly at 10 A.M. to affect our concentration. When I go to the Kmart or Wal-Mart, I am irritated by soft rock playing not too softly. When I phone my local bank or automobile shop, I am involuntarily entertained with music that I would not choose. Although I go to my doctor early in the morning so I get to see him on time, I cannot escape the late '60s rock that he loves. My visits to the fitness center are always accompanied by the resentment I feel about having to listen to loud music I dislike.

Indeed, I have to listen to very loud rap music before I can enjoy the basketball games I loyally attend. I am almost blown away by the decibels emanating from a souped-up Camaro as I walk down the street; my office is not even immune to the vibrations set off by the enormous auto sound systems that pass by on the street far below. To my consternation the management of the local soccer club thinks the spectators must be musically entertained *while* the game is going on. (This may be a harbinger of things to come. Music will surround us from the rising of the sun

Originally published in *The Cresset* (Christmas/Epiphany 1999–2000). Amended and reprinted with permission.

to the going down of the same! We will literally be entertained to death.)

Americans are hooked on music. And it seems that the younger the person, the more addicted. Students come to my classes with earphones around their necks, though no one has yet tried to put them on *during* my class. However, I have heard other faculty colleagues complain that indeed this has been attempted.

Indeed, music matters a great deal for the young. Too much. Not only can they not be without it, but it takes on too much gravity in their lives. It is not an original insight of mine that for many their music is a substitute for religion. It is a quasi-religion.

Young people who will not go across the street to attend their church will cross the country—repeatedly!—to attend concerts by the bands of their choice. Thousands of the young make pilgrimages to the holy sites at which their bands play. The concerts are a replacement for the summer church camps of yore.

The bands also dispense wisdom and ecstasy to their followers. The texts take the place of the hymn stanzas that an earlier generation knew by heart. The concert experience offers intense euphoria to the shimmering masses that are caught up in its rhythms. The bands take on godlike qualities and are given godlike obeisance by their adherents. The universal church of rock extends around the world and connects the young of almost every nation with one another and with the objects of their adoration. It is understandable that cultural and religious conservatives try to ban such music from earshot of their young. They rightly understand that it is a competitor for their souls.

All of this may seem overwrought, and it is. Most young people are not swept up completely by this quasi-religious phenomenon. Music remains a hobby, a sidelight in a varied and wholesome life. But the trends toward overdose on music are disturbing, especially when the quality of the music is taken into account.

Plato outlawed certain kinds of music in his *Republic* because he thought that highly energetic rhythms would encourage the passions to overcome the rationality he wanted to train in the developing young. Malcolm X and the early Martin Luther King Jr. believed that the blues and jazz would divert the young from developing the kind of disciplined intentionality that would overcome oppression. Indeed, anyone who watched *Soul Train* or *American Bandstand* with a critical eye over the years would not be surprised at the increasing incidence of premarital sex and its accompanying rise in births out of wedlock.

Allan Bloom, he of *The Closing of the American Mind* fame, argued that "rock gives children, on a silver platter, with all the public authority of the entertainment industry, everything their parents always used to tell them they had to wait for until they grew up and would understand later." But when it comes to unleashing and expressing raw passions, sex does not stand alone.

So much contemporary popular music is characterized by a driving but mindless energy bordering on violence. Can enough violence in the mind not finally issue into coarse and vulgar, if not violent, behavior? In too much pop music that violent attitude is directed toward women, persons of other races, the police, and other authority figures who present convenient targets. Certainly many rock groups have understood that their celebration of the darker passions has distinct anti-Christian implications. Surprisingly, this development seems to be taken in stride by a culture that doesn't know where to set limits or that doesn't have the courage to protest even if it knows.

Our culture in general is deep into what that old social philosopher Sorokin called its "sensate" phase. The intense, the raw, the immediate, the direct, the violent, the shocking, the flashy, and the flamboyant—anything that strongly stimulates the senses is valued. Pornographic sex and violence are a sensate culture's dead-end conclusion. Celebrities flourish in such a culture because their lives are calculated attempts to catch our eye and ear—for fifteen minutes or more. Music celebrities in particular stand close to the top of our sensate culture's pantheon.

Again, this is overwrought and exaggerated. There is good popular music around. Country music seems to be overtaking rock as the music of choice, though it seems to be adapting some of rock's characteristics as it does so. Most popular music is treasured because it connects the hearer with cherished memories, not for its intrinsic merit. (I listen to the music of the '50s for that reason and am increasingly aware of how trivial most of it was.) Most of the young seem to be able to adore the worst sorts of music yet remain responsible human beings. All is not lost.

But the kind and quality of music does matter. The sensate music of our time makes it difficult for the young to appreciate more complex, refined, and nuanced music. The young man who has his brain waves flattened by the ten thousand decibels emanating from his car's audio system will most likely never be able to appreciate Mozart or, for that matter, Andrew Lloyd Weber, let alone be able to read Immanuel Kant. His addiction to a narrow range of hammering passions will make it difficult to savor music of genuinely subtle or transcendent aspirations. Moreover, such music encourages and reinforces the unguided emotions that have made their contribution to the coarsening and vulgarization of our culture in general. Besides being a nuisance, it does have negative effects on our broader culture.

Any note of comfort to conclude these melancholy reflections? Sorokin thought that cultures went through cycles. Sensate cultures had their dead-ends because they led to such mindless, ugly, and destructive activities. Out of the charred stump of sensate culture, he argued, more noble aspirations would emerge. Maybe he was right. We will simply get sick and tired of all this. Popular music will again take its proper place as a diversion, not an obsession. Melody and beauty will return. Romantic instead of libidinous love will make a comeback. A diversity of music will again be appreciated by the young, and they will make a place for the great classical tradition that can nourish their spirits.

Indeed, many already have.

WHATEVER HAPPENED TO ACCOUNTABILITY?

Americans are big on the concept of freedom. If there is any "highest good" in the pantheon of American values, it is the freedom to choose. In most debates the freedom to choose can be used to trump almost any other value. When my students debate social issues in my classes, the conversation is often ended by one party claiming the right to choose. What can overcome such a trump card? I try to tell them that we do indeed have the right to choose—we do have freedom—but that the challenge of the moral life is to make the right choices. Beyond that, I argue, the life of freedom entails accountability for one's choices. Freedom cannot be sustained without a lot of people making right or at least tolerable choices, and it cannot live long without people being accountable for their choices, especially their wrong choices.

Increasingly, it seems to me, we have freedom only *before* the act. We prize that and hold it almost sacrosanct. But *after* the act, when we are obligated to be accountable for our actions, freedom disappears. We explain it away through psychological or

Originally published in *The Cresset* (Michaelmas 1999).
Amended and reprinted with permission.

sociological analyses. Accountability is shifted elsewhere, preferably to someone far in the past or to social institutions that have deep pockets.

Perhaps the most dramatic example of this accountability-shifting shell game is that regarding smoking. If anyone claims to be oblivious to the dangers of smoking since at least the mid-1960s, they have been living in never-never land. Indeed, cigarettes were called "coffin nails" far earlier than the 1960s.

For thirty years the rhetoric against smoking has gradually gained momentum. In recent years antismoking has become a cause of the "enlightened elite." Television commentators can speak contemptuously of "big tobacco" and roundly condemn the hapless members of the human community that go on smoking. Never mind that many people smoke lightly or moderately. They are "smokers," an almost ontological category. Even insurance companies refuse to make distinctions about the frequency of smoking. Thus few persons can claim that they are unaware that smoking is risky or that it is generally condemned by the larger culture. When a person smokes, he or she does so "against the grain" and should be willing to take the consequences of the action.

But the accountability has been dramatically shifted away from the smoker and toward the deep pockets of the tobacco industry. Billions have been ransacked from legal industries that offer a risky product. (Not that one should feel sorry for the tobacco companies. They irresponsibly denied for far too long the hazards of smoking, even after everyone else knew better. Further, they simply pass their litigation expenses on to the blue-collar folks who buy the cigarettes. Trial lawyers and state treasuries suck up another hidden tax on the working class.)

Our litigious trial lawyers will not stop with tobacco, I fear. Gun manufacturers are already in their sights, to use an unfortunate image. No doubt a likely next target will be brewing and distilling companies. Certainly the misuse of alcohol brings forth far more negative effects than even smoking. And drinking alcoholic beverages, like smoking, is looked upon as something of an addiction, something that goes beyond free choice. No matter that there are more ex-smokers than smokers and abstainers than drinkers. Accountability for the misuse of alcohol will soon be shifted to brewers and distillers, not the drinkers themselves. We have freedom only before the act, not after.

But let's get off smoking and drinking. Sex may be more interesting. Hillary Clinton has psychologized away husband Bill's gargantuan sexual appetites by attributing them to abuse he suffered when he was caught between the emotional claims of his mother and his grandmother. It is amazing, she avers, that he is as noble a man as he is. So Clinton's many willful and reckless adulteries have little to do with his own moral agency. He is not really accountable for them. We'll just have to "understand."

The church is wracked with legal actions against the sexual misconduct of a surprising number of its ministers. Those in leadership positions spend way too much of their time intervening in such cases and defending themselves against litigation. Again, accountability is not placed with the ministers and the sometimes willing "victims" of the misconduct. (Yes, I know, there are real victims in many cases.) It is shifted to the leaders and churches that supervise the ministers. Big sums are involved. Could it be that shifting accountability is a lucrative business?

The nation's violent episodes are also compelling cases in point. In all the commentary about the young men who shot so many fellow students and teachers in Littleton, Colorado, not one that I am aware of attributed their actions to a willful choice of evil. Great searches were mounted for "understanding" their actions. Could it be parental neglect? Could it be violent video games? Could it be fascist organizations? Could it be rejection by peers? Could it be the general youth culture? Could it be the availability of guns? There are similar ruminations about the day trader who went on a murderous rampage in Atlanta. Did he snap? Did losses in day trading lead him to morbid despair? Is there something in his family origins to account for his violent tendencies? Is it a male thing?

Of course all these factors are relevant. But they don't absolve the perpetrators of their moral agency. They chose their deeds, even as they chose their own deaths after doing their worst. They no doubt thought they were avoiding accountability for their deeds through suicide. But accountability does not end with this life; they have much for which to account as they meet their Maker. I hesitate to contemplate what may be in store for us as biological research finds more genetic "causes" for what we do. The biological sciences may make psychology and sociology look like pikers when it comes to absolving us of our accountability.

It all comes down, it seems to me, to the dominance of philosophical naturalism in our thinking about human agency. If all of reality—including human thought and action—can be understood in terms of a tight chain of natural cause and effect, then there is little room for freedom. Moral agency is an illusion we need to live without going totally mad. It is a fiction that comforts us into believing our choices are actually real.

But we know that is not the case. Philosophical naturalism is not reflexively adequate. That is, it cannot account for itself and its claims to be true. If everything is equally caused, then there are no true are false opinions. Further, it cannot account for the immediate sense of freedom we have when we are confronted with an agonizing choice in which we have to use our judgment about an ambiguous case. In those times we sometimes wish we were "determined." But our immediate experience is that we aren't. We have to decide. And, I hope, take accountability for our acts.

AMERICA THE OKAY?

THE STATE OF THE NATION
AT THE MILLENNIUM

G regg Easterbrook, a prolific and respected journalist who has
written widely about ecological matters and recently on religion and science, has a blockbuster article in the January 4 and
January 11, 1999, issue of *The New Republic*. He has given it the
same title as the title of this article, but he didn't add a question
mark. The thrust of his essay is captured in its subtitle: "Why life
in the U.S. has never been better."

In the same issue of *The New Republic*, Robert Brustein, its
veteran drama critic, reports on a recent trip to Las Vegas after
years of absence. He tells of the massive growth in gambling that
the expansion of Las Vegas represents. He marvels at the mega-
resorts that are devoted to entertaining the whole family, which
also serve as a strong come-on to attract even more gamblers. The
mega-resorts are characterized by ersatz replicas of other cultural
meccas—New York City, Egypt, Italy. He writes: "Nowhere is

Originally published in *The Cresset* (Lent 1999).
Amended and reprinted with permission.

America's obsession with instant wealth exploited more efficiently than in these trackless gambling wastes, where thousands of funereal characters, many of them women, huddle over machines like wraiths. I had visions of Dante's circles of Hell (*I had not thought death had undone so many.*)"

Both of these pictures of America are presented in the same journal by perceptive writers. Which one is true? Or are both true? What is the state of our nation as we wind down one millennium and begin another?

I.

First, we must admit that the good news that Easterbrook brings is pretty convincing. In section after section he marshalls empirical evidence for his thesis that things are not only good in America but also slowly getting better. Crime has fallen sharply. The economy continues to boom. Teen pregnancy is declining. The federal budget is running a surplus, as are many state budgets. The air and water are getting cleaner. Health is improving by almost every measure, including the first-ever decline in cancer incidence. Deaths from accidents are decreasing. Standards of living continue to improve. The use of drugs and cigarettes is waning. Levels of education keep rising. Women and minorities are acquiring an ever-larger slice of the national pie. Personal liberty is greater than ever, while American culture becomes more and more diverse. Even home runs are at an all-time high!

George Will, in a column appearing at nearly the same time, adds more good news from his conservative perspective. The number of welfare recipients is declining, as are illegitimacy and abortion. Americans saying that abortion should be "legal under any circumstances" has fallen from 34 percent to 22 percent since 1990. Church attendance is rising. Since the late '70s, the percentage of Americans who say that religion is "very important" in their lives has increased from 52 to 61. There has been a sharp increase in charitable service and giving.

Easterbrook argues that this good news is obfuscated by the left elite because it smacks of triumphalism, particularly on the part of those on the conservative right who have presided over many of the public and private agencies involved with these improvements. It is negated by the conservative elite because a good deal of these improvements have come through governmental policies, and besides, such good news can damage the right's commitment to the culture wars.

Easterbrook is not complacent. He thinks we have serious problems with the greenhouse effect on one front and poverty on the other. We also have great problems with world imbalances in wealth and well-being. But his point is that incremental reform has brought us a great distance in recent decades and that further commitment to reform will make us even better. So, he says, it is time to quit the doomsday rhetoric and commit ourselves to further reform.

I've never been captivated by doomsday analyses of the world nor by apocalyptic strains in Christianity. After all, being raised a Nebraskan protected me from the former and being raised a Lutheran inoculated me against the latter. So I find Easterbrook credible. But I also find the more somber and disturbing sensibilities of Brustein credible.

II.

Other indices reveal some darker elements in this American portrait. A recent *Washington Post* poll shows a precipitous drop in the trust of people for the government above all but also for other institutions. Seventy-one percent do not think their fellow countrymen and women lead as good a life as in the past. The exact percentage think that Clinton does not have high personal moral standards and only a slightly smaller percentage (61 percent) think they are about the same as others of his generation. Fifty-five percent believe the country is becoming too tolerant of behaviors harmful for society. One also is reminded that the promising drops in crime, illegitimacy, divorce, etc., mentioned by Easterbrook are departures from historic highs, and in comparison with many other countries and with earlier periods of our national life they remain high.

Yet I enjoy the good things that seem to be abundant as we close the twentieth century. I delight in seeing my pension accumulations grow. So many products and services are affordable. We enjoy peace and prosperity. Why knock it? Easterbrook is certainly describing part of our reality.

Nevertheless, a spirit of unease is unquenchable. At a basic level, I believe, our culture is weakening. Indeed, the very success of our society—its affluence mixed with large measures of freedom—is paradoxically at the root of our malaise. The virtues we need for continued humane existence are being eroded by our successes.

Robert Bellah's analysis of the drift of our culture seems eminently persuasive to me. He has argued for many years now that the two great traditions in American life—the biblical and the republican—are being undercut by two new lifestyles: utilitarian individualism and expressive individualism. Although both older traditions are characterized by "practices of commitment" (the former oriented to the will of God and the latter to the polis), the newer forms of individualism dispense with such practices altogether as they seek individual success or individual expression.

Although the two forms of individualism are parasitic on the older traditions for any substantive good, they also undercut them by instrumentalizing their practices or by turning them into vehicles of personal expression. Thus one has the unencumbered self, freed from the constraints of tradition and its practices and freed for the fulfillment of individual desire or expression. And one has to have a pretty sunny view of human nature to believe that the unencumbered self will automatically choose and express itself wisely or responsibly.

Our colleges experience the effects of these forms of individualism. Raised on entertainment—the epitome of the American commitment to freedom of choice in the search for one's pleasures—students increasingly find it difficult to master the practices of reading a challenging text, of analyzing the meaning of the text, and of constructing coherent arguments. Adeptness with computers doesn't help either. Computer exchanges seem too quick, fragmentary, biased, and protean to carry real intellectual weight. It is difficult to sort out the serious from the trivial on the burgeoning Internet. It takes far more savvy than most students have to make those distinctions.

Higher portions of our students seem to bear more impediments than those who have gone before. A surprising number come with learning disabilities for which colleges are obligated to compensate. Many are emotionally troubled; college counseling centers could expand dramatically and still not meet the demand. Indeed, expansion might stimulate demand. Troubles are often acted out in excessive drinking, though most students need no such excuses for binge drinking. Behind the troubles one frequently finds broken or turbulent homes. It is amazing how much "life" some of our students have already experienced, and they are definitely not better for the wear.

Enhanced utilitarian and expressive individualism also undercuts what Stephen Carter has called "civility." Defining the term as the willingness to sacrifice our own desire for the sake of living together in a common world, on the one hand, and the active helpfulness we offer to fellow citizens, on the other, Carter laments the loss of the lawfulness, modesty, manners, and considerateness that incivility breeds. Unrestrained individualism leads to more friction in all areas of human social intercourse; violence seems right around the corner, even when it does not flare up overtly. Add to these dynamics a strong dose of high decibel music and one gets an unpleasant combination.

Perhaps most disturbing is the waning of practices of commitment with regard to institutional life. Modern individualism eschews ongoing engagement with organized religious communities, with conventional patterns of marriage and family life, and with the community associations that have played such an important role in American civic life. Americans increasingly demand freedom from institutional bonds that cut down on their prized autonomy. We may lament the loss of such commitment, but perhaps we are not ready yet for recapturing it; it would leave us too few free evenings.

Although I am willing to accept and enjoy the okay-ness that Easterbrook and others describe, I find a sobering shadow at the heart of our culture. Can such high rates of individualism sustain the kind of economic and political success we currently enjoy? Can they do anything but diminish the already impoverished and decadent forms of popular culture we copiously consume and just as copiously export? Can they support the institutional life without which we risk confusion and chaos? Can they inspire the sort of common commitment needed to address the stubborn poverty that continues to plague a significant portion of our population and the world?

Rather than adapt a breezy optimism about the "happy" close to this century, it might be wiser to claim a more dialectical view, such as that proposed by Reinhold Niebuhr. He argued that the historical potentialities for evil grow in proportion to the expansion of the good. The prosperity of America the Okay may have nestled next to it the seeds of cultural and social decay. The complex technologies that drive our civilization have implicit in them the capacity for enormous malfunction and disaster. The larger world may yet collapse in a catastrophe that will encompass us too. Indeed, as Niebuhr argued, history may not solve but rather cumulate the problems of humankind.

As the millennium comes closer, it behooves us Christians to realize that we really cannot "read the signs of the times" with accuracy. We should not let our faith be swayed by either the anticipation of good times or the fear of bad. Indeed, good times do not guarantee a good reception of Christ or His followers. We know that the crucifixion of Jesus took place in "good" times, executed by the best and the brightest of the day. Good times are no guarantee of good faith. We ought to prefer the latter.

THE OBJECTIVE WORTH
OF HUMAN LIFE

The foundation of Western law is being shaken. The West's commitment to the objective worth of every human person is being challenged in debates about the beginning of life, the end of life, and the meaning of basic justice. Until this point in history, our law has reflected its Judeo-Christian foundations, but that is less and less the case. The grounds for human worth are being shifted from transcendent sources (God) to subjective and utilitarian sources (the human individual and the human community). We—both individually and collectively—are becoming the arbiters of human worth and dignity. A great shift is taking place.

Christians need to be aware of this and struggle against it because our faith makes comprehensive claims about the nature of truth and justice. Our faith does not simply claim that it is true for us and for our community of believers. On the contrary, the Christian faith believes in a God of the whole world whose will is to be obeyed by His followers and is to be reflected in the common law that governs the whole human community.

Originally published in *Lutheran Forum* (Winter 1998).
Amended and reprinted with permission.

Of course this does not mean that we have a clear reading of God's will in all issues of law and policy, but it does mean that we are given strong clues that shape our perspectives and arguments. It also does not mean that we refuse to argue in commonly shared concepts and language nor that we won't participate in compromise. The public square is precisely that arena where we must make intelligible arguments and compromises but at the same time draw upon religious grounds for our positions.

What are those religious grounds? What fundamental concepts shape uniquely Christian arguments in the public sphere about the worth of human life?

"Exalted Individuals" by Creation and Redemption

Glenn Tinder, an important and wise Christian political philosopher, has articulated those religious grounds in *The Political Meaning of Christianity*.[1] A distillation of his larger argument appeared in a famous article entitled "Can We Be Good without God?" which appeared in *The Atlantic Monthly*.[2] In those works Tinder not only elaborates the key biblical and theological concepts pertaining to human nature and dignity, but he does so in fresh language that penetrates our thinking anew. We listen to the old, old story in very new ways.

Tinder believes the key to objective human worth is the Christian concept of *agape* love, a love that does not judge but that loves unconditionally. This divine love makes us all "exalted individuals." Because of our basic affirmation by God's love, we are all elevated to royalty in the kingdom of God.

This divine love is not just an undifferentiated, inactive love that shines down on us like the sun. It is active and personal. First, God gives us a destiny. In this reworking of the Lutheran doctrine of the calling of all Christians, Tinder argues that a God-given destiny is not the same as fate. A destiny is more like an ongoing conversation between God and the creature; it is a drama. As such it can be refused, and many persons do in fact refuse their destiny.

A destiny, Tinder suggests, is the "unfoldment of our essential being." It is a search for those places in life where our talents, capacities, and interests intersect with the needs and possibilities of the created world. So we are given destinies in our work, our marriage and family life, our lives as citizens, and our lives in the church. In each of these places of responsibility, the Christian is given the opportunity to find and express his or her calling. In so doing we play our role in the larger divine drama that God is working out. We realize our essential being as creatures of God. We are blessed.

So the divine gift of a destiny bestows meaning on life. It also gives humans great dignity and worth because we all have parts to play in God's unfolding drama. The parts may be small and even insignificant in the world's view, but they, and the creatures who fulfill them, are cherished and prized in God's eyes. As participants in the present and coming kingdom of God, we are "exalted individuals."

Although we are sacred as creatures of God's love, we are not good. All are fallen. Instead of allowing God to exalt us with His unconditional love, we try to exalt ourselves. We elevate ourselves and our groups above others. This not only leads to idolatry but also to all the relational woes of our fallen condition. We oppress and are oppressed. We neglect and are neglected. We have a persisting and inevitable will to cling to the creature instead of the Creator.

Given this condition, then, God does another wondrous thing to lift us up to Him. In addition to being given a destiny at our birth, we are now given a Savior to release us from the bondage to sin, death, and the devil that we have strangely elected. God sends His Son into the world to identify with our condition and to achieve solidarity with us. Baptized into Christ, we are crucified and raised with Him. "In Christ" we are again freed from our shackles and elevated with Him to participate in the life of God.

Our justification through Christ enables us to receive the eternal dimension of our destiny that was given to us at birth but was frustrated by our refusal to accept it. Our temporal destiny is not all that there is. Indeed, as Augustine put it, God has created us for Himself, and we are restless until we are at home with Him. All are invited through their creation and redemption to take their royal place in the kingdom of God.

Each of these biblical and theological themes—that we are given a temporal and eternal destiny at our birth and that we are retrieved by God in His salutary work in Christ—ensures an objective worth for each human being. We are, as Tinder says, "exalted individuals." But this status is not ours by earning it; it is bestowed. No matter what we do, we cannot efface the dignity that God has given us in our creation and redemption.

Such theological affirmations undergird the Western conception of the dignity of the individual and have been ensconced in custom, law, and policy. They constitute, Tinder avers, the "spiritual center of Western politics." And that is good. Although we realize the full meaning of these affirmations only fragmentarily, they have given our societies benchmarks to judge our performance and ideals toward which to strive.

The question is, can we be good without God? Can we sustain these profound affirmations of the individual without preserving their religious roots? Can our moral and political principles survive without their religious grounding? Or are we more likely a "cut flower civilization" that will wither dramatically once the blooms are cut off from their roots?

DAMAGE AT THE ROOTS

We are now in the process of finding the answers to those questions. The Judeo-Christian roots of our civilization are indeed slowly being cut off. In their place we have moral and legal reasoning that takes place outside or below the grand Christian vision of life that has informed our reasoning in the past. Such reasoning assumes less and less the objective worth of the individual as created in the image of God. Rather, it judges lives according to subjective or utilitarian criteria. Let me illustrate.

THE OBJECTIVE WORTH OF HUMAN LIFE

Issues at the Beginning of Life

One of the clearest moves to qualify the objective worth of human life is by making the existence of that life subject to human preference. That is, many persons argue that the developing unborn human being's claim to life can be affirmed only if it is wanted or planned. Now there is room for argument about when such claims to life by the unborn become unqualified or inviolable. But, from a Christian point of view, it seems abhorrent to accept or reject God's great gift of life on the basis of whether we want it or not. If God has bestowed a destiny upon a developing human being, it is wicked to kill it.

Likewise, the Christian conviction that each life has objective value grounded in God's love augurs against too-easy abortion of "defective" fetuses. Again, there is room for argument about which defects are so horrendous that one cannot imagine the fetus having a human life. But increasingly we are seeing fetuses aborted on much less weighty grounds. Who has the right to say, for instance, that a developing human with Down Syndrome has no God-bestowed destiny?

Further, Christians have been properly resistant to the engineering of humans through cloning and gene manipulation. Such ventures inevitably carry the connotation that humans are "manufactured" or "made." And if we can make human beings, their worth is dependent on our wishes for them, not on whether they have a destiny and worth bestowed on them by God.

Issues at the End of Life

Traditional Western laws against suicide and active euthanasia have been founded on the notion that human life has a transcendent source. As such it belongs neither to the state nor to the individual. Our laws have reflected this larger scheme of meaning.

Recently, however, the question has become: "Whose life is this anyway?" And the answer is: "It's mine to do with as I choose." I might rightly choose to end it, or, if I don't have the courage or ability, I will ask someone else to help me end it. Thus the continuing existence of a human life depends on subjective grounds.

There are legitimate arguments about what to do about particularly anguished ends of life. No one wants to insist that persons suffer drawn-out and painful ends. Indeed, most Christians agree that passive voluntary euthanasia is morally permissible. We need not pursue heroic measures if the dying process is clearly underway. But that is far from intending to kill either oneself or someone else at their request. In such instances, one is playing God, determining the time and place that temporal destiny is transformed into eternal destiny. Christian doctors find such a role morally repugnant, with good reason.

ISSUES OF JUSTICE DURING LIFE

Our reflections thus far give comfort to religious and social conservatives who are disturbed by the relativizing of the worth of human life at its beginning and end. And properly so. But we must press on to issues that are more conducive to liberal sensitivities than conservative.

If we as Christians really believe in the objective worth of every human being, we must also believe in the moral claims that all human beings have for the basic necessities of life—protection, food, shelter, clothing, medical care, schooling, and opportunities for work. Can a dignified human life consonant with God's bestowed worth be led without human beings being assured access to these things? That seems unlikely. The essential equality and dignity of human beings dictate that we recognize objective worth by assuring access to these goods also.

This does not mean that we must agree on *how* these goods are made available to all. Many of us part company on the strategies for doing so. But we must agree on the principle that such moral claims are legitimate, even from those who have been improvident in their own lives, even from those who have refused their destinies. God does not give up on such folk—in fact He sent His Son for them as well as for us—so neither should we give up on them.

Such convictions move strongly against the current trend to measure the worth of every life by its capacity for pleasure and happiness. They resist the arguments put forth by such philosophers as Peter Singer that humans incapable of pleasure are essentially disposable.

Conclusion

It is no secret that the "Christian" West is undergoing powerful secularizing forces. Pope John Paul II spoke passionately about re-evangelizing the West. So it is no surprise that the religious notions undergirding the morality and politics of the West are weakening. Other sorts of arguments—egoistic and utilitarian—are trying to supply the rationale for both morality and politics. But their arguments are thinner and thinner, based on ever-dwindling moral capital.

It is time for Christians to awaken not only in their efforts at evangelism but also in their efforts to witness in the public sphere for the objective worth of human life.

NOTES

1. Glenn Tinder, *The Political Meaning of Christianity* (Baton Rouge: Louisiana State University Press, 1989).

2. Glenn Tinder, "Can We Be Good without God?" *The Atlantic Monthly* (December 1989).